Study Guide

to accompany

Edwards ◆ Wattenberg ◆ Lineberry

Government in America
People, Politics, and Policy
Fourteenth Edition

Prepared by

Charles S. Matzke
Michigan State University

Longman

New York   Boston   San Francisco
London   Toronto   Sydney   Tokyo   Singapore   Madrid
Mexico City   Munich   Paris   Cape Town   Hong Kong   Montreal

Study Guide to accompany *Government in America: People, Politics, and Policy, Fourteenth Edition*, by Edwards, Wattenberg, and Lineberry.

Copyright © 2009 Pearson Education, Inc.

2 3 4 5 6 7 8 9 10—11 10 09

Longman
is an imprint of

www.pearsonhighered.com   ISBN: 0-205-68436-X

Table of Contents

Forward

This Study Guide is designed to assist the student in understanding and learning the material presented in the text, *Government in America, People, Politics and Policy,* Fourteenth Edition by George C. Edwards III, Martin P. Wattenberg, and Robert L. Lineberry. Each chapter in the Study Guide is divided into eight sections: Chapter Outline, Learning Objectives, Key Terms, Using Your Understanding, Multiple Choice Questions, True/False Questions, Short Answer/Short Essay Questions, and Essay Questions.

The Chapter Outline section presents a brief summary of the chapter in outline form. Key terms in the chapter are presented in bold type. This section serves as a quick review of the major topics of the chapter. The outline is not meant to substitute for a thorough reading of the chapter.

Learning objectives are listed in the second section. After studying the chapter the student should be able to understand and discuss these objectives. Several exercises are presented to help the student better understand and meet these objectives.

The section on key terms provides a space to identify and describe each key term from the chapter and compare and contrast related terms. "Name that term" reverses "identify and describe" by presenting a definition or example of a term for the student to name.

The Using Your Understanding section is designed to give the student the opportunity to delve deeper into a subject presented in the text. Most of these exercises require some outside research beyond the information found in the text. These exercises may be used as the basis for a term paper.

The multiple choice, true/false, short answer/short essay, and essay questions are designed to help the student test their knowledge of the information presented in the text and prepare for exams. The answers to the multiple choice and true/false questions are listed in the back of the Study Guide.

CHAPTER 1

INTRODUCING GOVERNMENT IN AMERICA

CHAPTER OUTLINE

I. Introduction: Politics and Government Matter (pp. 3–8)
    A. Many Americans are apathetic about politics and government.
    B. Political knowledge fosters civic virtues, educates citizens on policy, and promotes participation.
    C. Voter turnout among the youth is lower than any other group.

II. Government (pp. 8–9)
    A. The institutions that make authoritative decisions for any given society are collectively known as **government.**
    B. Two fundamental questions about governing serve as themes of this book.
        1. How should we govern?
        2. What should government do?
    C. All national governments have certain functions in common:
        1. Governments maintain national defense.
        2. Governments provide public services called **public goods.**
        3. Governments preserve order.
        4. Governments socialize the young.
        5. Governments collect taxes.

III. Politics (pp. 9–10)
    A   **Politics** determines whom we select as our governmental leaders and what policies they pursue.
    B. The ways in which people get involved in politics make up their **political participation.**
    C. **Single-issue groups** are so concerned with one issue that their members will cast their votes on the basis of that issue only.

IV. The Policymaking System (pp. 10–13)
    A. People Shape Policy
        1. The **policymaking system** is the process by which policy comes into being and evolves over time. (See Figure 1.4)
        2. Political parties, elections, interest groups, and the media are key **linkage institutions** that transmit the preferences of Americans to the policymakers in government.
        3. The **policy agenda** consists of the issues that attract the serious attention of public officials and other people actively involved in politics at a given time.
        4. A **political issue** arises when people disagree about a problem or about a public policy choice made to fix a problem.

5.   Policymakers work within the three **policymaking institutions** (the Congress, the presidency, and the courts as established by the U.S. Constitution).

B.   Policies Impact People

    1.   Every decision that government makes—a law it passes, a budget it establishes, and even a decision not to act on an issue—is **public policy**. (See Table 1.1)

    2.   **Policy impacts** are the effects that a policy has on people and on society's problems.

V.   Democracy (pp. 13–23)

    A.   Defining Democracy

        1.   **Democracy** is a means of selecting policymakers and of organizing government so that policy reflects citizens' preferences.

    B.   Traditional Democratic Theory

        1.   Equality in voting

        2.   Effective participation

        3.   Enlightened understanding

        4.   Citizen control of the agenda

        5.   Inclusion

        6.   Democracies must practice **majority rule** and preserve **minority rights**.

        7.   The relationship between the few leaders and the many followers is one of **representation**.

    C.   Three Contemporary Theories of American Democracy

        1.   **Pluralist theory** states that groups with shared interests influence public policy by pressing their concerns through organized efforts.

        2.   **Elite and class theory** contends that societies are divided along class lines, and that an upper-class elite pulls the strings of government.

        3.   **Hyperpluralism** contends that many groups are so strong that government is unable to act.

    D.   Challenges to Democracy

        1.   Increased Technical Expertise

        2.   Limited Participation in Government

        3.   Escalating Campaign Costs

        4.   Diverse Political Interests (**policy gridlock**)

    E.   American Political Culture and Democracy

        1.   **Political culture** consists of the overall set of values widely shared within a society.

        2.   Liberty

        3.   Egalitarianism

        4.   Individualism

        5.   Laissez-faire

        6.   Populism

    F.   A Culture War? (Is America polarized into rival political camps with different political cultures?)

    G.   Preview Questions about Democracy

LEARNING   OBJECTIVES

After studying Chapter 1, you should be able to:

1.   Describe what government is and what governments do.

2.   Understand how politics is the struggle over "who gets what, when, and how."

3.   Identify the important features of the policymaking system and explain how public policies are the choices that government makes—and declines to make—in response to political issues.

4.   Understand the nature of democratic government and traditional democratic theory, and the key questions concerning democracy.

5.   Distinguish among the three contemporary theories of American democracy and politics (pluralist, elite and class, and hyperpluralist) and identify some of their strengths and weaknesses.

6.   Understand the nature of American political culture and identify the elements of the American creed.

7.   Understand the nature of the scope of government in America and the key questions concerning the scope of government.

The following exercises will help you meet these objectives:

Objective 1: Describe what government is and what governments do.

1.   Define the term "government."

2. What are the two fundamental questions about governing that serve as themes throughout the textbook?

   1.

   2.

3. List the five functions that all national governments perform.

   1.

   2.

   3.

   4.

   5.

Objective 2: Understand that politics is the struggle over "who gets what, when, and how."

   1. Define the term "politics."

   2. Give examples of the "who," "what," "when," and "how" of politics.

   1. Who:

   2. What:

   3. When:

   4. How:

Objective 3: Identify the important features of the policy system and explain how public policies are the choices that government makes, and declines to make, in response to political issues.

   1. Draw a diagram of how a policy system works.

2. List four key linkage institutions in a democratic society.

   1.

   2.

   3.

   4.

3. Define the term "policy agenda."

4. How does a government's policy agenda change?

5. List the four major policymaking institutions in the United States.

   1.

   2.

   3.

   4.

6. Define the term "policy impacts."

Objective 4: Understand the nature of democratic government, traditional democratic theory, and the key questions concerning democracy.

   1. Define the term "democracy" as used in this text.

2.   List the five cornerstones of an ideal democracy.

        1.

        2.

        3.

        4.

        5.

3.   Explain the principles of majority rule and minority rights.

Objective 5: Distinguish among the three contemporary theories of American democracy and politics (pluralist, elite and class, and hyperpluralist) and identify some of their strengths and weaknesses.

1.   Complete the following table comparing pluralist, elite and class, and hyperpluralist theories according to who holds the power and how policy is made.

Theory	Who Holds Power	How Policy is Made
Pluralist		
Elite and Class		
Hyperpluralist		

2.   List the major challenges facing American democracy.

        1.

        2.

        3.

        4.

Objective 6: Understand the nature of American political culture and identify the elements of the
    American creed.

    1.   What is 'political culture' and why is it crucial to understanding American
            government?

    2.   List and give an example of the five elements of the American creed according to
            Seymour Martin Lipset.

            1.

            2.

            3.

            4.

            5.

    3.   List three ways in which America might be experiencing a crisis of cultural values.

            1.

            2.

            3.

Objective 7: Understand the nature of the scope of government in America and the key questions concerning the scope of government.

    1.   Make a list of items that illustrate the scope of American government.

    2.   What is gross domestic product and how does the term illustrate the scope of American government?

KEY TERMS

Identify and describe:

government

public goods

politics

political participation

single-issue groups

policymaking system

linkage institutions

policy agenda

political issue

policymaking institutions

public policy

policy impacts

democracy

majority rule

minority rights

representation

pluralist theory

elite and class theory

hyperpluralism

policy gridlock

political culture

gross domestic product

Compare and contrast:

government and politics

policy agenda and public policy

policymaking system and linkage institutions

policymaking system and political issue

democracy and traditional democratic theory

majority rule and minority rights

democracy and representation

pluralist theory, elite and class theory, and hyperpluralism

Name that term:

1. Something in which any member of society can share without diminishing the supply to any other member of society.

   _____

2. It consists of subjects and problems getting the attention of government officials and their associates.

   _____

3. This is a choice that government makes in response to an issue on its agenda.

   _____

4. This arises when people disagree about a problem or about public policy choices made to combat a problem.

   _____

5. Political parties, elections, and interest groups are the main ones in the United States.

   _____

6. The effects a policy has on people and on society's problems.

   _____

7. The most fundamental aspect of democratic theory.

   _____

8. According to this theory of American government, many groups are so strong and numerous that the government is unable to act.

   _____

9. This problem is magnified when voters choose a president from one party and congressional majorities from the other party.

   _____

10.   A key factor hat holds American democracy together.

_____

11.   The total value of all goods and services produced annually by the United States.

_____

USING YOUR UNDERSTANDING

1.   Identify and discuss, in your own words, the important features of the policymaking system. Take a problem (such as AIDS, racial discrimination, or crime) and describe how it might be dealt with in this system, from how it becomes a political issue to the policies that could be made in response to it and their impact on people. Discuss different ways in which the problem could be dealt with based on beliefs about the appropriate role of government. State your own view as well.

2.   Collect some current examples of politics and policymaking that illustrate, support, or refute aspects of the three theories of American democracy. Use Internet news sources, newspapers, and/or news magazines in your search. Briefly describe what you discover. Based on your understanding of the three theories and the evidence you have collected make an initial judgment of the applicability of each theory to political and policy realities in America. As you continue to learn about American politics and policymaking, see how your perceptions change.

MULTIPLE CHOICE QUESTIONS
Circle the correct answer:

1. Which of the following statements is TRUE?
   a. There is no relationship between political knowledge and age.
   b. In the mid-1960s, there was virtually no relationship between political knowledge and age; now, in the early twenty-first century, political knowledge increases with age.
   c. In the mid-1960s, there was virtually no relationship between political knowledge and age; now, in the early twenty-first century, political knowledge decreases with age.
   d. Today, in the early twenty-first century, there is virtually no relationship between political knowledge and age; in the mid-1960s, political knowledge increased with age.
   e. Today, in the early twenty-first century, there is virtually no relationship between political knowledge and age; in the mid-1960s, political knowledge decreased with age.

2. Political scientists argue that higher levels of political knowledge
   a. foster tolerance.
   b. foster intolerance.
   c. promote partisanship.
   d. promote bipartisanship.
   e. increase wealth.

3. Despite their differences, all governments
   a. provide public services.
   b. maintain a national defense.
   c. collect taxes.
   d. All of the above
   e. C only

4. Which of the following is an example of a public good?
   a. Libraries
   b. Parks
   c. College education
   d. All of the above
   e. Both a and b

5. Single-issue groups
   a. aid effective policymaking for the public interest.
   b. are concerned with a wide range of problems.
   c. have very little influence on voters or politicians.
   d. tend to have a narrow interest and to dislike compromise.
   e. view politics as a vocation, rather than as an avocation.

6. Which of the following is NOT a component of the policymaking system?
   a. People
   b. Linkage institutions
   c. Policy agenda
   d. Criminal justice institutions
   e. Policymaking institutions

7. Which of the following is TRUE of the policymaking system?
   a. Linkage institutions transmit people's interests to government.
   b. Media investigate social problems and inform people about them.
   c. Elections enable Americans to make their opinions heard by choosing their public officials.
   d. People, linkage institutions, media, and elections all help to shape the policy agenda?
   e. All of the above

8. In a democratic society, parties, elections, interest groups, and the media are all examples of ____ between the preferences of citizens and the government's policy agenda.
    a. cross-pollination
    b. inputs and outputs
    c. ideological bridges
    d. obstacles
    e. linkage institutions

9. Karl Marx and Freidrich Engels published
    a. *The Communist Manifesto*
    b. *A Theory of Democracy*
    c. *The Federalist Papers*
    d. *Poor Richard's Almanac*
    e. *War and Peace*

10. Which of the following is NOT a type of public policy?
    a. Congressional statute
    b. Regulation
    c. Court decision
    d. Budgetary choices
    e. Mandate

11. The principle of "one person, one vote," is an expression of the principle of
    a. equality in voting.
    b. effective participation.
    c. enlightened understanding.
    d. inclusion.
    e. citizen control of the agenda.

12. The principle of traditional democracy theory guaranteeing rights to those who do not belong to majorities and allows that they might join majorities through persuasion and reasoned argument is called the principle of
    a. majority rule.
    b. minority rights.
    c. representation.
    d. pluralism.
    e. enlightened understanding.

13. Pluralists
    a. believe that the public interest will prevail through bargaining and compromise.
    b. depend on fragmented, decentralized, and dispersed power in the policy process.
    c. oppose the principle of majority rule.
    d. compete through a system of "minority rule" for influence.
    e. All of the above

14. Who referred to the U.S. as a "nation of joiners"?
    a. Thomas Jefferson
    b. Alexis de Tocqueville
    c. Robert Putnam
    d. Ronald Reagan
    e. George H. W. Bush

15. Increased technical expertise poses a potential challenge to democracy because
    a. it is difficult to have an informed "nontechnical" public debate on technical issues.
    b. it goes against the tenets of pluralist political theory.
    c. it violates the notion of one man, one vote.
    d. elected officials find it hard to understand technical experts.
    e. interest groups have a difficult time securing technical expertise.

16. A condition that occurs when no coalition is strong enough to form a majority and establish policy is
    a. PAC.
    b. policy gridlock.
    c. policy failure.
    d. policy impact.
    e. hyperpluralist policy.

17. The overall set of values widely shared within a society is called the society's
    a. political culture.
    b. public opinion.
    c. media influence.
    d. linkage institutions.
    e. popular culture.

18. America's bountiful frontier provides a partial explanation for which element of the American creed?
    a. Egalitarianism
    b. Populism
    c. Individualism
    d. Opportunism
    e. Liberty

19. Which of the following is NOT a possible way that Americans may be experiencing a crisis of culture values, according to Wayne Baker?
    a. A loss of traditional values, such as religion and family life
    b. An unfavorable comparison with citizens of other countries in terms of patriotism and/or support for moral principles
    c. The division of society into opposed groups with irreconcilable moral differences
    d. A decline in citizens' commitment to equal opportunity
    e. None of the above

20. Which of the following statements is TRUE?
    a. When expenditures grow, tax revenues must grow to pay the additional costs.
    b. When taxes do not grow as fast as spending, a budget deficit results.
    c. In 2009, the federal deficit was more than $400 billion.
    d. The national debt is more than $9 trillion.
    e. All of the above

TRUE FALSE QUESTIONS

Circle the correct answer:

1. The voter turnout rate among young Americans is consistently higher than among older Americans. T / F

2. Emergent communication technologies and the proliferation of television channels make it easier to avoid information about politics. T / F

3. All governments protect national sovereignty, frequently by maintaining a national defense and armed forces. T / F

4. The daily recitation of the Pledge of Allegiance in public schools is a tool of political socialization used to instill national values among the young. T / F

5. The courts are an example of a linkage institution. T / F

6. The policy agenda responds more to societal failures than it responds to societal successes. T / F

7. Most people around the world believe that democracy is the best form of government. T / F

8. Over one-third of the nation's wealth is held by just 1 percent of the population. T / F

9. The tax burden on Americans is small compared to other democratic nations. T / F

10. Lincoln's famous phrase, "government of the people, for the people, and by the people," is a classic expression of laissez-faire. T / F

SHORT ANSWER/ SHORT ESSAY QUESTIONS

1. Define and provide an example of a public good. How do public goods create circumstances that government must address?

2. What are the key linkage institutions in the United States and what roles do these institutions play in politics and policymaking?

3. What is meant by "representation"? How and why is representation vital to modern democracy?

4. When people talk about a culture war, what do they mean?

5. What tools and techniques does the U.S. government use to socialize the young?

ESSAY QUESTIONS

1. What is the relationship between age, on one hand, and political interest and knowledge on the other? Which age groups are most likely to be interested in and knowledgeable about politics? Which are most likely to be least interested and least knowledgeable? What kinds of explanations have political scientists offered to explain these relationships?

2. Thomas Jefferson believed that a politically ignorant people could never be free. What do you think Jefferson meant? How might Jefferson react to historically low levels of political knowledge among young Americans in the early twenty-first century?

3. What is the role of interest groups in the policymaking process? How is this role different from that played by political parties?

4. Define government and identify the functions that government performs. In this context, what is politics?

5. Compare, contrast, and critically evaluate the three theories of American democracy discussed in Chapter 1: pluralism, elite theory, and hyperpluralism. Which do you think most accurately depicts the reality of contemporary politics in the United States?

CHAPTER 2

The Constitution

CHAPTER OUTLINE

I. Politics in Action: Amending the Constitution (pp. 31–32)
    A. Flag desecration and Gregory Johnson
    B. A **constitution** is a nation's basic law.

II. The Origins of the Constitution (pp. 32–37)
    A.   The Road to Revolution
    B.   Declaring Independence
         1.   The **Declaration of Independence**
    C.   The English Heritage: The Power of Ideas
         1.   **Natural rights** are the rights inherent in human beings, not dependent on governments.
         2.   **Consent of the governed** means the people must agree on who their rulers will be.
         3.   **Limited government** means there must be clear restrictions on what rulers may do.
    D.   Jefferson's Handiwork: The American Creed
    E.   Winning Independence
    F.   The "Conservative" Revolution

III. The Government That Failed: 1776-1787 (pp. 37–40)
    A.   The **Articles of Confederation**
    B.   Changes in the States
    C.   Economic Turmoil
    D.   **Shays' Rebellion**
    E.   The Aborted Annapolis Meeting

IV. Making a Constitution: The Philadelphia Convention (pp. 41–42)
    A.   Gentlemen in Philadelphia
    B.   Philosophy into Action
         1.   Human Nature
         2.   Political Conflict (**Factions** arise from sources of conflict.)
         3.   Objects of Government
         4.   Nature of Government

V. The Agenda in Philadelphia (pp. 43–47)
    A.   The Equality Issues
         1.   Equality and Representation of the States
              a.   The **New Jersey Plan** had each state equally represented in Congress.

b.   The **Virginia Plan** made state representation in Congress based on population.

c.   The **Connecticut Compromise** created two houses of Congress.

2.   Slavery: Congress could limit the future importation of slaves and the three-fifths compromise settled how slaves would be represented.

3.   Equality in Voting

B.   The Economic Issues

1. The delegates were the nation's economic elite.

2. The delegates clearly spelled out the economic powers of Congress.

C.   The Individual Rights Issues

1.   The Constitution says little about personal freedoms.

2.   The Constitution prohibits suspension of the **writ of habeas corpus,** prohibits passing bills of attainder, passing *ex post facto* laws, prohibits imposing religious qualifications for office, outlines rules of evidence for treason, and upholds the right to trial by jury.

VI.   The Madisonian Model (pp. 48–51)

A.   Thwarting Tyranny of the Majority

1.   Limiting Majority Control

2.   Separating Powers (Under **separation of powers,** the three branches of government are relatively independent of each other and share powers.)

3.   Creating Checks and Balances (Under **checks and balances,** each branch of government requires the consent of the others for many of its actions.)

4.   Establishing a Federal System

B.   The Constitutional Republic

1.   A **republic** is a system based on the consent of the governed in which representatives of the public exercise power.

C.   The End of the Beginning

VII.   Ratifying the Constitution (pp. 51–55)

A.   Federalists and Anti-Federalists

1.   **Federalists** supported the Constitution and **Anti-Federalists** opposed it.

2.   The *Federalist Papers* were a series of articles supporting the Constitution.

3.   The **Bill of Rights** is made up of the first ten amendments to the Constitution which restrain the national government from limiting personal freedoms.

B.   Ratification

VIII.   Constitutional Change (pp. 55–61)

A.   The Formal Amending Process

1. Amendment consists of two stages, proposal and ratification.

2. The **Equal Rights Amendment (ERA)** was proposed but not ratified.

B.   The Informal Process of Constitutional Change

1.   Judicial Interpretation: In *Marbury v. Madison* (1803), the Supreme Court claimed the power of **judicial review,** giving courts the right to decide the constitutionality of government actions.

2. Changing Political Practice: includes political parties and the electoral college.
3. Technology
4. Increasing Demands on Policymakers
C. The Importance of Flexibility

IX. Understanding the Constitution (pp. 61–64)
   A. The Constitution and Democracy
   B. The Constitution and the Scope of Government

X. Summary (p. 65)

LEARNING OBJECTIVES

After studying Chapter 2, you should be able to:

1. Discuss the importance of the English philosophical heritage, the colonial experience, the Articles of Confederation, and the character of the Founding Fathers in shaping the agenda of the Constitution writers.

2. Identify the important principles and issues debated at the Constitutional Convention and describe how they were resolved.

3. Explain the Madisonian model of limiting majority control, separating powers, creating checks and balances, and establishing a federal system.

4. Understand the conflict between the Federalists and Anti-Federalists over the ratification of the Constitution.

5. Describe the formal and informal processes by which the Constitution is changed in response to new items on the policy agenda.

6. Evaluate the Constitution in terms of democracy and its impact on policymaking.

The following exercises will help you meet these objectives:

Objective 1: Discuss the importance of the English philosophical heritage, the colonial experience, the Articles of Confederation, and the character of the Founding Fathers in shaping the agenda of the Constitution writers.

1. Make a list of the major grievances of the colonists under British rule.

2. What are the major components of John Locke's political philosophy and how did they influence Thomas Jefferson's writings?

3.   Draw a schematic diagram of the American government under the Articles of Confederation.

4.   Make a list of the reasons why the Articles of Confederation failed.

5.   Briefly describe the general philosophical views of the founding fathers on the following issues:

Human Nature:

Political Conflict:

Objects of Government:

Nature of Government:

Objective 2: Identify the important principles and issues debated at the Constitutional Convention and describe how they were resolved.

1.   What were the three major equality issues at the Constitutional Convention? How were they resolved?
1.

2.

3.

2.   What were the major economic problems addressed at the Constitutional Convention? How were they resolved?

3. Why did the Founding Fathers believe it was not necessary to address individual rights issues specifically in the Constitution?

Objective 3: Explain the Madisonian model of limiting majority control, separating powers, and creating checks and balances.

1. Draw a schematic diagram of the Madisonian model of government.

2. Define the term "constitutional republic."

Objective 4: Understand the conflict between the Federalists and Anti-Federalists over the ratification of the Constitution.

1. Complete the following table summarizing the major differences between the Federalists and the Anti-Federalists on the issues of civil liberties, power of the states, and the economy.

Issues	Federalists	Anti-Federalists
Civil Liberties		
Power of the States		
Economy		

2.   Why did the Anti-Federalists believe the new Constitution was a class-based document?

Objective 5: Describe the formal and informal processes by which the Constitution is changed in response to new items on the policy agenda.

1.   What is an unwritten constitution?

2.   Describe the different ways in which a formal constitutional amendment might be adopted.

3.   The text examines four ways the Constitution changes informally. Complete the following table, listing these ways, defining them, and giving an example for each.

Informal Change	Definition	Example

Objective 6: Evaluate the Constitution in terms of democracy and its impact on policymaking.

1.   List and explain the five Constitutional amendments that expanded the right to vote.

1.

2.

3.

4.

5.

2.   In what ways does the Constitution expand and diminish the scope of government?

KEY TERMS

Identify and describe:

Constitution

Declaration of Independence

natural rights

consent of the governed

limited government

Articles of Confederation

Shays' Rebellion

U.S. Constitution

factions

New Jersey Plan

Virginia Plan

Connecticut Compromise

writ of habeas corpus

separation of powers

checks and balances

republic

Federalists

Anti-Federalists

Federalist Papers

Bill of Rights

Equal Rights Amendment

Marbury *v.* Madison

judicial review

Compare and contrast:

natural rights and consent of the governed

Constitution, Articles of Confederation, and U.S. Constitution

New Jersey Plan, Virginia Plan, and Connecticut Compromise

separation of powers and checks and balances

limited government and republic

Federalists and Anti-Federalists

Marbury v. *Madison* and judicial review

Name that term:

1. This was the first constitution of the United States.

   _____

2. This view contrasts sharply with the divine right of kings.

   _____

3. These were a series of armed attacks on courthouses in 1787 to protest farm foreclosures.

   _____

4. Today these would be called interest groups or parties.

   _____

5. This enables persons detained by authorities to secure an immediate inquiry into the causes of their detention.

   _____

6. This is a system of government based on the consent of the governed in which representatives of the public exercise power.

   _____

7. This was a series of articles published under the name "Publius."

   _____

8. This is made up of the first ten amendments to the Constitution.

   _____

9. First introduced in 1923, this constitutional amendment was passed by Congress in 1972 but never ratified by the states.

   _____

10. Not found in the Constitution, this power was given to the courts in the case of *Marbury* v. *Madison.*

    _____

USING YOUR UNDERSTANDING

1. Try your hand at sketching out a new Constitution for the contemporary United States. Be sure to indicate key governmental institutions and their functions. Also, include a Bill of Rights in your constitution. Keep in mind today's high-tech politics and the current policy agenda. Briefly discuss how the twenty-first century Constitution you envision is similar to or different from the eighteenth century Constitution of the Founders. Evaluate how well the Founders did in terms of these similarities or differences.

2. Locate the written constitution of your state or that of another modern democratic system, such as France, Germany, or Japan. In reading the document or parts of it, look for similarities or differences with the American Constitution. Take note of the governmental institutions it creates, the functions they perform, and whether or not something comparable to the Bill of Rights is included. Describe briefly what you have found. Use this exercise to write a term paper comparing different types of constitutions and their effectiveness.

MULTIPLE CHOICE QUESTIONS

Circle the correct answer:

1. In setting the broad rules of the game of politics, constitutions
    a. are never neutral; they give some participants advantages over others.
    b. are fair and impartial.
    c. allow all participants the same political opportunities.
    d. have no effect on the distribution of power in society.
    e. are constantly changing.

2. Which body issued the Declaration of Independence?
    a. The Constitutional Convention of 1776
    b. The First Continental Congress
    c. The first thirteen colonial legislatures
    d. General George Washington's army
    e. The British Parliament

3. What are natural rights?
    a. Rights inherent in human beings not dependent on governments.
    b. The laws of humans, which are superior to those of nature.
    c. Laws that only exist when people are in a state of nature.
    d. Laws that enabled the British to proclaim their rule over the colonies.
    e. The rights given by a government to a people regardless of their consent.

4. Reflecting Lockean natural rights philosophy, the Declaration of Independence declared that governments derive their just powers from
    a. God.
    b. the consent of the governed.
    c. tradition.
    d. elected leaders.
    e. a Constitution.

5. Which of the following phrases is found in the Declaration of Independence?
    a. "Life, liberty, and property"
    b. "Men being by nature all free, equal, and independent"
    c. "The history of the present King of Great Britain is a history of repeated injustices and usurpations"
    d. "The people shall be the judge...Oppression raises ferments and makes men struggle to cast off an uneasy and tyrannical yoke"
    e. Both a and c

6. Which of the following was NOT a problem with the national government under the Articles of Confederation?
    a. The states were unwilling to send money requisitioned by the national government.
    b. The executive lacked the authority to lead the nation.
    c. The state legislatures had too little power.
    d. The national government was unable to regulate foreign trade or the national economy.
    e. All of the above

7. Which of the following is TRUE based on data presented in **Table 2.02**?
    a. Before the American Revolution, both northern and southern state legislatures were dominated by wealthy and well-to-do individuals.
    b. After the American Revolution, increasing numbers of moderate income individuals and farmers entered state legislatures.
    c. After the American Revolution, in northern states, moderate-income individuals and farmers comprised a majority of office holders in state legislatures.
    d. All of the above
    e. None of the above

8. Shay's Rebellion was a significant event in that it
    a. heightened elites' fears that people were ignoring the law and violating property rights of others.
    b. demonstrated the weakness of Congress to raise a militia that would have stopped Shays and his followers.
    c. fueled dissatisfaction with the Articles of Confederation.
    d. All of the above
    e. None of the above

9. What was the original purpose of the Constitutional Convention?
   a. To write the Declaration of Independence.
   b. To revise the Articles of Confederation.
   c. To draft an entirely new constitution.
   d. To elect the first president of the United States.
   e. To negotiate a peace treaty with Great Britain.

10. The _____, offered as a proposal at the Constitutional Convention, called for each state to be equally represented in Congress.
   a. New Jersey Plan
   b. Connecticut Plan
   c. Virginia Plan
   d. Rhode Island Plan
   e. New York Plan

11. In 1787, slavery was legal in all states except?
   a. New Jersey
   b. New York
   c. Pennsylvania
   d. Massachusetts
   e. Virginia

12. Which issue concerning equality did the delegates to the Constitutional Convention deal with in drafting the constitution?
   a. Equality of the states
   b. Equality in voting
   c. Slavery
   d. All of the above
   e. None of the above

13. Historian Charles Beard argued that the Constitution is best understood in terms of
   a. the propertied upper-class men who drafted it to serve their own elite interests.
   b. the farmers and middle-class men who comprised the Anti-Federalists.
   c. a battle between Federalists and Anti-Federalists.
   d. a battle between state and national power.
   e. the religious ideologies of delegates to the Constitutional Convention.

14. The Anti-Federalists believed that the new constitution
   a. was a thinly disguised attempt to abolish a federal form of government in the United States.
   b. was an enemy of freedom and designed to give control of the government to a rich elite.
   c. created a new government too weak to be effective, and they preferred a monarchy to ensure stability.
   d. was too democratic and would lead to tyranny of the masses against the wealthy.
   e. with whatever faults it might have, was the young nation's best hope for a workable government.

15. Which was the first state to ratify the Constitution?
   a. Delaware
   b. New Jersey
   c. Pennsylvania
   d. Rhode Island
   e. New York

16. Which of the following statements about judicial interpretation is FALSE?
   a. Judicial interpretation can profoundly affect how the Constitution is understood.
   b. The power of judicial review gives courts the right to decide whether legislative actions are in accord with the Constitution.
   c. The power of judicial interpretation is explicitly stated in the Constitution.
   d. In the case of *Marbury v. Madison*, the Supreme Court decided it would be the one to decide constitutional disputes.
   e. None of the above

17. When did the two-party system first appear as part of presidential elections?
   a. 1800
   b. 1787
   c. 1776
   d. 1865
   e. 1920

18. In what ways does the Constitution encourage stalemate?
   a. By providing access for so many interests
   b. Through the separation of powers
   c. By protecting individual rights
   d. By limiting the scope of government
   e. A and b

19. The Supreme Court decision in *United States v. Eichman*
   a. ruled that the Flag Protection Act, which outlawed the desecration of the American flag, was unconstitutional.
   b. ruled that the Flag Protection Act, which outlawed the desecration of the American flag, was constitutional.
   c. ruled that "die-ins" intended to dramatize the consequences of nuclear war were unconstitutional.
   d. ruled that "die-ins" intended to dramatize the consequences of nuclear war were constitutional.
   e. Both b and d

20. The Constitution created a
   a. class-based society.
   b. democracy.
   c. republic.
   d. government of the "rich, well-born, and able".
   e. majoritarian society.

TRUE/FALSE QUESTIONS

Circle the correct answer:

1. The Declaration of Independence mainly focused on King George's abuses. T / F

2. Most delegates to the Constitutional Convention in 1787 believed that human nature was fundamentally self-interested. T / F

3. The Connecticut Compromise gives more power to people who live in heavily populated states. T / F

4. The founders believed that state governments, where most of the governmental activity was expected to take place, would act as checks on the power of the national government. T / F

5. Among the powers given to Congress in the Constitution is the power to establish post offices and postal roads. T / F

6. The Anti-Federalists feared that the national government designed in the constitution would be far too weak. T / F

7. Since the Bill of Rights was ratified, 26 additional amendments have been added to the Constitution. T / F

8. The Bill of Rights had to be added to the Constitution before any states would ratify it. T / F

9. The Court's power of judicial review was first articulated in *Marbury v. Madison*. T / F

10. The U.S. Constitution created a democracy. T / F

SHORT ANSWER/SHORT ESSAY QUESTIONS

1. Briefly describe the political philosophy of John Locke and point to ways in which this philosophy is evident in the Declaration of Independence.

2. Describe the main features of the Articles of Confederation and explain why the Articles failed.

3. What is a faction, according to James Madison? How does the Constitution resolve the problems stemming from factions, according to Madison.

4. Describe the personal characteristics of the delegates to the Philadelphia Convention. What were their basic philosophical views and how did those views shape the convention?

5. Explain the constitutional amendment process.

ESSAY QUESTIONS

1. What are the multiple historical and ideological origins of American national government?

2. The Connecticut Compromise created a bicameral Congress that reflected parts of both the Virginia Plan and the New Jersey Plan. How and why did the Constitution create distinct roles for the House and the Senate? What were the framers' motivations in designing a bicameral Congress with different methods of selecting representatives?

3. What were the Anti-Federalists' main objections to the proposed Constitution? In what ways were their worries prescient with respect to contemporary politics?

4. According to Thomas Jefferson, "the Constitution belongs to the living and not to the dead." What do you think Jefferson meant by this? Was he right? Why or why not?

5. *Marbury v. Madison* (1803) established the principle of judicial review, making the judiciary a coequal branch of government. Does judicial review violate the Constitution? Where and how did the court claim its power?

CHAPTER 3

Federalism

CHAPTER OUTLINE

I.   Politics in Action: Aiding Disaster Victims (pp. 71–72)
   A.   The government response to Hurricane Katrina illustrates the importance of understanding American federalism.
   B.   The relationships between local, state, and national governments often confuse Americans.

II. Defining Federalism (pp. 72–75)
   A.   What Is Federalism?
       5.   **Federalism** is a way of organizing a nation so that two or more levels of government have formal authority over the same area and people.
       6.   **Unitary governments** place all power in the central government.
       7.   Confederations place all or most power in the hands of the components while the national government is weak.
       8.   **Intergovernmental relations** refers to the entire set of interactions among national, state, and local governments.
   B.   Why Is Federalism So Important?
       1.   Federalism decentralizes politics in America.
       2.   Federalism decentralizes policies in America.

III. The Constitutional Basis of Federalism (pp. 75–81)
   A.   The Division of Power
       1.   The **supremacy clause** establishes the Constitution, laws of the national government, and treaties as the supreme law of the land.
       2.   The **Tenth Amendment** states that "powers not delegated to the United States by the Constitution, nor prohibited by it to the states, are reserved to the states respectively, or to the people."
   B.   Establishing National Supremacy
       1.   Implied Powers: *McCulloch v. Maryland* established the principle of **implied powers,** powers that go beyond the **enumerated powers** of the Constitution, on the basis of the **elastic clause.**
       2.   Commerce Power: *Gibbons v. Ogden* defined commerce very broadly.
       3.   The Civil War
       4.   The Struggle for Racial Equality
   C.   States' Obligations to Each Other
       1.   **Full Faith and Credit**
       2.   **Extradition**
       3.   **Privileges and Immunities**

IV.   Intergovernmental Relations Today (pp. 82–90)
    A.   From Dual to Cooperative Federalism
        1.   In **dual federalism** the states and the national government each remain supreme within their own spheres.
        2.   In **cooperative federalism** powers and policy assignments are shared between states and the national government.
            a.   Shared costs
            b.   Federal guidelines
            c.   Shared administration
    B.   Devolution?
        1.   During the mid 1990s, Republicans favored **devolution,** the transfer of policy responsibilities to state and local governments.
        2.   Today Republicans have adopted a pragmatic approach to federalism.
    C.   **Fiscal Federalism** is the pattern of spending, taxing, and providing grants in the federal system.
        1.   The Grant System: Distributing the Federal Pie
            a.   **Categorical grants** are the main source of federal aid to state and local governments.
                (1)   **Project grants** are awarded on the basis of competitive applications.
                (2)   **Formula grants** are distributed according to a formula.
            b.   **Block grants** are given more or less automatically to states or communities that have discretion in deciding how to spend the money.
        2.   The Scramble for Federal Dollars
        3.   The Mandate Blues

V.   Understanding Federalism (pp. 90–95)
    A.   Federalism and Democracy
        1.   Advantages for Democracy
        2.   Disadvantages for Democracy
    B.   Federalism and the Scope of the National Government

III.   Summary (p. 96)

LEARNING OBJECTIVES

After studying Chapter 3, you should be able to:

1.   Define federalism and explain why it is important to American government and politics.

2.   Describe how the Constitution divides power between the national and state governments and understand why the supremacy of the national government is the central principle of American federalism.

3.   Explain the nature of the states' obligations to each other.

4.   Explain how federalism in the United States has shifted from dual federalism to cooperative federalism.

5.   Describe the nature of fiscal federalism and how states and cities compete for federal grants and aid.

6.   Explain the relationship between federalism and democracy, and how federalism contributes to and detracts from democracy.

7.   Understand how federalism has contributed to the scope of the national government.

The following exercises will help you meet these objectives:

Objective 1: Define federalism and explain why it is important to American government and politics.

    1.   Define the three ways of organizing a nation that were discussed in the text.

        1.

        2.

        3.

    2.   In what ways does federalism decentralize politics and policies?

Objective 2: Describe how the Constitution divides power between the national and state governments and understand why the supremacy of the national government is the central principle of American federalism.

    1.   List the three items that are considered the supreme law of the land.

        1.

        2.

        3.

2.   What is the significance of the Tenth Amendment?

3.   List the four key events that have largely settled the issue of how national and state powers are related.

    1.

    2.

    3.

    4.

4.   Explain the difference between enumerated powers and implied powers.

Objective 3: Explain the nature of the states' obligations to each other.

    1.   Describe the three general obligations that each state has to every other state under the Constitution.

        1.

        2.

        3.

Objective 4: Explain how federalism in the United States has shifted from dual federalism to cooperative federalism.

    1.   How is dual federalism analogous to a layer cake and cooperative federalism analogous to a marble cake?

    2.   Explain the three general standard operating procedures of cooperative federalism.

        1.

2.

3.

3.   Explain how the Republican Party's view of federalism changed in the 1990s.

Objective 5: Describe the nature of fiscal federalism and how states and cities compete for federal grants and aid.

1.   What do the terms "cross-over sanctions" and "cross-cutting requirements" mean?

Cross-over Sanctions:

Cross-cutting Requirements:

2.   Explain the two types of categorical grants.

1.

2.

3.   For what reasons might a state or locality not want to receive federal aid?

Objective 6: Explain the relationship between federalism and democracy, and how federalism contributes to and detracts from democracy.

1.   List four advantages of federalism for democracy.

1.

2.

3.

4.

2.   List four disadvantages of federalism for democracy.

    1.

    2.

    3.

    4.

Objective 7: Understand how federalism has contributed to the scope of the national government.

1.   How did industrialization increase the role of the national government?

2.   Why don't the states handle more issues?

KEY TERMS

Identify and describe:

federalism

unitary governments

intergovernmental relations

supremacy clause

Tenth Amendment

McCulloch v. Maryland

enumerated powers

implied powers

elastic clause

Gibbons v. Ogden

full faith and credit

extradition

privileges and immunities

dual federalism

cooperative federalism

devolution

fiscal federalism

categorical grants

project grants

formula grants

block grants

Compare and contrast:

federalism and unitary government

intergovernmental relations and fiscal federalism

supremacy clause and Tenth Amendment

enumerated powers and implied powers

McCulloch v. Maryland and *Gibbons v. Ogden*

full faith and credit, extradition, and privileges and immunities

dual federalism and cooperative federalism

categorical grants and block grants

project grants and formula grants

Name that term:

1. In this type of system, the national government can redraw the boundaries of local governments or change their form.

    _____

2. The supremacy of the national government over the states was established by this court case.

    _____

3.   Examples of this include the power of Congress to coin money, regulate its value, and impose taxes.

_____

4.   In this case, the Supreme Court broadly defined commerce to include virtually every form of commercial activity.

_____

5.   When a state returns a person charged with a crime in another state to that state for trial or imprisonment, they are practicing this constitutional requirement.

_____

6.   This type of federalism has been likened to a "marble cake."

_____

7.   This was at the center of the Republican revolution of the mid-1990s to transfer more responsibility for policies from the national government to the state and local governments.

_____

8.   These grants are awarded on the basis of competitive applications.

_____

9.   This was a response to state and local governmental unhappiness with cumbersome and tedious categorical grants.

_____

USING YOUR UNDERSTANDING

1. Try to identify all of the governments that have authority and policymaking responsibilities in your area, from the federal and state governments to the various types of local government. At the same time, identify the types of public policies for which they are responsible. Briefly discuss your impressions of the federal system from your own vantage point. Indicate whether or not you found what you expected, based on your understanding of the American federal system.

2. Contact your local Chamber of Commerce and find out what strategies your community is pursuing in order to compete with other communities, including its efforts to win federal aid. You may even be able to find some brochures that "sell" your community to prospective residents and industries. Describe what you found in terms of how well you think your community is doing in the economic growth game. Try devising some marketing strategies for your community based on its location and other advantages.

MULTIPLE CHOICE QUESTIONS

Circle the correct answer:

1. A unitary system is a way of organizing government so that
   a. all power resides in a central government.
   b. both national and state levels of government have authority over the same land and people.
   c. all power resides in state and local governments.
   d. national and state governments have separate powers over different areas and people.
   e. the president is the central power of the government.

2. The United States began as a(n)
   a. confederation.
   b. federalist nation.
   c. series of unitary governments.
   d. strong national government, which weakened over time.
   e. series of weakened states that slowly gained strength.

3. From clean-air legislation to welfare reforms, the states constitute a _____ to develop and test public policies and share the results with other states and the national government.
   a. major roadblock
   b. national laboratory
   c. neglected resource
   d. last chance
   e. severe reluctance

4. Which of these is not a power attributed to the states according to the Constitution?
   a. Coin money
   b. Establish local governments
   c. Conduct elections
   d. Ratify amendments to the Constitution
   e. Create taxes

5. The supremacy clause of the Constitution states that all of the following are the supreme law of the land, EXCEPT
   a. laws of the national government (when consistent with the Constitution).
   b. the United States Constitution.
   c. state constitutions.
   d. treaties of the national government (when consistent with the Constitution).
   e. Both c and d

6. The primary thrust of the original intent and wording of the Tenth Amendment is that
   a. state legislatures have the ultimate authority to determine what a state government's powers are.
   b. states have certain powers that the national government cannot encroach upon.
   c. the national government can take control of a state government during a national emergency.
   d. national laws override state laws when there is a conflict between the two.
   e. both the states and national government are bound by the limitations in the Bill of Rights.

7. Which amendment prohibits individual damage suits against state officials?
   a. Ninth
   b. Tenth
   c. Eleventh
   d. Twelfth
   e. Thirteenth

8. The principle that the national government has certain implied powers that go beyond its enumerated powers was first elaborated in the Supreme Court's decision in
   a. *United States v. the States.*
   b. *Gibbons v. Ogden.*
   c. *Miranda v. Arizona.*
   d. *McCulloch v. Maryland.*
   e. *Marbury v. Madison.*

9. Which of the following federal policies exemplifies the implied powers of Congress?
   a. Environmental protection law
   b. Income tax
   c. The regulation of interstate commerce
   d. The provision of an army and a navy
   e. All of the above

10. The Supreme Court case of *Gibbons v. Ogden*
    a. defined the meaning of the elastic clause.
    b. settled the contested presidential election of 1824.
    c. defined commerce as virtually every form of commercial activity.
    d. established the principle of implied powers.
    e. established the supremacy of the national government.

11. A tuition difference between in-state and out-of-state students is an example of
    a. dual federalism.
    b. federal exceptions to the full faith and credit provision.
    c. the extension of full faith and credit to all students from all states.
    d. an example of an exception to the privileges and immunities clause.
    e. project grants to the states.

12. The constitutional requirement that the states return a person charged with a crime in another state to that state for trial or imprisonment is known as
    a. forfeiture.
    b. extradition.
    c. privileges and immunities.
    d. full faith and credit.
    e. the elastic clause.

13. In _____ federalism, the powers and policy assignments of different levels of government are like a marble cake, with mingled responsibilities and blurred distinctions between layers of government.
    a. fiscal
    b. mixed
    c. dual
    d. cooperative
    e. tripartite

14. An example of a direct order from the federal government to the states is the
    a. Equal Employment Opportunity Act of 1982.
    b. Equal Rights Amendment.
    c. Americans with Disabilities Act.
    d. No Child Left Behind Act.
    e. Brady Act.

15. If a university violates Title VI of the 1964 Civil Right Act, which bars discrimination in the use of federal funds on account of race, national origin, gender, or physical disability, by discriminating in athletics, it risks losing its federal funding in all of its programs. This is an example of
    a. crossover sanctions.
    b. crosscutting requirement.
    c. devolution.
    d. cooperative federalism.
    e. intergovernmental relations.

16. Programs such as Medicaid and Aid for Families with Dependent Children, where applicants automatically qualify for aid if they meet the requirements, are examples of
    a. dual federalism.
    b. project grants.
    c. formula grants.
    d. block grants.
    e. welfare.

17. A broad program for community development would most likely be supported through a(n)

    a. formula grant.
    b. enterprise zone.
    c. project grant.
    d. categorical grant.
    e. block grant.

18. What are mandates?
    a. Requirements that direct states or local governments to comply with federal rules under threat of penalties or as a condition of receipt of a federal grant
    b. A grant awarded on the basis of competitive applications
    c. The use of federal dollars in one program to influence state and local policy in another program
    d. When a condition on one federal grant is extended to all activities supported by federal funds, regardless of the source
    e. A general rule of federalism involving the principle that there will be "something for everyone"

19. Which of the following is NOT a standard operating procedure of cooperative federalism today?
    a. Distinctly separated powers of state and national governments
    b. Federal grants-in-aid
    c. Shared administration of programs
    d. Shared financing of government
    e. Federal guidelines imposed on states

20. Which of the following is true of the politics of federalism during the twentieth century?
    a. In general, Democrats supported increasing the power of the federal government, while Republicans favored increasing state responsibilities.
    b. In general, Republicans supported increasing the power of the federal government, while Democrats favored increasing states responsibilities.
    c. In general, both Republicans and Democrats favored increasing the power of the national government and weakening the power of the state governments.
    d. In general, both Republicans and Democrats favored increasing the power of the state governments and weakening the power of the national government.
    e. In general, the presidency favored a strong national government, while Congress favored stronger state governments.

TRUE/FALSE QUESTIONS

1. The federal government immediately took responsibility for its anemic response to Hurricane Katrina. T / F

2. The United Nations is an example of a confederation. T / F

3. The word federalism is absent from the Constitution. T / F

4. The Tenth Amendment is sometimes called the supremacy clause, because it reinforces the power of the national government over the state governments. T / F

5. The powers to tax and borrow money, to establish courts, and to make and enforce laws are powers given by the Constitution to both the national and state governments. T / F

6. *U.S. v. Lopez* signaled a shift in federalism, in that the Supreme Court limited Congress's use of the commerce power. T / F

7. Dual federalism refers to a situation in which the national government and state governments remain supreme within their own spheres. T / F

8. Project grants are awarded and distributed according to a formula. T / F

9. Only school districts in the poorest communities receive federal assistance. T / F

10. Over the course of the twentieth century, intergovernmental relations increasingly leaned toward greater national power. T / F

SHORT ANSWER/SHORT ESSAY

1. Define the term federalism and compare and contrast it with unitary and confederation governments. Give examples of each.

2. Describe authority relations across the three systems of government—unitary, confederate, and federal.

3. Explain what happened in the Supreme Court case, *Gibbons v. Ogden*? What is the importance of this case to the distribution of powers between the states and the national government?

4. How does the Defense of Marriage Act challenge contemporary understandings of full faith and credit?

5. What is a categorical grant, and how is it different from a block grant?

ESSAY QUESTIONS

1. How does the failed government response to Hurricane Katrina—at federal, state, and local levels—reflect the politics of federalism? What kinds of changes are necessary to prevent similar failures in the future? What constraints does the Constitution set on possible solutions to failed coordination across multiple levels of government?

2. How has federalism evolved or changed since the writing of the Constitution, particularly in terms of the establishment of national supremacy? What are the causes and consequences of these changes?

3. What is the proper boundary of Congress's commerce power? How has the Court interpreted the Commerce Clause in the past? What do recent cases such as *U.S. v. Lopez* (1995) and *U.S. v. Morrison* (2000) suggest about the direction of a new politics of federalism?

4. Given the growth of the scope and power of the national government, are state governments still necessary in the American political process?

5. Does federalism create a more democratic political system? Why or why not, and how?

CHAPTER 4

Civil Liberties and Public Policy

CHAPTER OUTLINE

I. Politics in Action: Free Speech on Campus (pp. 101–102)
    A. The University of Wisconsin case represents the complex controversy that shapes civil liberties.
    B. **Civil liberties** are individual legal and constitutional protections against the government.
    C. Americans' civil liberties are set down in the **Bill of Rights**, the first ten amendments to the Constitution.

II. The Bill of Rights—Then and Now (pp. 103-105)
    A. The **First Amendment** is the source of Americans' freedom of religion, speech, press, and assembly.
    B. The Bill of Rights and the States
        1. ***Barron v. Baltimore*** determined that the Bill of Rights restrained only the national government.
        2. ***Gitlow v. New York*** relied on the **due process clause** of the **Fourteenth Amendment** to rule that a state government must respect some First Amendment rights.
        3. The **incorporation doctrine** is a legal concept under which the Supreme Court has nationalized the Bill of Rights by making most of its provisions applicable to the states through the Fourteenth Amendment.

III. Freedom of Religion (pp. 105–110)
    A. The **Establishment Clause** dictates that "Congress shall make no law respecting an establishment of religion." (***Lemon v. Kurtzman, Zelman v. Simmons-Harris, Engel v. Vitale,*** and ***School District of Abington Township, Pennsylvania v. Schempp***)
    B. The **Free Exercise Clause** prohibits the abridgment of the citizens' freedom to worship, or not to worship, as they please.

IV. Freedom of Expression (pp. 111–119)
    A. **Prior Restraint,** or governmental actions that prevent material from being published (censorship), has been consistently struck down by the Supreme Court (***Near v. Minnesota***).
    B. Free Speech and Public Order: the right to protest has been protected to varying extent depending on the political climate (***Schenck v. United States***).
    C. Free Press and Fair Trials
        1. Press coverage may interfere with a fair trial.

2. Reporters do not always like to open their files to the courts; shield laws may protect reporters from revealing their sources. (***Zurcher v. Stanford Daily***)

D. Obscenity has not been regarded as a fully constitutionally protected area of free speech and press, but remains controversial. (***Roth v. United States*** and ***Miller v. California***)

E. **Libel** and Slander:

1. The Supreme Court has held that statements about public figures are libelous only if made with malice and reckless disregard for the truth (***New York Times v. Sullivan***).

F. **Symbolic Speech** is an action that does not consist of speaking or writing but that expresses an opinion (***Texas v. Johnson***).

V. Commercial Speech (pp. 119–120)

A. **Commercial Speech** is restricted far more extensively than other expressions of opinion.

B. Regulation of the Public Airwaves

1. The Federal Communications Commission regulates the content, nature, and very existence of radio and television broadcasting (***Miami Herald Publishing Co. v. Tornillo*** and ***Red Lion Broadcasting Co. v. Federal Communication Commission***).

VI. Freedom of Assembly (pp. 121–122)

1. Right to Assemble: The right to gather together in order to make a statement.

B. Right to Associate: The right to associate with people who share a common interest, including an interest in political change (***NAACP v. Alabama***).

VII. Right to Bear Arms (pp. 122–123)

A. Many communities have passed restrictions on handguns.

B. *District of Columbia v. Heller* (2008) held that the Second Amendment protects an individual right to possess a firearm.

VIII. Defendants' Rights (pp. 123–133)

A. Interpreting Defendants' Rights

B. Searches and Seizures

1. Before making an arrest, police need **probable cause** to believe that someone is guilty of a crime.

2. The Fourth Amendment forbids **unreasonable searches and seizures.**

3. The Constitution requires that probable cause exist before issuing a **search warrant.**

4. The **exclusionary rule** prevents illegally seized evidence from being introduced in the courtroom (***Mapp v. Ohio***).

C. **Self-incrimination:** The **Fifth Amendment** forbids self-incrimination and *Miranda v. Arizona* set guidelines for police questioning.

D. The Right to Counsel: The **Sixth Amendment** ensures the right to counsel and *Gideon v. Wainwright* extended this right to those who can not afford counsel.

E. Trials: Most cases are settled through **plea bargaining.**

F. **Cruel and Unusual Punishment**
  1. The **Eighth Amendment** forbids cruel and unusual punishment.
  2. Almost all of the constitutional debate over cruel and unusual punishment has centered on the death penalty (***Gregg v. Georgia*** and ***McClesky v. Kemp***).

IX. The Right To Privacy (pp. 133–137)
  A. Is There a **Right to Privacy?**
  B. Controversy over Abortion
    1. ***Roe v. Wade*** defined the conditions under which abortions are allowed.
    2. ***Planned Parenthood v. Casey*** permitted more regulation of abortions.

X. Understanding Civil Liberties (pp. 137–138)
  A. Civil Liberties and Democracy
  B. Civil Liberties and the Scope of Government

XI. Summary (pp. 138–139)

LEARNING OBJECTIVES

After studying Chapter 4, you should be able to:

  1. Understand the constitutional basis of civil liberties and the Supreme Court's role in defining them.

  2. Discuss the religious liberties guaranteed in the First Amendment.

  3. Explain the nature of and the issues involving freedom of expression, freedom of assembly, and the right to bear arms in America.

  4. Identify the rights of individuals accused of crimes.

  5. Evaluate and discuss the issue of the right to privacy.

  6. Understand the impact of civil liberties on democracy and the scope of government.

The following exercises will help you meet these objectives:

Objective 1: Understand the constitutional basis of civil liberties and the Supreme Court's role in defining them.

  1. Define the term "civil liberties."

2.   What was the most important difference between the Supreme Court's decision in *Barron v. Baltimore* and the one in *Gitlow v. New York*?

3.   Explain the importance of the Fourteenth Amendment.

4.   What is the incorporation doctrine?

Objective 2: Discuss the religious liberties guaranteed in the First Amendment.

1.   List four Supreme Court cases concerning the establishment clause and comment on the significance of each.

        1.

        2.

        3.

        4.

2. Compare and contrast the Supreme Court case of *Employment Division v. Smith* (1990) with the Religious Freedom Restoration Act of 1993.

Objective 3: Explain the nature of and the issues involving freedom of expression, freedom of assembly, and the right to bear arms in America.

1.   Define the term "prior restraint."

2.   List and explain the significance of three Supreme Court cases concerning free speech and public order.

   1.

   2.

   3.

3.   What is a shield law?

4.   How did the Supreme Court define obscenity in the case of *Miller v. California*?

5.   How are the standards for winning libel lawsuits different for public figures and private individuals?

6.   Define the term "symbolic speech."

7.   Who regulates commercial speech?

8.   What is the function of the Federal Communications Commission (FCC)?

9.   Explain the two facets of the freedom of assembly.

   1.

   2.

10.   Explain the Supreme Court ruling in *District of Columbia v. Heller* (2008).

Objective 4: Identify the rights of individuals accused of crimes.

1.   Draw a diagram of the criminal justice system as a series of funnels.

2.   How are the following terms interrelated: probable cause, unreasonable search and seizure, search warrant, and exclusionary rule?

3.   What are the three guidelines for police questioning of suspects as set forth in *Miranda v. Arizona* (1966)?
       1.

       2.

       3.

4.   What is the significance of the Supreme Court case of *Gideon v. Wainwright* (1963)?

5.   What are the pros and cons of plea bargaining?

6. List and explain the importance of three Supreme Court cases concerning the death penalty.

1.

2.

3.

Objective 5: Evaluate and discuss the issue of the right to privacy.

1. Explain how the Constitution implies a right to privacy.

2. List and explain the importance of four Supreme Court cases concerning abortion.

1.

2.

3.

4.

Objective 6: Understand the impact of civil liberties on democracy and the scope of government.

1. In your opinion are the rights guaranteed in the Fourth, Fifth, Sixth, Seventh, and Eighth Amendments more beneficial to criminals or to society at large?

2. In what ways do civil liberties limit the scope of government? In what ways do they expand the scope of government?

KEY TERMS AND CASES

Identify and describe: key terms

civil liberties

Bill of Rights

First Amendment

Fourteenth Amendment

due process clause

incorporation doctrine

establishment clause

free exercise clause

prior restraint

libel

symbolic speech

commercial speech

probable cause

unreasonable searches and seizures

search warrant

exclusionary rule

Fifth Amendment

self-incrimination

Sixth Amendment

plea bargaining

Eighth Amendment

cruel and unusual punishment

right of privacy

Identify and describe: key cases

Barron v. Baltimore (1833)

Gitlow v. New York (1925)

Lemon v. Kurtzman (1971)

Zelman v. Simmons-Harris (2002)

Engel v. Vitale (1962)

School District of Abington Township, Pennsylvania v. Schempp (1963)

Near v. Minnesota (1931)

Schenk v. United States (1919)

Zurcher v. Stanford Daily (1976)

Roth v. United States (1957)

Miller v. California (1973)

New York Times v. Sullivan (1964)

Texas v. Johnson (1989)

Miami Herald Publishing Co. v. Tornillo (1974)

Red Lion Broadcasting Co. v. Federal Communications Commission (1969)

NAACP v. Alabama (1958)

Mapp v. Ohio (1961)

Miranda v. Arizona (1966)

Gideon v. Wainwright (1963)

Gregg v. Georgia (1976)

McCleskey v. Kemp (1987)

Roe v. Wade (1973)

Planned Parenthood v. Casey (1992)

Compare and contrast:

civil liberties and Bill of Rights

First Amendment and Fourteenth Amendment

Barron v. Baltimore and *Gitlow v. New York*

Gitlow v. New York and Fourteenth Amendment

establishment clause and free exercise clause

Lemon v. Kurtzman and *Zelman v. Simmons-Harris*

Engel v. Vitale and *School District of Abington Township, Pennsylvania v. Schempp*

prior restraint and *Near v. Minnesota*

Roth v. United States and *Miller v. California*

libel and *New York Times v. Sullivan*

Texas v. Johnson and symbolic speech

Miami Herald Publishing Company v. Tornillo and *Red Lion Broadcasting Company v. Federal Communications Commission*

probable cause, unreasonable searches and seizures, and search warrant

unreasonable searches and seizures and *Mapp v. Ohio*

unreasonable searches and seizures and exclusionary rule

Fifth Amendment and self-incrimination

Fifth Amendment and *Miranda v. Arizona*

Sixth Amendment and *Gideon v. Wainwright*

Eighth Amendment and cruel and unusual punishment

Gregg v. Georgia and *McCleskey v. Kemp*

right of privacy and *Roe v. Wade*

Name that term:

1. The legal doctrine through which the Bill of Rights has been made applicable to the states.

    _____

2. This part of the First Amendment forbids the government from having an official church.

    _____

3. A government's actions that prevent material from being published in the first place.

    _____

4. This 1973 Supreme Court case attempted to clarify the meaning of obscenity by spelling out what would and would not be obscene.

    _____

5. The publication of knowingly false or malicious statements that damage someone's reputation.

    _____

6. Actions that do not consist of speaking or writing, but that express an opinion.

    _____

7. This type of speech is restricted far more extensively than expressions of opinion on religious, political, or other matters.

    _____

8. This case established the principle of "clear and present danger."

    _____

9. This case upheld the right to associate.

    _____

10. The Constitution requires that no court may issue one of these unless probable cause exists to believe that a crime has occurred or is about to occur.

   _____

11. This case extended the exclusionary rule to the states.

   _____

12. This case set strict guidelines for police questioning of suspects.

   _____

13. Most criminal cases are settled through this process.

   _____

14. Undefined by the Eighth Amendment, this has been the basis of the controversy over the death penalty.

   _____

15. This right is implied, but not directly stated, in the Bill of Rights.

USING YOUR UNDERSTANDING

1. Select one of the Supreme Court cases discussed in this chapter that is of interest to you. Find and read the opinions presented in the case, including any dissenting opinions, and briefly describe what you found. Identify the social values that were in conflict in the case. Based on your understanding, state whether or not you are persuaded by the arguments presented in justification of the decision.

2. How have the terrorist attacks of September 11, 2001 affected civil liberties in the United States? List and explain the various restrictions put in place and laws passed by the government since September 11, 2001, such as the Patriot Act, that have had an impact on our personal freedoms. In your opinion, are these restrictions worth the tradeoff? Does the reality of international terrorism require a reevaluation of an unconditional commitment to civil liberties? In your opinion, how far should we go?

MULTIPLE CHOICE QUESTIONS

Circle the correct answer:

1. Americans' civil liberties are detailed in
    a. the Declaration of Independence.
    b. the Bill of Rights.
    c. Article I of the Constitution.
    d. no written document or law.
    e. the Preamble to the Constitution.

2. Which of the following statements about the Bill of Rights is FALSE?
    a. The Bill of Rights was written by the First Congress of the United States.
    b. The Bill of Rights consists of the first ten amendments to the Constitution.
    c. Most state constitutions did not have a bill of rights at the time of the Constitutional Convention.
    d. Many states made adoption of a bill of rights a condition of ratification of the Constitution.
    e. The Constitution of 1787 contained no bill of rights.

3. In literal terms, the First Amendment pertains to
    a. the states.
    b. Congress.
    c. the courts.
    d. all units of government.
    e. All of the above

4. The significance of *Gitlow v. New York* (1925) was that
    a. a provision of the Bill of Rights was applied to the states for the first time.
    b. the national government was prevented from violating the Bill of Rights.
    c. a state constitution had precedence over the United States Constitution within that state.
    d. the Bill of Rights was interpreted as restraining only the national government and not cities or states.
    e. the U.S. Constitution has precedence over the state constitution within the state.

5. Federal aid for parochial or private religious school raises questions about
    a. the government's involvement in promoting, or favoring, particular religions.
    b. violating the "wall of separation" between church and state.
    c. the No Child Left Behind Act.
    d. the conflict between evolution and creationism.
    e. Both a and b

6. In 2005, the Supreme Court found that two Kentucky counties violated the establishment clause of the First Amendment by
    a. establishing English as the "official first language of the state of Kentucky."
    b. posting the Ten Commandments as a way of promoting religion.
    c. banning "intelligent design" from the curriculum.
    d. providing an "inefficient" system of public education.
    e. requiring students to say the Pledge of Allegiance.

7. In regard to the free exercise clause, the Supreme Court has made each of the following rulings EXCEPT
    a. polygamy may be justified for Mormons on religious grounds.
    b. the Air Force can enforce its dress code even against religiously based dress choices.
    c. Amish parents may take their children out of school after the eighth grade.
    d. people could become conscientious objectors to war on religious grounds.
    e. public schools cannot require Jehovah's Witnesses to attend flag saluting ceremonies.

8. Freedom of expression
    a. has sometimes been limited when it conflicts with other rights and values.
    b. is protected by the Fourth and Fifth Amendments.
    c. is an absolute right protected by the First Amendment.
    d. includes freedom of speech and press, but not actions.
    e. would not protect a political rally to attack an opposition candidate's stand on issues.

9. In *Schenck v. United States* (1919), Justice Holmes said that speech can be restricted when it
    a. is uttered by government officials in an effort to establish a religion.
    b. provokes "a clear and present danger" to people.
    c. advocates the violent overthrow of the United States.
    d. is spoken rather than nonverbal or symbolic.
    e. is expressed on private property.

10. The Supreme Court ruled in *Branzburg v. Hayes* (1972) that in the absence of shield laws,
    a. the right of a free trial preempts the reporter's right to protect sources.
    b. newspaper files are protected by the First Amendment.
    c. reporters have more rights than other citizens.
    d. judges can bar cameras from the courtroom.
    e. None of the above

11. In *Miller v. California* (1971), the Court ruled that decisions regarding whether or not material was obscene should generally be made by
    a. Congress, through statutory law.
    b. lower federal judges as they see fit, but in conformance with the First Amendment.
    c. local communities, with some guidelines provided by the Court itself about how to make such judgments.
    d. the Supreme Court itself, on a case-by-case basis.
    e. individual persons in their own private lives.

12. Symbolic speech
    a. consists of speech criticizing the symbols of government.
    b. cannot be prohibited because it is too vague for government to legislate against.
    c. has been ruled as disruptive and as a criminal activity.
    d. consists of action that expresses an opinion.
    e. is prohibited under the First Amendment.

13. In *District of Columbia v. Heller* (2008) the Supreme Court
    a. held that the Second Amendment protects an individual's right to posses a firearm unconnected with service in a militia.
    b. held that the Second Amendment protects an individual's right to use a firearm for traditionally lawful purposes.
    c. held that a District of Columbia law requiring lawful firearms in homes to be disassembled or bound by a trigger lock was unconstitutional because it makes it impossible for citizens to use arms for the core lawful purpose of self-defense.
    d. All of the above
    e. None of the above

14. Unreasonable searches and seizures are specifically forbidden in the
    a. Sixteenth Amendment.
    b. Fifth Amendment.
    c. Second Amendment.
    d. Tenth Amendment.
    e. Fourth Amendment.

15. The exclusionary rule, which was applied to state governments, as well as the federal government in *Mapp v. Ohio* (1961), meant that
    a. federal agents may make arrests for state crimes.
    b. state governments are excluded from prosecuting federal crimes.
    c. searches by police could not be made without a legal search warrant.
    d. probable cause must be established prior to arrest.
    e. unlawfully obtained evidence could not be used in court.

16. Which of the following is TRUE about the Supreme Court's decision in *Miranda v. Arizona*?
    a. Miranda's innocence or guilt was not at issue; his rights had been violated, so his conviction was overturned.
    b. The Court's decision greatly relieved members of police departments around the country.
    c. The Court ruled that Miranda was innocent, and Miranda later became a famous public defender in the local courts.
    d. The Court ruled that Miranda's constitutional rights had not been violated and that he could be legally executed.
    e. The Court concluded that Miranda was innocent, overturned his conviction, and ordered him freed from prison.

17. Which of the following is NOT included in protections provided in the Sixth Amendment?
    a. The right to counsel
    b. The right to confront witnesses
    c. The right to a speedy trial
    d. The right to a public trial
    e. The right to remain silent

18. The vast majority of criminal cases in the United States are settled through/by
    a. the Supreme Court.
    b. plea bargaining.
    c. municipal and county courts.
    d. district court.
    e. the jury room.

19. In its 2008 ruling in *Boumedine v. Bush*, the Supreme Court
    a. held that foreign terrorism suspects held at Guantanamo Bay have constitutional rights to challenge their detention in U.S. court.
    b. held that foreign terrorism suspects held at Guantanamo Bay do not have constitutional rights to challenge their detention in U.S. court.
    c. overturned part of the Military Commissions Act that permitted the government to detain aliens indefinitely without prosecuting them in any manner.
    d. held that "the laws and Constitution are designed to survive, and remain in force, in extraordinary times."
    e. A, c, and d

20. The abortion decision in *Roe v. Wade* (1973) was justified by the Supreme Court largely on the grounds of
    a. the freedom of religion clause of the First Amendment.
    b. the free exercise clause of the First Amendment.
    c. the right of privacy implied in the Bill of Rights.
    d. our constitutional right to life.
    e. new advances in medical technology.

TRUE/FALSE QUESTIONS

Circle the correct answer:

1. The legal constitutional protections against government are collectively referred to as civil rights. T / F

2. In 1833, in *Barron v. Baltimore*, the Supreme Court ruled that the Bill of Rights applied only to the national government. T / F

3. The legal concept under which the Supreme Court has nationalized the Bill of Rights is called the incorporation doctrine. T / F

4. In most cases, courts have ruled that teachers cannot discuss creationism as an alternative to evolution, but they can discuss "intelligent design." T / F

5. Prior restraint refers to unlawful arrest without probable cause. T / F

6. The publication of false or malicious statements that damage someone's reputation is called libel. T / F

7. The Supreme Court has permitted communities to use time, place, and manner restrictions to stifle free expression. T / F

8. *Mapp v. Ohio* (1961) incorporated the Fourth Amendment to the states. T / F
   Bloom's level: Knowledge

9. In the decades since the *Miranda* decision, the Supreme Court has made no exceptions to its requirements. T / F

10. The laws governing abortions for women under the age of 18 vary from state to state. T / F

SHORT ANSWER/SHORT ESSAY QUESTIONS

1. What are civil liberties? What defines and protects civil liberties?

2. Why is free speech essential to democracy?

3. What is the incorporation doctrine? Which amendments have not been incorporated, or fully incorporated?

4. What is the principle of clear and present danger? How has the Court applied this principle to balance First Amendment rights with public order and national security?

5. What is meant by symbolic speech? Provide some examples and explain how the Supreme Court has balanced competing interests surrounding symbolic speech.

ESSAY QUESTIONS

1. How would you characterize the first ten amendments to the Constitution? Why, taken together, are these so significant? Do you consider them too narrow, too broad, or about right? Explain.

2. Should public school children be forced to repeat the Pledge of Allegiance? Should public schools permit a recitation of the Pledge of Allegiance, even if it violates some students' religious beliefs?

3. In what ways has the U.S. government's detention of 1,200 persons following 9/11, and its subsequent detention and treatment of prisoners at Guantanamo Bay, Cuba, raised important questions about Bill of Rights protections for the criminally accused? Which amendments and civil liberties are at stake in these cases? What has the Court said, to date, about the government's actions?

4. Most modern, industrialized democracies (including all member nations of the European Union) have abolished the death penalty. Should the U.S. abolish the death penalty?

5. Your text, *Government in America*, notes, "civil liberties are both the foundation for and a reflection of our emphasis on individualism." What is meant by this statement? Do you agree or disagree, and why?

CHAPTER 5

Civil Rights and Public Policy

CHAPTER OUTLINE

I. Politics in Action: Launching the Civil Rights Movement (pp. 145–147)
    A. The civil rights movement was launched in 1955 when Rosa Parks refused to give up her seat on a bus in Montgomery, Alabama.
    B. **Civil rights** are policies that extend basic rights to groups historically subject to discrimination.
    C. Debates on inequality in America center on racial discrimination, gender discrimination, and discrimination based on age, disability, sexual orientation, and other factors.

II. Racial Equality: Two Centuries of Struggle (pp. 147–149)
    A. Conceptions of Equality
        1. Equality of opportunity: everyone should have the same chance.
        2. Equal results or rewards: everyone should have the same rewards.
    B. The Constitution and Inequality:
        The **Fourteenth Amendment** provides for **equal protection of the laws,** resulting in expansive constitutional interpretation.

III. Race, the Constitution, and Public Policy (pp. 149–161)
    A. The Era of Slavery
        Scott v. Sandford (1857) upheld slavery.
        The Civil War and the **Thirteenth Amendment** ended slavery.
    B. The Era of Reconstruction and Resegregation
        Jim Crow laws (segregation laws) were established in the South.
        Plessy v. Ferguson justified segregation through the "equal but separate" doctrine.
    C. The Era of Civil Rights
        1. *Brown v. Board of Education* (1954) overturned *Plessy* and ended legal segregation.
        2. The civil rights movement organized to end the policies and practice of segregation.
        3. The **Civil Rights Act of 1964** made racial discrimination illegal in places of public accommodation and in employment.
    D. Getting and Using the Right to Vote
        1. **Suffrage** was guaranteed to African Americans by the **Fifteenth Amendment** in 1870.
        2. Southern practices to deny African American suffrage (literacy tests, grandfather clause, **poll taxes,** and the **White primary**) were gradually struck down by the Supreme Court and the **Twenty-fourth Amendment.**

3. The **Voting Rights Act of 1965** prohibited any government from using voting procedures that denied a person the vote on the basis of race or color.
E. Other Minority Groups
   1. Native Americans
   2. Hispanic Americans: ***Hernandez v. Texas*** (1954) extended protection against discrimination to Hispanics.
   3. Asian Americans: ***Korematsu v. United States,*** 1944 upheld the internment of Japanese Americans during World War II.
   4. Arab Americans and Muslims

IV. Women, the Constitution, and Public Policy (pp. 162–169)
   A. The Battle for the Vote
   The **Nineteenth Amendment** gave women the right to vote.
   B. The "Doldrums": 1920–1960
   Public policy toward women was dominated by protectionism.
   The **Equal Rights Amendment** was first introduced in Congress in 1923.
   C. The Second Feminist Wave
   Reed v. Reed (1971) ruled that any "arbitrary" sex-based classification violated the Fourteenth Amendment.
   Craig v. Boren (1976) established a "medium scrutiny" standard.
   D. Women in the Workplace:
   Congressional acts and Supreme Court decisions have reduced sex discrimination in employment and business activity.
   E. Wage Discrimination and Comparable Worth:
   Women should receive equal pay for jobs of "**comparable worth.**"
   F. Women in the Military
   Only men must register for the draft.
   Statutes and regulations prohibit women from serving in combat.
   G. Sexual Harassment
   The Supreme Court has ruled that sexual harassment that is so pervasive as to create a hostile or abusive work environment is a form of sex discrimination.

V. Newly Active Groups Under the Civil Rights Umbrella (pp. 169–172)
   A. Civil Rights and the Graying of America
   B. Civil Rights and People with Disabilities: the **Americans with Disabilities Act of 1990** required employers and public facilities to make reasonable accommodations and prohibited employment discrimination against the disabled.
   C. Gay and Lesbian Rights

VI. Affirmative Action (pp. 172–175)
   A. **Affirmative action** involves efforts to bring about increased employment, promotion, or admission for members of groups that have suffered invidious discrimination.
   B. In ***Regents of the University of California v. Bakke*** (1978), the Court rul[ed] against the practice of setting aside a quota of spots for particular groups.
   C. Until 1995, the Court was more deferential to Congress than to local governmer[t] upholding affirmative action programs.

D. In ***Adarand Constructors v. Peña*** (1995), the Court ruled that federal programs that classify people by race are constitutional only if they are "narrowly tailored" to accomplish a "compelling governmental interest."

E. Opponents view affirmative action as reverse discrimination.

VII. Understanding Civil Liberties and the Constitution (pp. 175–177)

A. Civil Rights and Democracy
Equality favors majority rule that may threaten minority rights.

B. Civil Rights and the Scope of Government
Civil rights laws increase the scope and power of government.

VIII. Summary (pp. 177–178)

LEARNING   OBJECTIVES

After studying Chapter 5, you should be able to:

1. Understand the historical and constitutional basis of the struggle for equal rights.

2. Discuss the struggle for equality for African Americans in terms of three historical eras, the Constitution, and public policy.

3. Explain how women have gained civil rights and what equality issues remain important for women today.

4. Describe the new groups in the civil rights movement.

5. Explain the controversy over the issue of affirmative action.

6. Understand the impact of civil rights on democracy and the scope of government.

The following exercises will help you meet these objectives:
Objective 1: Understand the historical and constitutional basis of the struggle for equal rights.

1. What are the three key types of inequality in America?

   1.

   2.

   3.

2.   Explain the two major conceptions of equality.

       1.

       2.

3.   What is the only mention of the idea of equality in the Constitution?

4.   Explain the Supreme Court's three standards for classifications under the equal protection clause and give an example of each.

       1.

       2.

       3.

Objective 2: Discuss the struggle for equality for African Americans in terms of three historical eras, the Constitution, and public policy.

       1.   Complete the following table listing the three eras of the struggle for African American equality, the major policy focus during each era, major court cases and their importance in each era, and any acts of Congress or constitutional amendments passed during each era.

Historical Era	Policy Focus	Court Cases	Acts/Amendments

2. Compare and contrast the significance of the Supreme Court cases of *Scott v. Sandford* (1857), *Plessy v. Ferguson* (1896), and *Brown v. Board of Education* (1954).

3. What is the difference between *de jure* segregation and *de facto* segregation?

4. List the six major provisions of the Civil Rights Act of 1964.

    1.

    2.

    3.

    4.

    5.

    6.

5. List and explain four ways in which the southern states denied African Americans the right to vote.

    1.

    2.

    3.

    4.

6.   What was the impact of the Voting Rights Act of 1965?

7.   List four other minority groups that have faced discrimination similar to that experienced by African Americans.

        1.

        2.

        3.

        4.

Objective 3: Explain how women have gained civil rights and what equality issues remain important for women today.

1.   Explain the policy of "protectionism."

2.   What was the Equal Rights Amendment?

3.   List and explain the significance of four Supreme Court cases dealing with sex-based discrimination.

        1.

        2.

        3.

        4.

4.   How has Congress attempted to end sex discrimination in the area of employment?

5.   What is meant by "comparable worth"?

6.   In what two ways are women legally treated differently in the military?

        1.

        2.

7.   How has the Supreme Court dealt with the issue of sexual harassment?

Objective 4: Describe the new groups in the civil rights movement.

        1.   In what ways are the elderly discriminated against in American society?

        2.   What are the main provisions of the Rehabilitation Act of 1973 and Americans with Disabilities Act of 1990?

        3.   Why might gays and lesbians face the toughest battle for equality?

Objective 5: Explain the controversy over the issue of affirmative action.

        1.   Define the term "affirmative action."

2.   List four cases in which the Supreme Court seems to support affirmative action and four cases in which it seems to oppose affirmative action.

Support   Oppose

1.   1.

2.   2.

3.   3.

4.   4.

Objective 6: Understand the impact of civil rights on democracy and the scope of government.

1.   How does equality threaten liberty?

2.   How do civil rights laws increase the scope and power of government?

KEY TERMS AND KEY CASES

Identify and describe: key terms

civil rights

Fourteenth Amendment

equal protection of the laws

Thirteenth Amendment

Civil Rights Act of 1964

Suffrage

Fifteenth Amendment

poll taxes

White primary

Twenty-fourth Amendment

Voting Rights Act of 1965

Nineteenth Amendment

Equal Rights Amendment

comparable worth

Americans with Disabilities Act of 1990 (ADA)

affirmative action

Identify and describe: key cases

    Scott v. Sandford (1857)

    Plessy v. Ferguson (1896)

    Brown v. Board of Education (1954)

    Hernandez v. *Texas* (1954)

    Korematsu v. United States (1944)

    Reed v. Reed (1971)

    Craig v. Boren (1976)

    Regents of the University of California v. Bakke (1978)

    Adarand Constructors v. Peña (1995)

Compare and contrast:

    Fourteenth Amendment and equal protection of the laws

    Dred Scott v. Sandford and Thirteenth Amendment

Plessy v. Ferguson and *Brown v. Board of Education*

Civil Rights Act of 1964 and Voting Rights Act of 1965

suffrage and Fifteenth Amendment

poll taxes and White primary

Twenty-fourth Amendment and poll taxes

Nineteenth Amendment and Equal Rights Amendment

Reed v. Reed and *Craig v. Boren*

affirmative action and *Regents of the University of California v. Bakke*

affirmative action and *Adarand Constructors v. Peña*

Name that term:

1.   Policies that extend basic rights to groups historically subject to discrimination.

        _____

2.   The Fourteenth Amendment forbids the state from denying this to their citizens.

        _____

3.   This Supreme Court case justified segregation.

_____

4.   This law made racial discrimination illegal in hotels, motels, restaurants, and other places of public accommodations.

_____

5.   This device permitted political parties in the heavily Democratic South to exclude blacks from primary elections.

_____

6.   This case upheld the internment of Japanese Americans in encampments during World War II.

_____

7.   This case extended protection against discrimination to Hispanics.

_____

8.   "Equality of rights under the law shall not be denied or abridged by the United States or by any state on account of sex."

_____

9.   This idea suggests that women should receive equal pay with men for jobs demanding similar skills.

_____

10.   This law requires employers and public facilities to make reasonable accommodations for disabled people.

_____

USING YOUR UNDERSTANDING

1. Investigate the policy that your college or university follows with regard to the admission of minority and women students. Also find out about its employment practices, and whether or not it has an affirmative action program. Collect statistics on the percentage of minorities enrolled and employed by the school. Does your college or university offer special academic programs for minorities and women? Evaluate whether or not you believe your school is doing too much or too little in addressing equality issues. Include a recommendation as to how you believe the school's policy might be improved, describing what consequences your recommendation would have.

2. The onslaught of the AIDS epidemic has raised new issues of equality in the United States. Examine this issue. Should AIDS victims receive the same protections as other handicapped people? How has AIDS affected the gay rights movement? Compile a list of state and local ordinances concerning homosexuals. Do most of these laws protect or discriminate against homosexuals? Also compile survey research results on public opinion towards gays and lesbians. Has the public become more or less tolerant of gays and lesbians? How has AIDS affected public attitudes? Compare the gay rights movement with the civil rights and women's movements. How are they similar and how are they different?

REVIEW QUESTIONS

Circle the correct answer:

1. "Equal protection of the laws," as provided in the Fourteenth Amendment, is understood to mean
    a. all states must treat everybody exactly alike.
    b. every state must promote equality among all its people.
    c. "equal protection of life, liberty, and property," for all.
    d. equality of results for all Americans.
    e. equality of outcomes for all Americans.

2. Classifications by race and ethnicity have now been ruled by the Court to be acceptable only in
    a. matters wherein certain races or ethnic groups show greater talent or less aptitude.
    b. laws passed by Congress, not those passed by the individual states.
    c. regard to rules and regulations of the armed forces.
    d. laws seeking to remedy previous discrimination.
    e. matters involving national security.

3. In the case of *Dred Scott v. Sandford,* the United States Supreme Court
   a. voted unanimously to declare slavery unconstitutional and barbaric, thus causing the southern states to secede.
   b. ruled that all adult African American men had a right to vote under the Constitution.
   c. outlawed segregation laws that separated Blacks and Whites in all public places.
   d. ruled that a Black man, slave or free, was "chattel," and upheld slavery itself as constitutional.
   e. for the first time placed a geographic limit on the expansion of slavery, banning it west of the Mississippi River.

4. Jim Crow laws
   a. imposed legal segregation on African Americans in the South after the Civil War.
   b. were an attempt to reimpose slavery in the South after the Civil War.
   c. gave African Americans the right to vote in local elections in the South.
   d. granted former slaves free land in compensation for their years of unpaid labor.
   e. allowed African Americans to hold state and federal offices in the South after the Civil War.

5. Which president sent troops to Little Rock, Arkansas, to desegregate Central High School?
   a. Franklin D. Roosevelt
   b. Harry Truman
   c. Dwight Eisenhower
   d. Richard Nixon
   e. John F. Kennedy

6. The Supreme Court's ruling in *Brown v. Board of Education* was based on the legal argument that segregation violated the _____ Amendment.
   a. Fourteenth
   b. First
   c. Twenty-sixth
   d. Nineteenth
   e. Equal Rights

7. In the case of _____, the Supreme Court upheld federal court rulings ordering busing of students to achieve racially balanced schools.
   a. *Craig v. Boren*
   b. *Plessy v. Ferguson*
   c. *Brown v. Board of Education*
   d. *Unified Transportation Co. v Madison County*
   e. *Swann v. Charlotte-Mecklenberg County Schools*

8. The Civil Rights Act of 1964
   a. made racial discrimination illegal in motels, restaurants, and other public accommodations.
   b. forbid employment discrimination on the basis of race, color, religion, national order, or sex.
   c. permitted the withholding of federal grants to states and localities that practiced racial discrimination.
   d. All of the above
   e. None of the above

9. To render African American votes ineffective, several southern states used the _____, a device that permitted political parties to choose their nominees in elections off limits to Blacks.
   a. suffrage
   b. grandfather clause
   c. poll tax
   d. hidden ballot
   e. White primary

10. Which of the following resulted from the Supreme Court's decision in *Thornburg v. Gingles* (1982)?
    a. State legislatures and the Justice Department interpreted the Court's ruling as a mandate to create majority-minority districts.
    b. Fourteen new U.S. House districts were redrawn to help elect African Americans to Congress.
    c. Six U.S. House districts were redrawn to help elect new Hispanic members to Congress.
    d. All of the above
    e. None of the above

11. Native Americans were made citizens of the United States in
    a. 1964.
    b. 1924.
    c. 1789.
    d. 1868.
    e. They were never made citizens of the United States.

12. Hispanic Americans make up about _____ percent of the U.S. population.
    a. two
    b. ten
    c. fifteen
    d. twenty
    e. twenty-five

13. Coverture refers to
    a. the combination of electric shock therapy and drugs once used to "cure" homosexuals of their homosexuality.
    b. the legal doctrine that deprived married women of any identity separate from that of their husbands.
    c. a term used to describe the time when minority groups will outnumber Caucasians of European descent.
    d. the principle used to justify the internment of Japanese Americans during World War II.
    e. the legal doctrine used to discriminate against Native Americans by placing them in reservations.

14. The _____ gave women the constitutional right to vote.
    a. Bill of Rights
    b. Fifteenth Amendment
    c. Twenty-fourth Amendment
    d. Equal Rights Amendment
    e. Nineteenth Amendment

15. The Civil Rights and Women's Equity in Employment Act of 1991
    a. banned sex discrimination in employment.
    b. forbade sex discrimination in federally subsidized education programs.
    c. shifted the burden of proof in justifying hiring and promotion practices to employers.
    d. made it illegal for employers to exclude pregnancy and childbirth from their health benefits plans.
    e. made it illegal for employers to include pregnancy and childbirth in their health benefits plans.

16. Which of the following statements about the Equal Rights Amendment (ERA) is FALSE?
    a. The ERA was ratified in 1982.
    b. The ERA battle stimulated vigorous feminist activity.
    c. The ERA battle stimulated vigorous antifeminist activity.
    d. The ERA was first introduced in the 1920s.
    e. Congress passed the ERA in 1972.

17. In 1990, Congress enacted the _____, a far-reaching law to protect a particular group of Americans from discrimination, ignoring those who claimed the price tag would be too high.
    a. Gay and Lesbian Civil Rights Bill
    b. Native Americans Inclusion Act
    c. Americans with Disabilities Act
    d. Children's Rights Act
    e. Immigrant Grant Act

18. Which of the following best describes affirmative action?
    a. A policy designed to give special attention to a previously disadvantaged group.
    b. A law that forces employers to have an equal number of employees from all racial groups.
    c. A law that makes hiring men over women illegal.
    d. A Supreme Court decision that makes school segregation illegal.
    e. A law that makes homosexual activity illegal in some states.

19. Which of the following statements is FALSE?
    a. Equality is a basic principle of democracy.
    b. The principle of equality can invite the denial of minority rights.
    c. Civil rights laws and court decisions tell groups and individuals that there are certain things they may and may not do.
    d. Current civil rights policies conform to the eighteenth century idea of limited government.
    e. Civil rights laws restrict the scope of government.

20. Equality tends to favor
    a. minority rule.
    b. elitism.
    c. pluralism.
    d. majority rule.
    e. hyperpluralism.

TRUE/FALSE QUESTIONS

Circle the correct answer:

1. The word equality does not appear in the original Constitution. T / F

2. *Dred Scott v. Sandford* was the Supreme Court's landmark decision that declared slavery was unconstitutional in all the United States. T / F

3. *De jure* segregation is that which is done by law. T / F

4. The Supreme Court has ruled that state legislative redistricting plans must create the greatest possible number of majority-minority districts possible. T / F

5. *Hernandez v. Texas* (1954) extended protection from discrimination to Hispanics. T / F

6. The Supreme Court has ruled that classifications based on gender are subject to a lower level of scrutiny than classifications based on race. T / F

7. The Supreme Court has been consistent over the years in supporting the principle of affirmative action, interpreted primarily as the use of quotas in hiring and promotion. T / F

8. Sexual harassment is prohibited by the Civil Rights Act of 1964. T / F

9. The Supreme Court ruled in *Romer v. Evans* that a state could not deny homosexuals protection against discrimination. T / F

10. In *Parents Involved in Community Schools v. Seattle School District No. 1* (2007), the Supreme Court argued that the districts' use of race in voluntary integration plans violated the Fourteenth Amendment. T / F

SHORT ANSWER/SHORT ESSAY QUESTIONS

1. Briefly explain the primary significance of the Fourteenth Amendment.

2. Explain the three standards of review that the Supreme Court uses in determining whether discrimination is reasonable and constitutional.

3. Compare and contrast the Supreme Court cases of *Plessy v. Ferguson* and *Brown v. Board of Education.*

4. Summarize the arguments for and against affirmative action.

5. Summarize growing questions surrounding the role of women in the military and their current exemption from compulsory registration for the draft.

ESSAY QUESTIONS

1. How do Americans understand the concept of equality? What does equality entail? How has its meaning changed throughout U.S. history? Have we truly achieved equality in contemporary political and social life?

2. Describe the three eras that delineate African Americans' struggle for equality in America. Explain how the roles of the court and Congress changed through the three eras.

3. The Supreme Court upheld the constitutionality of the United States government's decision to remove the Japanese Americans from the west coast and place them in internment camps during World War II in *Korematsu v. United States.* What was the basis for the Court's rationale? In your estimation, did the Supreme Court make the right or wrong decision? Why?

4. What questions about civil rights are raised by the government's treatment of Arab Americans and Muslims after 9/11. Were the government's actions justified?

5. Explain the Supreme Court's ruling in *Adarand Constructors v. Pena*. How did this decision differ from earlier ones? To what extent did this decision void federal affirmative action programs?

CHAPTER 6

Public Opinion and Political Action

CHAPTER OUTLINE

I.   Politics in Action: A Rare Moment of Consensus in Public Opinion (pp.183-184)
    A.   September 11 revealed a rare example of consensus in public opinion.
    B.   The study of American **public opinion** aims to understand the distribution of the population's belief about politics and policy issues.

IV.   The American People (pp. 184–191)
    A.   **Demography** is the science of human populations. The Constitution requires a **census,** "an actual enumeration" of the population, every ten years.
    B.   The Immigrant Society: There have been three great waves of immigration.
    C.   The American Melting Pot
        1.   A **melting pot** refers to a mixture of cultures, ideas, and peoples.
        2.   The United States will soon experience a **minority majority,** where white Anglo-Saxons will no longer be a majority.
        3.   The Simpson-Mazzoli Act required employers to document the citizenship of their employees.
        4.   Americans share a common **political culture**—an overall set of values widely shared within a society.
    D.   The Regional Shift
        1.   Over the last 60 years, the Sunbelt has had the greatest population growth.
        2.   **Reapportionment** occurs after every census. House seats are reallocated to the states based on population changes.
    E.   The Graying of America
        1.   Citizens over 65 compose the fastest growing age group.

V.   How Americans Learn About Politics: Political Socialization (pp. 191–195)
    A.   **Political socialization** is the process through which an individual acquires his or her particular political orientations.
    B.   The Process of Political Socialization
        1.   The Family
        2.   The Mass Media
        3.   School
    C.   Political Learning over a Lifetime

IV.   Measuring Public Opinion and Political Information (pp. 195–201)
    A.   How Polls are Conducted
        1.   A **sample** of the population is a relatively small proportion of people who are chosen as representative of the whole.
        2.   **Random sampling** operates on the principle that everyone should have an equal probability of being selected.

3. **Sampling error** depends on the size of the sample.
4. Most polling is done on the telephone with samples selected through **random-digit dialing.**
- B. The Role of Polls in American Democracy
  1. Polls help political candidates detect public preferences.
  2. Polls may make politicians followers rather than leaders.
  3. Polls can distort the election process.
  4. **Exit polls** may discourage people from voting.
  5. Polls can be manipulated by altering the wording of questions.
- C. What Polls Reveal about Americans' Political Information
  1. Americans are not well informed about politics.
- D. The Decline of Trust in Government

V. What Americans Value: Political Ideologies (pp. 201–206)
- A. A **political ideology** is a coherent set of values and beliefs about public policy.
- B. Who are the Liberals and Conservatives?
  1. More Americans consistently choose the ideological label of conservative over liberal.
  2. Liberals generally like to see the government do more.
  3. Groups with political clout tend to be more conservative than groups whose members have often been shut out from political power.
  4. Ideological differences between men and women have led to the **gender gap,** where women are more likely to support Democratic candidates.
  5. The role of religion in influencing political ideology has changed greatly in recent years.
- C. Do People Think in Ideological Terms?
  1. For most people, the terms liberal and conservative are not as important as they are for the political elite.

VI. How Americans Participate in Politics (pp. 206–210)
- A. **Political participation** encompasses the many activities used by citizens to influence the selection of political leaders or the policies they pursue.
- B. Conventional Participation: The majority of Americans participate only by voting in presidential elections.
- C. Protest as Participation
  1. **Protest** is designed to achieve policy change through dramatic and unconventional tactics.
  2. **Civil disobedience** is consciously breaking a law thought to be unjust.
- D. Class, Inequality, and Participation: Lower rates of political participation among minority groups are linked with lower socioeconomic status.

VII. Understanding Public Opinion and Political Action (pp. 210–211)
- A. Public Attitudes toward the Scope of Government
- B. Democracy, Public Opinion, and Political Action

VI. Summary (p. 211)

LEARNING OBJECTIVES

After studying Chapter 6, you should be able to:

1. Describe how demographic factors shape who we are politically.

2. Identify the processes through which people learn about politics.

3. Define public opinion, identify how it is measured, explain its role in shaping public policy, and discuss the nature of political information in America.

4. Understand the concept of political ideology in American politics and government.

5. Explain the ways in which people participate in politics and in the policymaking process, and discuss the implications of unequal political participation.

6. Understand the relationship between the scope of government, democracy, public opinion, and political action.

The following exercises will help you meet these objectives:

Objective 1: Describe how demographic factors shape who we are politically.

1. What were the three great waves of immigration to the United States?

    1.

    2.

    3.

2. What is meant by the term "minority majority"?

3. What was the goal of the Simpson-Mazzoli Act?

4.   How have the following demographic changes affected political changes?

1. Immigration

2. Regional Shifts

3. Aging Population

Objective 2: Identify the processes through which people learn about politics.

1.   Explain the significance of each of the following as sources for political learning:

1. Family

2. Mass media

3. Schools

2.   Name two ways in which aging affects political behavior.

1.

2.

Objective 3: Define public opinion, identify how it is measured, explain its role in shaping public policy, and discuss the nature of political information in America.

1.   What is the key to the accuracy of opinion polls?

2.   Explain the technique of random-digit dialing.

3. List three criticisms of public opinion polling.

1.

2.

3.

4. What is the "paradox of mass politics," according to Russell Neuman?

5. What is the largest impact of declining trust in government since the 1960s?

Objective 4: Understand the concept of political ideology in the context of American politics and government.

1. Fill in the following table concerning political ideology.

Ideology	General Beliefs	Typical Demographic Characteristics
Liberals		
Conservatives		

2.   Explain how the role of religion influences political ideology in the United States.

3.   Fill in the following table on the classification of the ideological sophistication of American voters according to the study *The American Voter*.

Ideological Classification	Definition	Percent

Objective 5: Explain the ways in which people participate in politics and in the policymaking process, and discuss the implications of unequal political participation.

1.   List five activities of conventional political participation, placing a star next to the most common activity.

        1.

        2.

        3.

        4.

        5.

2. Define civil disobedience and give an example.

3. How does minority group status affect political participation?

Objective 6: Understand the relationship between the scope of government, democracy, public opinion, and political action.

1. What is the public's general attitude about the scope of government?

2. Comment on how Americans' lack of political knowledge and low participation rate affects democracy.

KEY TERMS

Identify and describe:

public opinion

demography

census

melting pot

minority majority

political culture

reapportionment

political socialization

sample

random sampling

sampling error

random-digit dialing

exit poll

political ideology

gender gap

political participation

protest

civil disobedience

Compare and contrast:

demography and census

melting pot and minority majority

public opinion and political ideology

sample, random sampling, and sampling error

random-digit dialing and exit poll

protest and civil disobedience

Name that term:

1. This is the mixing of cultures, ideas, and peoples.

    _____

2. This is an overall set of values widely shared within a society.

    _____

3. This occurs when the 435 seats in the House of Representatives are reallocated to the states based on population changes.

    _____

4. The process through which an individual acquires his or her particular political orientations.

    _____

5.   The distribution of the population's beliefs about politics and policy issues.

    _____

6.   This technique is the key to the accuracy of public opinion polls.

    _____

7.   This is the most criticized type of poll.

    _____

8.   In American politics, this is usually characterized by the liberal-conservative dimension.

    _____

9.   Ideological differences between men and women have led to this.

    _____

10.   Voting, running for office, and even violent protest are examples of this.

    _____

USING YOUR UNDERSTANDING

1.   Locate the published results of an opinion poll by Gallup, Harris, or one of the news organizations on a topic that is of interest to you. You may want to use polls that focused on the 2008 presidential election, social or economic issues, the war on terrorism, or the war in Iraq. Assess the results in terms of the demographic distributions, if any, that are reflected in the results. See if males differed from females, whites from non-whites, and so on. If the results are compared with the findings of an earlier poll, see if public opinion on the topic is changing. Briefly describe what you found and what its implications are for policymaking. Alternatively, design a small questionnaire for your class dealing with questions of information, ideology, and political participation. Have the respondents to your survey provide demographic information. Summarize your findings in a table or two presenting the overall responses and those for particular demographic groups. Keep in mind that you will probably face the problems of a limited sample size and a lack of representativeness for the general population.

2. Conduct a study on the role of unconventional political participation in the United States. Compare and contrast the different types of unconventional political participation. Identify examples of historical events in the United States that exemplify unconventional political participation. Present an analysis of these events in terms of the number of people involved, the type of activity, the target of the activity, and the short-term and long-term results of the activity. In particular, you might want to analyze the protest movements against the war on Iraq. Critically evaluate the effectiveness of unconventional political participation as compared to conventional political participation.

MULTIPLE CHOICE QUESTIONS

Circle the correct answer:

1. Which of the following statements is TRUE?
    a. Normally, American public opinion reveals conflicting attitudes and ambivalence.
    b. Immediately after 9/11, American public opinion was nearly unanimous on responding immediately and by force to the terrorist attacks.
    c. More than 80 percent of Americans viewed 9/11 as an act of war.
    d. Both a and b
    e. All of the above

2. The distribution of the population's beliefs about politics and policy issues is called
    a. demography.
    b. ideology.
    c. public opinion.
    d. the public agenda.
    e. the U.S. census.

3. By constitutional requirement, the government conducts the United States Census every
    a. two years.
    b. year.
    c. five years.
    d. presidential election year.
    e. ten years.

4. The 2000 census indicated that the largest minority population is comprised of
    a. illegals.
    b. African Americans.
    c. Asian Americans.
    d. Hispanics.
    e. Native Americans.

5. Approximately what percent of African Americans live below the poverty line?
    a. 28
    b. 42
    c. 24
    d. 6
    e. 17

6. The Simpson-Mazzoli Act
    a. represented a crackdown on illegal aliens by requiring that employers document the citizenship or legitimate immigrant status of workers or pay stiff fines.
    b. requires that states keep their polls open for at least ten hours on election day in order to facilitate participation.
    c. established federal guidelines and regulations for taking public opinion polls.
    d. reformed the jury procedures in felony cases, particularly the unanimous verdict requirement.
    e. required that the homeless be counted in the 1990 census.

7. _____ occurs after every census to reallocate the 435 seats in the United States House of Representatives, reflecting shifts in the population of the states and, thus, how many seats each state is allotted.
    a. Equalization
    b. Restructuring
    c. Political socialization
    d. Reapportionment
    e. Demography

8. Political socialization is defined as
    a. the distribution of the population's beliefs about politics and policy issues.
    b. the various political roles that individuals play in society.
    c. a coherent set of values and beliefs about public policy.
    d. the process through which an individual acquires his or her particular political orientations.
    e. the activities used by citizens to influence the selection of political leaders or the policies they pursue.

9. The most obvious intrusion of the government into America's socialization is through
    a. political parties.
    b. the family.
    c. schooling.
    d. the mass media.
    e. criminal laws.

10. The level of confidence about a public opinion poll is referred to as   .
     a. the confidence index.
     b. sampling error.
     c. the sample.
     d. random sampling.
     e. demographic certainty.

11. Which of the following is NOT a criticism of modern polling?
     a. Careful attention to polls is unwise, as polls only reflect the passive attitudes of voters.
     b. Politicians use polls to follow the crowd rather than to assert bold leadership.
     c. Polls can distort the election process by creating a bandwagon effect, where people want to follow the crowd.
     d. Polls are subject to very wide margins of error, yet are treated as accurate measurements of public opinion.
     e. All of the above

12. A _____ is a coherent set of values and beliefs about public policy.
     a. policy agenda
     b. political ideology
     c. demography
     d. public opinion
     e. political socialization

13. In general, liberal ideology supports
     a. a strong central government that sets policies to promote equality.
     b. individuals responding generously to each other to solve society's problems without looking to government to do so.
     c. a small, less active government that gives freer reign to the private sector.
     d. public and government ownership of the means of production.
     e. strong local and state governments that are closer to the people.

14. Which of the following statements is TRUE?
     a. Americans consistently choose the ideological label of liberal over conservative.
     b. Americans consistently choose the ideological label of conservative over liberal.
     c. Young people are more likely than older people to be conservative.
     d. Both a and c
     e. Both b and c

15. One of the effects of growing older on political learning and political behavior is that
     a. political participation increases with age.
     b. the strength of one's party attachment declines with age.
     c. people become more liberal with age.
     d. interest in politics decreases with age.
     e. single-issue voting increases with age.

16. The *American Voter* study on ideological sophistication among voters in the 1950s showed that only a small percentage of Americans
    a. had no coherent political ideology.
    b. identified with groups reflecting their own interests.
    c. had a coherent political ideology.
    d. had ever taken a government or civics course.
    e. linked their own economic well-being with the party in power.

17. Recent presidential elections have shown
    a. a sharp turn in public thinking to more conservative positions on issues.
    b. that voters are less interested in ideology or issue positions than in candidate traits such as competence and integrity.
    c. a sharp turn in public thinking to more liberal positions on issues.
    d. a dramatic growth of ideological voters.
    e. that voters are more interested in issue positions than in candidate ideology.

18. Sidney Verba and his colleagues found that while voter turnout declined between 1967 and 1987,
    a. writing letters to the editor and contacting government officials increased.
    b. participating in nonpolitical activities increased.
    c. protesting and giving money to candidates increased.
    d. contacting government officials and giving money to candidates increased.
    e. none of the above

19. There is evidence that when incomes and educational levels are equal
    a. members of the majority tend to be more politically active than minorities.
    b. members of minority groups tend to participate more than members of the majority.
    c. Hispanics participate more than whites and African Americans participate less than whites.
    d. Hispanics, African Americans, and women tend to be less politically active than white males.
    e. the political participation of members of minority groups and the majority are also equal.

20. To say that Americans are ideological conservatives, but operational liberals is to say that Americans
    a. oppose big government in principle, but want it to do more in practice.
    b. favor big government in principle, but want it to do less in practice.
    c. favor divided government.
    d. oppose divided government.
    e. believe, following Reagan, that government is the source of their problems.

TRUE/FALSE QUESTIONS

Circle the correct answer:

1. Americans hold a diversity of views and conflicting attitudes. T / F

2. The census is mandated by the U.S. Constitution. T / F

3. Over the second part of the twentieth century, the greatest population growth occurred east of the Mississippi. T / F

4. The family plays little significant role in an individual's political socialization. T / F

5. Voter turnout is related to age. T / F

6. The level of confidence in the findings of a public opinion poll is called sampling error. T / F

7. Americans' trust in government has increased in recent decades. T / F

8. More Americans call themselves liberals than moderates. T / F

9. The gender gap refers to the regular pattern by which women are more likely than men to support Democratic candidates. T / F

10. Public opinion surveys show that acceptance of gays and lesbians is increasing among liberals but decreasing among moderates and conservatives. T / F

SHORT ANSWER/SHORT ESSAY QUESTIONS

1. What is the census and why is it so politically important?

2. Explain the process of reapportionment. Why is it important in American politics?

3. What factors influence an individual's political socialization?

4. What is the gender gap? Where does it come from? What are its consequences?

5. Define protest and why it is employed in the political process. What is civil disobedience? Should it be tolerated in American politics or strictly curtailed? How can civil disobedience be defended? Explain.

ESSAY QUESTIONS

1. What is demography, and why is it important to understanding political changes? What demographic changes have occurred in the United States and what are their political and public policy consequences?

2. Explain how public opinion is measured. What scientific techniques are used to measure public opinion? What are the arguments against public opinion polling?

3. What challenges are raised by recent patterns of immigration in the U.S.? What particular challenges are states facing with respect to illegal immigration? How should states respond to these challenges? In answering, consider a variety of responses, including granting "amnesty" to illegal immigrants, refusing to grant public benefits (including, for example, welfare, education, medical care) to illegal immigrants, and so on. How should we respond as a nation to these issues?

4. To what extent does political participation reflect a bias in favor of the privileged? Should this matter? What are the consequences for democracy?

5. What is meant by the claim that Americans are ideological conservatives in principle, but ideological liberals in practice? Why do you think this is the case? What are the consequences for democracy of our "split" personality in this case?

CHAPTER 7

THE MASS MEDIA AND
THE POLITICAL AGENDA

CHAPTER OUTLINE

I.   Politics in Action: How Television has brought a Sense of Immediacy to Governing (pp. 217–218)
   A.   **High-tech politics** is a politics in which technology increasingly shapes the behavior of citizens and policymakers, as well as the political agenda itself.
   B.   The **mass media** consist of television, radio, newspapers, magazines, and other means of popular communication that reach, and profoundly influence, not only the elites but also the masses.

II. The Mass Media Today (pp. 218–219)
   A.   A **media event** is staged primarily for the purpose of being covered.
   B.   Image making is critical to campaigning and day-to-day governing.

III. The Development of Media Politics (pp. 220–230)
   A.   Introduction
      1.   Franklin D. Roosevelt practically invented media politics, holding two **press conferences** (presidential meetings with reporters) a week.
      2.   The Vietnam War and the Watergate scandal soured the press on government.
      3.   **Investigative journalism** is the use of detective-like reporting methods to unearth scandals.
   B.   The **Print Media**
      1.   "Yellow journalism" characterized the early history of newspapers in the United States.
      2.   The press has a pecking order.
      3.   The political content of leading magazines is slim.
   C.   The **Broadcast Media**
      1.   During World War II, radio went into the news business in earnest.
      2.   Since the 1960s, television has had a profound impact on politics.
   D.   Government Regulation of the Broadcast Media
      1.   The Federal Communications Commission (FCC) regulates communications via radio, television, telephone, cable, and satellite.
      2.   The FCC regulates airwaves to prevent near-monopolies, license stations, and ensure fair treatment.
   E.   From Broadcasting to **Narrowcasting**: The Rise of Cable News Channels
      1.   Rather than appealing to a general audience, cable news channels focus on a narrow particular interest.

      2.   Many scholars feel that cable news has reduced the overall quality of political journalism.

  F.   The Impact of the Internet

      1.   The Internet provides vast amounts of information at one's fingertips.

      2.   The impact of the Internet on politics has been more subtle than revolutionary.

  G.   Private Control of the Media

      1.   Unlike many other countries, virtually all American media outlets are in private hands, allowing freedom in journalistic content.

      2.   Major metropolitan newspapers are mostly owned by **chains**.

IV.   Reporting the News (pp. 230–236)

  A.   News is what is timely and different.

  B.   Finding News

      1.   Most news organizations assign reporters to **beats,** specific locations where news frequently happens.

      2.   **Trial balloons** consist of information leaked to discover the political reaction.

  C.   Presenting the News

      1. News coverage has become less complete as technology has enabled the media to pass along information with greater speed.

      2. **Sound bites** are more common.

  D.   Bias in the News

      1.   News reporting is not systematically biased toward a particular ideology or party.

      2.   Television is biased toward stories that generate good pictures. The **talking head** is considered boring.

V.   The News and Public Opinion (pp. 236–238)

  A.   Although studies show that the media do not affect how people vote, they do affect what they think about and the priorities they attach to problems.

  B.   People's opinions shift with the tone of news coverage.

VI.   The Media's Agenda-Setting Function (pp. 238–239)

  A.   The **policy agenda** is the list of subjects or problems to which government officials, and people outside of government closely associated with those officials, are paying some serious attention at any given time.

  B.   **Policy entrepreneurs** are people who invest their political "capital" in an issue.

  C.   The media can be used by the poor and downtrodden as well as the elite.

VII.   Understanding the Mass Media (pp. 239–241)

  A.   The Media and the Scope of Government

  B.   Individualism and the Media

  C.   Democracy and the Media

VIII. Summary (p. 241)

LEARNING OBJECTIVES

After studying Chapter 7, you should be able to:

1. Describe the characteristics of the mass media today.

2. Explain the development of the print and broadcast media from a historical perspective.

3. Understand how news is found and reported by the media.

4. Describe how the news media affect public opinion.

5. Discuss the concepts of policy agenda and policy entrepreneur and the media's importance to each.

6. Understand how the media affect the scope of government and the democratic process.

The following exercises will help you meet these objectives:

Objective 1: Describe the characteristics of the mass media today.

1. Explain the purpose of a media event.

2. List the seven principles of news management as practiced in the Reagan White House.

    1.

    2.

    3.

    4.

    5.

    6.

    7.

Objective 2: Explain the development of the print media and the broadcast media from a historical perspective.

1. Explain two media techniques used most effectively by President Franklin Roosevelt.

    1.

    2.

2. What is meant by the term "investigative journalism"?

3. Explain the significance of the "yellow journalism" era to the print media.

4. Explain how television affected the political career of Richard Nixon.

5. What effect did television have on the war in Vietnam?

6. Explain the three ways in which the Federal Communications Commission has regulated the airwaves.

    1.

    2.

    3.

7. What impact has cable TV had on news reporting?

8.   List four findings of the Columbia University's Project for Excellence in Journalism on cable news programming.

     1.

     2.

     3.

     4.

9.   What makes news reporting on the Internet particularly different from news reporting on television?

10.   Explain two consequences of private control of the media in the United States.

     1.

     2.

Objective 3: Understand how news is found and reported by the media.

     1.   Where does most news come from?

     2.   What is meant by a "sound bite" and what does it tell us about news coverage?

     3.   Explain how the news media tend to be biased.

Objective 4: Describe how the news media affect public opinion.

     1.   In experiments by Shanto Iyengar and Donald Kinder, what effect did manipulating TV stories have on viewers?

2.   Give examples of how the media have had an effect on the public's evaluation of specific events.

Objective 5: Discuss the concepts of policy agenda and policy entrepreneur and the media's importance to each.

        1.   Define the term "policy agenda."

        2.   List five items in the policy entrepreneur's "arsenal of weapons."

                1.

                2.

                3.

                4.

                5.

Objective 6: Understand how the media affect the scope of government and the democratic process.

        1.   How do the media act as a "watchdog"?

        2.   What is the difference between the "information society" and the "informed society"?

KEY TERMS

Identify and describe:

high-tech politics

mass media

media event

press conferences

investigative journalism

print media

broadcast media

narrowcasting

chains

beats

trial balloons

sound bites

talking head

policy agenda

policy entrepreneurs

Compare and contrast:

high-tech politics and mass media

media event and press conference

print media and broadcast media

sound bite and talking head

policy agenda and policy entrepreneur

Name that term:

1. It reaches the elite as well as the masses.

   _____

2. These are staged primarily for the purpose of being covered.

   _____

3. This tends to pit reporters against political leaders.

   _____

4. These control newspapers with most of the nation's circulation.

   _____

5. The primary mission of cable and Internet news.

   _____

6. Specific locations from which news frequently emanates.

7. Information leaked to see what the political reaction would be.

   _____

USING YOUR UNDERSTANDING

1. Choose one of the three major networks, CBS, NBC, or ABC, and watch the evening news every day for a week. While watching, write down the topic of each news story, the amount of time spent on the story, and an assessment of the story's content and the issues it raises. Read a daily newspaper (preferably the *New York Times* or another major paper) for the same days. Compare the television and newspaper coverage of the same news stories. Analyze the differences between these media in terms of how the stories were presented, depth of coverage, and issue orientation. Evaluate how the print media and the broadcast media might differ in their influence on public opinion.

2.   Based on your understanding of the role of the media in the agenda-building process, critique a news item or article that concerns a policy issue. Your critique should begin by asking how well the item identified the policy issue, the policy entrepreneurs, and people in government concerned about the issue. Assess the news item as both a source of information and a source of influence on your perceptions of politics, government, and policy. Consider how policymakers might use the news item as well. Put yourself in the position of the reporter and consider how the story might have been improved. In light of your critique, discuss your impressions of the media as unofficial but important sources of influence on public opinion and the policy agenda.

MULTIPLE CHOICE QUESTIONS

Circle the correct answer:

1. Which of the following statements is FALSE?
   a. There was virtually no daily press when the Constitution was written.
   b. The daily newspaper is largely a product of the mid-nineteenth century.
   c. Television has been around since the first half of the twentieth century.
   d. Reporters submitted questions in writing to presidents as late as Herbert Hoover's presidency, 1929-1933.
   e. None of the above

2. Prior to the 1930s,
   a. press conferences were held twice a week.
   b. the president was rarely directly questioned by the media.
   c. the media was dominated by a few influential newspapers.
   d. image building was essentially built around radio broadcasting.
   e. the president catered to the local, rather than the national, press.

3. Investigative journalism
   a. uses in-depth reporting to unearth scandal among political leaders.
   b. frequently pits reporters against political leaders.
   c. may contribute to greater public cynicism and negativity about politics, according to some analysts.
   d. All of the above
   e. None of the above

4. The two primary kinds of media that scholars distinguish between are
   a. online media and hard media.
   b. new media and old media.
   c. print media and broadcast media.
   d. biased media and objective media.
   e. news media and entertainment media.

5. At the turn of the century, newspaper magnates Joseph Pulitzer and William Randolph Hearst ushered in the era of
   a. yellow journalism.
   b. nickel tabloids.
   c. newspaper chains.
   d. penny press.
   e. political advertising.

6. Which of these is not an example of broadcast media?
   a. Magazines
   b. The Internet
   c. Television
   d. Radio
   e. None of the above; all are examples of broadcast media.

7. The Associated Press is an example of a
   a. high-technology medium.
   b. newspaper chain.
   c. massive media conglomerate.
   d. wire service.
   e. trade association acting as an interest group for newspapers.

8. A major metropolitan newspaper averages roughly 100,000 words per day; a typical broadcast of the nightly news on TV amounts to about _____ words.
   a. 3,600
   b. 150,000
   c. 200,000
   d. 250,000
   e. 300,000

9. Television coverage of the war in Vietnam had the effect of
   a. generating popular support for the president and the war.
   b. hiding the true horrors of the war and the number of casualties from the American people.
   c. exposing governmental naiveté and lies about the progress of the war.
   d. duping the public into believing the war would soon end.
   e. simultaneously undermining support for the war in North Vietnam while boosting public morale in South Vietnam.

10. The FCC regulates communications via
    a. radio.
    b. television.
    c. telephone.
    d. cable.
    e. All of the above

11. Since 1996, no single owner can own more than _____ percent of the broadcast market.
    a. five
    b. ten
    c. twenty
    d. thirty-five
    e. fifty

12. Which of the following is an example of a narrowcasting outlet?
    a. MTV
    b. ESPN
    c. ABC
    d. All of the above
    e. Both a and b

13. To a large extent, television networks define news as what is _____ to viewers.
    a. informative
    b. vital information
    c. entertaining
    d. thought-provoking
    e. yet unknown

14. The bottom line that shapes how journalists define the news, where they get the news, and how they present it is
    a. their personal ideology.
    b. the First Amendment right to freedom of the press.
    c. government regulations.
    d. profits.
    e. their professional values.

15. A trial balloon is a
    a. method used by the media to force a politician or public official to admit to lying to a reporter.
    b. piece of information leaked to politicians from a reporter in order to confirm another source.
    c. sensational criminal trial that attracts inflated media coverage.
    d. directive by judges to deny access to reporters in certain sensitive cases.
    e. method used by public figures of leaking certain stories to reporters to see what the political reaction will be.

16. A news beat is a(n)
    a. location from which news frequently emanates, such as Congress or the White House.
    b. successful angle for covering a story.
    c. approach to investigative journalism.
    d. story that has passed its time and is no longer interesting.
    e. description of the pace and rhythm of journalism.

17. In 2004, the average sound bite of a presidential candidate shown talking on the nightly news averaged
    a. less than ten seconds.
    b. about thirty seconds.
    c. about two minutes.
    d. about ninety seconds.
    e. about a minute.

18. Which of the following statements is TRUE?
    a. The vast majority of studies have found that reporting in the news media is systematically liberally biased.
    b. The vast majority of studies have found that reporting in the news media is systematically conservatively biased.
    c. The vast majority of students have found that reporting in the news media is not systematically biased toward one ideology or party.
    d. Most stories in the news media present only one point of view, thus painting an unbalanced view for readers and/or viewers.
    e. Few reporters actually believe in journalistic expectations about objectivity.

19. Comprehensive surveys of American journalists between 1971 and 2002 have found that reporters are
    a. more likely to classify themselves as liberal than as conservative.
    b. more like to classify themselves as conservative than as liberal.
    c. more like to classify themselves as independent, or having no ideological preference.
    d. evenly split between conservatives and liberals.
    e. Both c and d

20. Which of the following is FALSE?
    a. The media's watchdog function helps keep politicians in check.
    b. Americans consistently rate the media's watchdog role in positive terms.
    c. A majority of Americans believe that press criticism of political leaders does more harm than good.
    d. Journalists frequently hold disparaging views of public officials.
    e. Journalists rate the watchdog as an important role for the media.

TRUE/FALSE QUESTIONS

Circle the correct answer:

1. A media event is staged primarily for the purpose of being covered by reporters, cameras, etc. T / F

2. Ronald Reagan was the first president to hold frequent press conferences and give fireside chats to reassure the public. T / F

3. Prior to the 1960s, the relationship between politicians and the press was one of skepticism and distrust. T / F

4. Investigative journalism has contributed to greater public cynicism and negativism about politics. T / F

5. Gradually, the broadcast media has replaced the print media as our principal source of news and information. T / F

6. Using the broadcast media, Lyndon Johnson was successful in persuading the public that America was winning the war in Vietnam. T / F

7. In Canada and most of Europe, the major networks are government owned. T / F

8. To a large extent, television networks define news as what is entertaining to the average viewer. T / F

9. An intentional news leak for the purpose of assessing the political reaction to that news leak is called a trial balloon. T / F

10. The majority of studies have shown that the media, especially newspapers, tend to have a liberal bias. T / F

SHORT ANSWER/SHORT ESSAY QUESTIONS

1. Explain the importance of the 1960 presidential debate.

2. Explain the historical development of the print and broadcast media in the U.S. Use examples to illustrate your answer.

3. What is the difference between broadcasting and narrowcasting?

4. How do reporters and journalists "find" the news?

5. How does television define what is newsworthy? Explain where television finds its news stories and how they are presented to the American public.

ESSAY QUESTIONS

1. Describe the relationship between the mass media and the president, and how it has changed over the last several decades. Include examples of how various presidents such as George Bush, Ronald Reagan, Richard Nixon, and Franklin Roosevelt have interacted with the media, i.e., how much and under what circumstances.

2. Has the increase in information technologies in society created a more informed citizenry? Why or why not? What claims do the commercial media make regarding why citizens are or are not informed?

3. What role do the media play in defining the policy agenda? How can the media be used by policy entrepreneurs to achieve their objectives? Is such use a problem or a virtue in America's democratic system? Explain.

4. Evaluate the role of the FCC? Does the FCC exert too much influence over the media? Not enough?

5. Is the news media biased?

CHAPTER 8

CHAPTER OUTLINE

I. Introduction (pp. 247-248)
   A. Political Parties have contributed greatly to American democracy.
   B. **Party competition** is the battle between Democrats and Republicans for the control of public offices.

II. The Meaning of Party (pp. 248–251)
   A. Introduction
      1. A **political party** is, according to Anthony Downs, a "team of men [and women] seeking to control the governing apparatus by gaining office in a duly constituted election."
      2. Political parties are viewed as "three-headed political giants."
         a. The *party-in-the-electorate*
         b. The *party as an organization*
         c. The *party-in-government*
   B. Tasks of the Parties
      1. Parties act as **linkage institutions**, translating inputs from the public into outputs from the policymakers.
      2. Parties perform many functions.
         a. Parties pick candidates.
         b. Parties run campaigns.
         c. Parties give cues to voters.
         d. Parties articulate policies.
         e. Parties coordinate policymaking.
   C. Parties, Voters, and Policy: The Downs Model
      1. **Rational-choice theory** "seeks to explain political processes and outcomes as consequences of purposive behavior."
      2. The wise party selects policies that are widely favored.

III. The Party in the Electorate (pp. 251–253)
   A. **Party images** help shape people's **party identification,** the self-proclaimed preference for one party or the other.
   B. **Ticket-splitting,** voting with one party for one office and another for other offices is near an all-time high.

IV. The Party Organizations: From the Grassroots to Washington (pp. 253–256)
   A. Local Parties
      1. Urban political parties were once dominated by **party machines.**
      2. **Patronage** is one of the key inducements used by party machines.

B. The 50 State Party Systems
   1. American national parties are a loose aggregation of state parties.
   2. States limit who can participate in their nomination contests by using **closed primaries, open primaries,** or **blanket primaries.**
C. The National Party Organizations
   1. The supreme power within each of the parties is the **national convention.**
   2. The **national committee** keeps the party operating between conventions.
   3. The **national chairperson** is responsible for the day-to-day activities of the national party.

V. The Party in Government: Promises and Policy (pp. 257–258)
   A. The party in control ultimately determines who gets what, where, when, and how.
   B. A **coalition** is a set of individuals and groups supporting a party.
   C. Parties have done a fairly good job of translating their platform promises into public policy.

VIII. Party Eras in American History (pp. 258–266)
   A. Introduction
      1. **Party eras** are long periods of time when one party has been the dominant majority party.
      2. Party eras are punctuated by a **critical election.**
      3. **Party realignment** is a rare event when the party system is transformed.
   B. 1796–1824: The First Party System
   C. 1828–1856: Jackson and the Democrats versus the Whigs
   D. 1860–1928: The Two Republican Eras
      1. 1850s–1896, Republican Party as the antislavery party.
      2. 1896–1928, Republican Party as the party of the new working class and moneyed interests.
   E. 1932–1964: The **New Deal Coalition**
      1. Following the Great Depression, a new Democratic coalition remained dominant for decades.
   F. 1968–Present: Southern Realignment and the Era of Divided Party Government
      1. Since 1968 the South has gradually realigned with the Republican Party.
      2. **Party dealignment** means that people are moving away from both parties.

VII. **Third Parties:** Their Impact on American Politics (pp. 266–268)
   A. Parties that promote certain causes.
   B. Splinter parties.
   C. Parties that are an extension of a popular individual with presidential hopes.

VIII. Understanding Political Parties (pp. 268–271)
   A. Democracy and Responsible Party Government
      1. The **responsible party model** would make it easier to convert party promises into governmental policy.
   B. American Political Parties and the Scope of Government
   C. Is the Party Over?
IX. Summary (p. 271)

LEARNING OBJECTIVES

After studying Chapter 8, you should be able to:

1.   Discuss the meaning and functions of a political party.

2.   Discuss the nature of the party-in-the-electorate, party organizations, and the party-in-government.

3.   Describe the party eras in American history and how parties realign and dealign.

4.   Evaluate the two-party system, its consequences, and the place of third parties in the system.

5.   Identify the challenges facing the American political parties and explain their relationship to American democracy and the scope of government.

The following exercises will help you meet these objectives:

Objective 1: Discuss the meaning and functions of a political party.

1.   Define the term "political party."

2.   Explain the three heads of the political party in the expression "a three-headed political giant."

   1.

   2.

   3.

3.   What are the five tasks political parties should perform if they are to serve as effective linkage institutions?

        1.

        2.

        3.

        4.

        5.

4.   Draw a graph or diagram depicting Anthony Downs' rational-choice model of political parties.

Objective 2: Discuss the nature of the party-in-the-electorate, party organizations, and the party-in-government.

    1.   What two clear patterns regarding party identification have been evident in recent elections?

        1.

        2.

    2.   What is meant by "ticket-splitting"?

    3.   Draw an organizational chart of an American political party and then mark where most of the power actually exists.

    4.   What is meant by a "party machine"?

5.   What are the differences between the following types of party primaries?

   1. closed primaries

   2. open primaries

   3. blanket primaries

6.   What is the function of each of the following national party organizations?

   1. National Convention

   2. National Committee

   3. National Chairperson

7.   What is the relationship between party promises and party performance?

Objective 3: Describe the party eras in American history and how parties realign and dealign.

   1.   List four elections that might be considered "critical" or "realigning." Explain why.

      1.

      2.

      3.

      4.

2.   Complete the following table on party eras.

Party Era	Major Party	Major Party Coalition	Minor Party	Minor Party Coalition	Prominent President(s)
1796–1824					
1828–1856					
1860–1892					
1896–1928					
1932–1964					

3.   List the six presidents since 1968 and complete the following table on divided government.

President and Party Affiliation	Number Of Years With Republican Congress	Number Of Years With Democratic Congress

Objective 4: Evaluate the two-party system, its consequences, and the place of third parties in the system.

1.   What are the three basic varieties of third parties?

       1.

       2.

       3.

2.   What are two ways in which third parties can have an impact on American politics?

       1.

       2.

3.   What is the most important consequence of two-party governance in the United States?

Objective 5: Identify the challenges facing the American political parties, and explain their relationship to American democracy, individualism, and the scope of government.

1.   List the four conditions that advocates of the responsible party model believe the parties should meet.

       1.

       2.

       3.

       4.

2.   How does the American party system affect the scope of government?

3.   What is the key problem of the American political parties today?

KEY TERMS

Identify and describe:

party competition

political party

linkage institutions

rational-choice theory

party image

party identification

ticket-splitting

party machines

patronage

closed primaries

open primaries

blanket primaries

national convention

national committee

national chairperson

coalition

party eras

critical election

party realignment

New Deal coalition

party dealignment

third parties

winner-take-all system

proportional representation

coalition government

responsible party model

Compare and contrast:

political party and linkage institutions

party identification and ticket-splitting

party machines and patronage

closed primaries, open primaries, and blanket primaries

national convention, national committee, and national chairperson

party eras and critical election

party realignment and party dealignment

party realignment and New Deal coalition

winner-take-all system and proportional representation

Name that term:

1.   This is the battle between the parties for the control of public offices.

   _____

2.   This is the perception of what the Republicans and Democrats stand for.

   _____

3.   This seeks to explain political processes and outcomes as consequences of purposive behavior.

   _____

4.   This is voting with one party for one office and another for other offices.

   _____

5.   This is one of the key inducements used by political machines.

   _____

6.   This is a set of individuals and groups who support a political party.

   _____

7.   Political party eras are punctuated by these.

   _____

8.   Often a consequence of proportional representation, many European governments are ruled by these.

      _____

9.   Examples of these include the Free Soil Party, the Jobless Party, and the American Independent Party.

      _____

10.   Advocates of this reform believe that this would make it easier for party promises to be turned into governmental policy.

      _____

USING YOUR UNDERSTANDING

1.   Investigate the party system of another Western democratic political system that is of interest to you, such as the United Kingdom. Try to identify the major features of the political parties in the system in terms of the party-in-the-electorate, the party as organization, and the party-in-government. Briefly describe what you found in comparison to the two-party system in the United States. Include a discussion of whether the party system is experiencing realignment, dealignment, or another form of change.

2.   Gerald Pomper's study of party platforms covered the years 1944–1976. Follow up on this study by examining the Republican Party platforms for 1980, 1984, 1988, 2000, and 2004, and the Democratic Party platforms for 1992 and 1996. Make a list of the promises made in the Republican platforms and compare them to the accomplishments of the Reagan, George H.W. Bush, and George W. Bush administrations. Make a list of the promises of the 1992 and 1996 Democratic platform and compare them to the policy initiatives of the Clinton administration. For the party not occupying the presidency, you might compare legislative initiatives by that party in Congress with their party platform. Evaluate the degree to which the parties keep the policy promises they set forth. If possible, look at public opinion polls to see if public opinion supports platform positions on key issues. Develop an analysis of the importance of party platforms in the electoral process and in making public policy.

MULTIPLE CHOICE QUESTIONS

Circle the correct answer:

1. The largest segment of an American political party is described as
   a. the party out of power.
   b. the party in the electorate.
   c. the party in government.
   d. the party volunteers.
   e. the party organization.

2. A political party is best defined as
   a. a group of men and women organized for the sole purpose of influencing public policy.
   b. an organized team of men and women with a political agenda.
   c. any group of men and women with a formal membership and a political or social purpose stated in their by-laws.
   d. a team of men and women seeking control of the governing apparatus by gaining office in a duly constituted election.
   e. a coalition of interests trying to influence government policies for their benefit.

3. Political parties perform all of the following tasks EXCEPT
   a. pick policymakers and run campaigns.
   b. enforce rigid adherence to their policy positions.
   c. advocate public policies.
   d. coordinate policymaking.
   e. give cues to voters.

4. Rational-choice theory asserts that
   a. the parties should not be expected to differentiate themselves in any way.
   b. more extremist party positions give the public a sense that things can really be changed, and usually win elections.
   c. the wise party selects policies in which it truly believes, and gives the voters a chance to vote them up or down on principle.
   d. the wise party selects policies that are widely favored.
   e. None of the above

5. Voting with one party for one office and the other party for another office is known as
   a. ticket splitting.
   b. treason.
   c. party competition.
   d. party identification.
   e. a rational choice.

6. A political party machine is a kind of local party organization that
    a. uses specific and material inducements to win party loyalty and power.
    b. remains strong in most large American cities.
    c. threatens the efficiency of state and national party organizations.
    d. has recently come to depend heavily on ethnic group support.
    e. only appeared after World War II.

7. In closed primaries,
    a. voters may vote for candidates from either party.
    b. voters may choose on election day which party primary they want to participate in.
    c. only voters who have registered in advance with the party can vote.
    d. voters may vote for multiple candidates.
    e. None of the above

8. If you are registered as a Democrat, you can vote in a(n)
    a. Democratic closed primary.
    b. Republican closed primary.
    c. open primary.
    d. blanket primary.
    e. a, c, and d

9. American national parties are best described as
    a. controlled from the bottom (local level) up.
    b. loose aggregations of state parties.
    c. bicameral in nature.
    d. centralized organizations based in Congress.
    e. powerful, centralized organizations based in Washington, D.C.

10. What is the primary duty of the national party chairperson?
    a. Hiring staff
    b. Raising money
    c. Paying bills
    d. Attending to the daily dues of the party
    e. All of the above

11. Every political party depends upon what the text calls a _____ , meaning a set of individuals or groups supporting it.
    a. system of patronage
    b. coalition
    c. set of superdelegates
    d. power base
    e. linkage institution

12. A critical election involves and accelerates a process called
    a. partisan transformation.
    b. electoral examination.
    c. proportional representation.
    d. party realignment.
    e. democratic rejuvenation.

13. The Democratic-Republicans were also known as the
    a. Jeffersonians.
    b. Madisonians.
    c. Whigs.
    d. Federalists.
    e. Hamiltonians.

14. Why did the framers fear a political party system?
    a. They thought that parties would be a forum for corruption and divisiveness.
    b. They were concerned that parties would make government too user friendly for ordinary voters.
    c. They thought that there was room for more than two parties and feared that only two would create a stalemate.
    d. They were concerned that the party system would be used to bring down the new government.
    e. They believed that a two-party system would end up making the country resemble Great Britain too much.

15. Which of the following is TRUE?
    a. Andrew Jackson founded the modern American political party.
    b. Jackson was initially a Democratic-Republican, but his party became known as the Democratic Party soon after he became president.
    c. Jackson's causes included broadening political opportunity for average citizens.
    d. A and b
    e. All of the above

16. The election of 1896 is considered a watershed because it
    a. entrenched western farmers and silverites in the Republican party.
    b. shifted the party coalitions and entrenched the Republicans in power for another generation.
    c. gave Republicans control of the South.
    d. marked the rise of the Populist Party, which dominated American politics until the Depression.
    e. brought the industrial working classes and Wall Street interests together into the Democratic fold.

17. Who was the president who brought together the original New Deal coalition in support of his candidacy?
     a. Woodrow Wilson
     b. Lyndon Johnson
     c. John F. Kennedy
     d. Franklin D. Roosevelt
     e. Herbert Hoover

18. In 1968, the Democratic party was torn apart, leaving the door to the presidency open for Republican Richard Nixon primarily due to
     a. the failure of President Johnson's war on poverty.
     b. the sudden evaporation of the New Deal coalition.
     c. the abandonment of the Democratic party by African Americans.
     d. President Johnson's Vietnam War policies.
     e. the severity of the mid-1960's recession.

19. Party dealignment is symbolized by
     a. the 1992 election of a president and Congress of the same party.
     b. the recent pattern of one-party control.
     c. a renewed commitment to America's two major political parties.
     d. the recent pattern of divided government.
     e. the Republican takeover of Congress in 1994.

20. The "responsible party" model holds that parties should
     a. not use wedge issues that cause the other party's supporters to fight with each other during the campaign.
     b. avoid making promises.
     c. keep to middle-of-the-road positions.
     d. present clear alternatives to voters.
     e. avoid ideological stands.

TRUE/FALSE   QUESTIONS

Circle the correct answer:

1. The party in the electorate is the largest component of an American party. T / F

2. Institutions that translate inputs from the public into outputs from policymakers are called linkage institutions. T / F

3. Rational-choice theory seeks to explain political processes and outcomes as consequences of purposive behavior. T / F

4. The only thing that you have to do to join a political party in the U.S. is to pay a one-time membership fee. T / F

5. Organizationally, state parties are on the upswing throughout the country. T / F

6. Progressive reforms, including the merit system, are partially responsible for the weakening of party machines. T / F

7. Each party holds a national convention every two years to bring delegates together, hear speeches, pass the party platform, attempt to project a certain image, and, during presidential election years, to nominate candidates for president and vice president. T / F

8. Coalition governments are relatively rare in European democracies. T / F

9. Andrew Jackson is often remembered as the founder of the modern political party. T / F

10. The Republican Party emerged as an antislavery party prior to the Civil war. T / F

SHORT ANSWER/SHORT ESSAY QUESTIONS

1. What is rational choice theory? How does it explain the behavior of voters and of political parties?

2. Describe the three major components of an American political party, and what the major tasks of a party are. Why is our political system so reliant on parties to organize public opinion? Explain.

3. What is patronage, and how was it used?

4. What was the New Deal coalition? Who were its leaders? How and why was the New Deal coalition significant?

5. Why have third parties been largely unsuccessful and so short-lived in the U.S.?

ESSAY QUESTIONS

1. Why do some scholars believe that political parties exercise waning influence over American politics? What are the consequences of this waning influence?

2. Evaluate the claim that in a democracy candidates should say what they mean to do if elected and be able to do what they promised once they are elected. To what extent do party promises result in public policy? What changes do the advocates of the "responsible party model" suggest in order to ensure that party promises be turned into public policy?

3. Describe the significance of a critical election, party realignment, and what is meant by a "party era." Do you think 1992 was a critical election? Why, or why not?

4. Some have argued that America's winner-take-all system fails to adequately represent differences of opinion in government. Would you prefer to see proportional representation? What are its strengths and weaknesses? Explain.

5. *Government in America* notes that "the lack of disciplines and cohesive European-style parties in American goes a long way to explain why the scope of governmental activity in the United States is not as broad as it is in other established democracies." Explain what this statement means. Then, evaluate the notion that the U.S.'s two party system limits the demands we can make to increase the scope of government. Is this a good or bad thing and why?

CHAPTER 9

NOMINATIONS AND CAMPAIGNS

CHAPTER OUTLINE

I. Introduction (pp. 277–287)
   A. Campaigning for any major office is a massive undertaking.
   B. Someone somewhere is always running for office in the United States.

II. The Nomination Game (pp. 278–287)
   A. Introduction
      1. A **nomination** is a party's official endorsement of a candidate for office.
      2. **Campaign strategy** is the way in which candidates attempt to manipulate money, media, and momentum to achieve the nomination.
   B. Deciding to Run
   C. Competing for Delegates: The goal of the nomination game is to win the majority of delegates' support at the **national party convention.**
      1. The Caucus Road
         a. A **caucus** is a meeting of state party leaders.
         b. Caucuses usually are organized like a pyramid.
      2. The Primary Road
         a. In **presidential primaries,** voters in a state go to the polls and vote for a candidate or delegates pledged to one.
         b. The **McGovern-Fraser Commission** had a mandate to make Democratic Party conventions more representative.
         c. The proliferation of presidential primaries has transformed politics.
         d. Politicians who are awarded convention seats on the basis of their position are known as **superdelegates.**
         e. More states have moved their primaries up in the calendar in order to capitalize on media attention (**frontloading**).
      3. Evaluating the Primary and Caucus System
         a. Disproportionate attention goes to the early caucuses and primaries.
         b. Prominent politicians find it difficult to take time out from their duties to run.
         c. Money plays too big a role in the caucuses and primaries.
         d. Participation in primaries and caucuses is low and unrepresentative.
         e. The system gives too much power to the media.
   D. The Convention Send-off
      1. Conventions are no longer dramatic; the winner is a foregone conclusion.
      2. Conventions orchestrate a massive send-off for the candidates.
      3. Conventions develop the party's policy positions (**party platform**) and promote representation.

VIII. The Campaign Game (pp. 287–291)
  A. The High-Tech Media Campaign
    1. The Internet and candidate websites have contributed greatly to campaigning and fundraising.
    2. The technique of **direct mail** helps identify potential supporters and contributors.
    3. Candidates use their advertising budget.
    4. Candidates get free attention as newsmakers.
  B. Organizing the Campaign
    1. Get a campaign manager.
    2. Get a fund-raiser.
    3. Get a campaign counsel.
    4. Hire media and campaign consultants.
    5. Assemble a campaign staff.
    6. Plan the logistics.
    7. Get a research staff and policy advisors.
    8. Hire a pollster.
    9. Get a good press secretary.
    10. Establish a Web site.

IV. Money and Campaigning (pp. 292–298)
  A. The Maze of Campaign Finance Reforms
    1. The **Federal Election Campaign Act** was passed in 1974.
      a. It created the **Federal Election Commission (FEC)**.
      b. It created the **Presidential Election Campaign Fund**.
      c. It provided partial public financing for presidential primaries (**matching funds**).
      d. It provided full public financing for major party candidates in the general election.
      e. It required full disclosure.
      f. It limited contributions.
      g. 1979 amendments placed no limits on **soft money.**
      h. The McCain-Feingold Act (2002) banned soft money, increased the amounts individuals could contribute, and barred certain "issue ads."
      i. **527 groups** are not subject to contribution restrictions because they do not directly seek the election of particular candidates.
  B. The Proliferation of **Political Action Committees (PACs)**
  C. Are Campaigns Too Expensive?

V. The Impact of Campaigns (p. 298)
  A. Campaigns have three potential effects: reinforcement, activation, and conversion.
  B. Factors that weaken campaigns' impact on voters include: **selective perception,** party identification, and incumbency.

VI.   Understanding Nominations and Campaigns (pp. 298–300)
    A.   Are Nominations and Campaigns Too Democratic?
    B.   Do Big Campaigns Lead to an Increased Scope of Government?

VII.   Summary (p. 300)

LEARNING OBJECTIVES

After studying Chapter 9, you should be able to:

1.   Explain the nomination process and the role of the national party conventions.

2.   Discuss the role of campaign organizations and the importance of the media in campaigns.

3.   Understand the role of money in campaigns, campaign finance reform, and the impact of political action committees.

4.   Explain the impact of campaigns on the voters.

5.   Understand how campaigns affect democracy, public policy, and the scope of government.

The following exercises will help you meet these objectives:

Objective 1: Explain the nomination process and the role of the national party conventions.

1.   List the three elements needed for success in the nomination game.

    1.

    2.

    3.

2.   Draw a diagram depicting the pyramid structure of the typical state party caucus.

3.   What reforms did the McGovern-Fraser Commission bring to the Democratic Party?

4.   List five criticisms of the primary and caucus systems.

1.

2.

3.

4.

5.

5.   What are the primary functions of the national party conventions?

Objective 2: Discuss the role of campaign organizations and the importance of the media in
 campaigns.

1.   What are the two factors that determine media coverage of a campaign?

1.

2.

2.   Using a rating system of strong, medium, and weak, rate campaign advertisements
        and campaign news coverage in terms of their attention to candidate image, issues,
        and the campaign itself.

	Campaign Advertisements	Campaign News Coverage
Image		
Issues		
Campaign		

3.   List ten things candidates must do to effectively organize their campaigns.

       1.

       2.

       3.

       4.

       5.

       6.

       7.

       8.

       9.

       10.

Objective 3: Understand the role of money in campaigns, campaign finance reform, and the impact of political action committees.

1.   What were the main features of the Federal Election Campaign Act of 1974?

       1.

       2.

       3.

       4.

       5.

       6.

2.   What were the three main provisions of the McCain-Feingold Act (2002)?

       1.

       2.

       3.

3.   Present an argument that political action committees are essential to a successful campaign.

Objective 4: Explain the impact of campaigns on the voters.

    1.   What are the three effects campaigns can have on voters?

        1.

        2.

        3.

    2.   What three factors tend to weaken campaigns' impacts on voters?

        1.

        2.

        3.

Objective 5: Understand how campaigns affect democracy, public policy, and the scope of government.

    1.   What is meant by the "permanent campaign"?

    2.   How might campaigns affect the scope of government?

KEY TERMS

Identify and describe:

nomination

campaign strategy

national party convention

caucus

presidential primaries

McGovern-Fraser Commission

superdelegates

frontloading

national primary

regional primaries

party platform

direct mail

Federal Election Campaign Act

Federal Election Commission (FEC)

Presidential Election Campaign Fund

matching funds

soft money

527 groups

political action committees (PACs)

selective perception

Compare and contrast:

nomination and national party convention

caucus and presidential primaries

McGovern-Fraser Commission and superdelegates

national primary and regional primaries

Federal Election Campaign Act and Federal Election Commission

Presidential Election Campaign Fund and matching funds

Soft money and 527 groups

Name that term:

1. This is the way in which candidates attempt to manipulate resources to achieve their party's nomination.

    _____

2. This is a meeting of state party leaders.

    _____

3. Moving a state primary earlier in the calendar year to take advantage of media attention is known by this term.

    _____

4. This bipartisan body that administers the campaign finance laws.

    _____

5. These party contributions include money raised for voter registration drives and the distribution of campaign material.

    _____

6.   These independent groups seek to influence the political process but are not subject to contribution restrictions.

_____

7.   These organizations must register with the FEC and make meticulous reports about their expenditures.

_____

8.   When people pay most attention to things they already agree with and interpret events according to their own predispositions, it is an example of this.

_____

USING YOUR UNDERSTANDING

1.   Present an analysis of the 2008 presidential campaign in terms of what you have learned in this chapter. In particular, compare the candidates in terms of their campaign organizations, their access to and use of money, their use of the media, and their attention to the issues. Did PAC money make a difference in the campaign? Which candidate received the most PAC money? Did the media treat the candidates differently? Which candidate do you believe was able to use the media most effectively and why? How did the campaign of independent candidates Ralph Nader and Bob Barr compare to that of Barak Obama and John McCain, who had political party organizations behind them?

2.   Find out which political action committees contribute to the member of Congress from your district and the two senators from your state and how much they contribute. Which PACs contributed to the representative's campaign in the 2008 congressional election? Determine what issues these PACs are most concerned with and investigate how your representative and senators voted on policies that would be relevant to the PACs' interests. Make a table or graph to illustrate your findings and use your results as the basis for a discussion of the relationship between members of Congress and Political Action Committees.

MULTIPLE CHOICE QUESTIONS

Circle the correct answer:

1. Anthony King's concept of "running scared" suggests that politicians
   a. do too little governing because they are perpetually campaigning.
   b. do too little campaigning because they are constantly governing.
   c. work constantly to avoid media coverage.
   d. make every effort to avoid public opinion.
   e. Both c and d

2. In most advanced industrialized countries, national campaigns
   a. are even less dignified than in the United States.
   b. occur once every four years.
   c. are limited by law to no more than two months.
   d. are longer than American elections.
   e. occur only once every seven years.

3. The first presidential caucus of the campaign season is traditionally held in
   a. Delaware.
   b. California.
   c. Minnesota.
   d. New Hampshire.
   e. Iowa.

4. Today, most delegates to each major party's national convention are chosen by
   a. state party chairpersons prior to any caucus or presidential primary.
   b. state presidential primaries.
   c. the previous national convention.
   d. state presidential caucuses.
   e. a lottery system.

5. The opening up of the process to choose delegates to the Democratic National Convention in the immediate aftermath of 1968 was spearheaded by
   a. the McGovern-Fraser Commission.
   b. the Kerner Commission.
   c. an act of Congress.
   d. President Johnson.
   e. the Warren Commission.

6. Superdelegates
   a. are special delegates chosen by popular election.
   b. are each able to cast three votes at their national convention rather than the standard one vote.
   c. are delegates uncommitted to a specific candidate.
   d. have helped make the delegation more representative of the population.
   e. have helped restore an element of peer review to the process of choosing a presidential candidate.

7. Which of the following is NOT a criticism of the current system of presidential primaries and caucuses?
   a. Prominent officeholders find it difficult to take time out from their current duties to run.
   b. The media do not have enough of a role in this process.
   c. Too much attention is paid to the early ones.
   d. Money plays too big a role.
   e. Many candidates drop out early before most states have held their primary or caucus.

8. Proponents of a national primary argue that it would do each of the following EXCEPT
   a. bring directness and simplicity to the nomination process.
   b. no longer allow votes in one state to have more political impact than votes in another.
   c. lengthen the time of the campaign.
   d. concentrate media coverage and increase interest and understanding.
   e. increase interest in more states.

9. Over the years, television coverage of national party conventions has
   a. received increasingly high Nielsen ratings.
   b. become more dramatic.
   c. shifted to local affiliate reporters focusing on their state delegations and away from the national network anchors.
   d. been scaled back.
   e. steadily increased.

10. The Federal Election Commission
    a. administers all elections in the United States from school board to president with a staff of 160,000.
    b. tabulates and certifies the votes in all federal elections.
    c. is a bipartisan body responsible for administering campaign finance laws and enforcing compliance with those laws.
    d. is a nonpartisan political organization that has sought for over fifty years to reform campaign financing.
    e. is the Republican Party's watchdog organization, which monitors fundraising and spending by Democratic candidates.

11. In the 1976 case of *Buckley v. Valeo*, the Supreme Court ruled that
    a. the limitation on the amount of money persons could contribute to their own election campaigns violated free speech, and was unconstitutional.
    b. presidential election campaigns could not be paid for by tax dollars.
    c. the forced disclosure of contributions to federal elections violated freedom of association, and was therefore unconstitutional.
    d. the limitation on the amount of money people could contribute to their own election campaigns was not a violation of free speech, and was constitutional.
    e. congressional and state legislative districts must be of equal population and reapportioned every ten years.

12. What does a presidential candidate have to do to qualify for federal matching funds?
    a. Raise $5,000 on their own in at least 20 states.
    b. Raise $50,000 on their own in all states collectively.
    c. Win three primaries.
    d. Win the nomination.
    e. Get 100,000 signatures in their support in at least five states.

13. The McCain-Feingold Act of 2002 did all of the following EXCEPT
    a. barred groups from running "issue ads" within 60 days of a general election if they refer to a federal candidate and are not funded through a PAC.
    b. banned soft money contributions.
    c. increased the amount that individuals could give to candidates from $1,000 to $2,000.
    d. indexed the limit on individual contributions to inflation in future years.
    e. None of the above

14. Soft money consists of money
    a. provided through public financing.
    b. for voter registration drives and campaign material at the grass-roots level.
    c. that is illegally given to a campaign.
    d. that individuals contribute to their own campaign.
    e. given directly to a candidate.

15. In its 2004 ruling the FEC ruled that 527 groups
    a. were subject to strict contribution restrictions.
    b. were not subject to strict contribution restrictions so long as their political messages did not make explicit endorsements of candidates using phrases like "vote for" or "vote against."
    c. were permitted to make explicit endorsements of candidates so long as they were not in the form of negative ads.
    d. Both a and c
    e. Both b and c

16. Critics of the PAC system are concerned that
    a. PACs are not regulated.
    b. they tend to support only Republican candidates.
    c. PACs are too weak and ineffective to contribute to a strong democracy.
    d. only the largest and most powerful interest groups can afford to form PACs.
    e. PACs may control what the electoral winners do once in office.

17. According to Herbert Alexander's "doctrine of sufficiency,"
    a. there is a minimum amount of money that candidates must spend to have a chance at winning.
    b. candidates with large personal fortunes are almost guaranteed victory, unless their opponent is of roughly equal net worth.
    c. in order to win, a candidate must have more money than his or her opponent.
    d. the wealthier candidate always wins.
    e. a candidate's sense of self-worth, not money, is most important to a successful campaign.

18. Campaigns strengthen voter commitment to the usual party or the candidate they previously supported by emphasizing _____ as part of their campaign strategy.
    a. conversion
    b. reinforcement
    c. activation
    d. persuasion
    e. direct mail

19. Which of the following is true of modern campaigns?
    a. They involve much less communication between candidates and voters than America's founders ever imagined.
    b. They involve much more communication between candidates and voters than America's founders ever imagined.
    c. Candidates in modern campaigns make numerous promises during nominations and elections that would have jarred with the founders' notions of the public interest.
    d. Both b and c
    e. All of the above

20. The "candidate-centered age" refers to a system of modern campaigns that allows politicians to
    a. decide on their own to run for office.
    b. raise their own campaign funds.
    c. build their own personal campaign organizations.
    d. make individual promises about what they will do once they are in office.
    e. All of the above

TRUE/FALSE QUESTIONS

Circle the correct answer:

1. Traditionally, Iowa holds the first presidential primary to choose delegates to each party's national conventions. T / F

2. The national party convention functions to select presidential and vice presidential candidates and to write a party platform. T / F

3. Unlike party convention delegates prior to 1968, most of today's delegates to Democratic conventions have few ties to experienced politicians or the party organization. T / F

4. The Democratic Party has been more preoccupied since 1968 with party efficiency and winning elections rather than with broadening representation in the party and opening up its process. T / F

5. The recent tendency of states to hold primaries early in the calendar year in order to capitalize on media attention is called frontloading. T / F

6. Candidates' policy positions receive more media attention than does their campaign strategy. T / F

7. A political party's statement of its goals and policies over the next four years is called the party platform. T / F

8. The Internet has had its greatest impact on campaigns in the area of advertising. T / F

9. The Federal Election Campaign Act of 1974 was extremely effective in limiting the influence of money on campaigns and elections. T / F

10. 527 groups cannot explicitly urge citizens to vote for or against a candidate. T / F

SHORT ANSWER/SHORT ESSAY QUESTIONS

1. Describe the process through which candidates are nominated for the presidency.

2. Why is the New Hampshire presidential primary so important?

3. Compare and contrast a caucus and a primary.

4. What was the purpose of the McGovern-Fraser Commission? What did it accomplish in the Democratic national convention and how?

5. Describe the various staff members necessary for a modern presidential campaign. What do many of these tasks say about the importance of issues as opposed to the importance of image?

ESSAY QUESTIONS

1. For what purpose do America's major parties hold national conventions? How have they changed over the last few decades, and why? Are they still worth holding? Why, or why not? Explain.

2. Describe the significance of money in a modern presidential election campaign. How does the government regulate the fundraising and expenditures of presidential campaigns? Is the government regulation adequate? Explain.

3. What role have 527 groups played in recent elections? Are groups such as MoveOn.org and Swift Boat Veterans for Truth an aid to democracy, or a hindrance to democracy, in this context of campaigns?

4. Describe the three key effects campaigns can have on voters, and note which two of the three are most significant, and why. If you were running a campaign, what would be your emphasis? Why?

5. What does it mean to suggest that modern campaigns promote individualism? Is this a positive or negative feature of our electoral process?

CHAPTER 10

Elections and Voting Behavior

CHAPTER OUTLINE

I.   Introduction (pp. 305-306)
    A.   It is difficult for elections to be a faithful mechanism for expressing the public's desires concerning what government should do.
    B.   Elections socialize and institutionalize political activity and provide regular access to political power, thus establishing **legitimacy.**

II. How American Elections Work (pp. 306–307)
    A.   A **referendum** gives voters the chance to approve or disapprove some legislative act or constitutional amendment.
    B.   **Initiative petitions** enable voters to put proposed legislation on the ballot.

III. A Tale of Three Elections (pp. 307–311)
    A.   1800: The First Electoral Transition of Power
        1.   This campaign focused on state legislatures.
    B.   1896: A Bitter Fight over Economic Interests
        1.   This campaign entrenched Republicans as the majority party.
    C.   2008: An Election about Change

IV. Whether To Vote: A Citizen's First Choice (pp. 312–317)
    A.   **Suffrage** is the legal right to vote.
    B.   Deciding Whether to Vote
        1.   The costs of voting may rationally outweigh the benefits.
        2.   People who see policy differences in the parties are more likely to vote.
        3.   People with a high sense of **political efficacy** are more likely to vote.
        4.   People with a high sense of **civic duty** are more likely to vote.
    C.   Registering to Vote
        1.   **Voter registration** procedures currently differ greatly from state to state.
        2.   The 1993 **Motor Voter Act** requires states to permit people to register at the same time they apply for driver's licenses.
    D.   Who Votes?
        1.   People with a higher education vote more regularly.
        2.   Older people vote more regularly than younger people.
        3.   African Americans and Hispanics vote less regularly.
        4.   Women vote slightly more regularly than men.
        5.   Married people are more likely to vote than nonmarried.
        6.   Government employees vote more regularly.

V.   How Americans Vote: Explaining Citizens' Decisions (pp. 317–321)
     A.   The **mandate theory of elections** suggests that the winner has a mandate to carry out promised policies.
     B.   Party Identification
          This provides a perspective through which voters can view the political world.
     C.   Candidate Evaluations: How Americans see the Candidates
     D.   **Policy voting** occurs when people base their choices in an election on their own issue preferences.

VI. The Last Battle: The **Electoral College** (pp. 322–323)
     A.   The founders created the electoral college so that the president would be chosen by the nation's elite.
     B.   The electoral college introduces a bias into the campaign.

VII. Understanding Elections and Voting Behavior (pp. 323–325)
     A.   Democracy and Elections
          1.   The greater the policy differences between the candidates, the more likely voters will be able to steer government policies by their choices.
          2.   People who feel better off than before will vote for candidates who pledge to continue the status quo; those who feel worse off will vote for the opposition (**retrospective voting**).
     B.   Elections and the Scope of Government

VIII. Summary (pp. 325–326)

LEARNING OBJECTIVES

After studying Chapter 10, you should be able to:

1.   Explain the functions and unique features of American elections.

2.   Describe how American elections have evolved using the presidential elections of 1800, 1896, and 2008 as examples.

3.   Discuss the factors that affect a citizen's choice of whether or not to vote.

4.   Explain how Americans vote and what factors influence how they vote.

5.   Explain how the electoral college works and what biases it can introduce.

6.   Understand how elections affect democracy, public policy, and the scope of government.

The following exercises will help you meet these objectives:

Objective 1: Explain the functions and unique features of American elections.

List three major functions of elections in American society.

1.

2.

3.

2. List the three kinds of elections found in the United States and their purpose.

1.

2.

3.

3. What is the difference between an initiative petition and a referendum?

Objective 2: Describe how American elections have evolved using the presidential elections of 1800, 1896, and 2008.

    1.   Complete the following table on the elections of 1800, 1896, and 2008.

Year	Candidates and Party	WINNER	MAJOR ISSUES	Campaign Style	Significance of Election
1800					
1896					
2008					

    2.   What were the major reasons why people voted for either Barack Obama or John McCain in the 2008 presidential election?

Barack Obama:

John McCain:

Objective 3: Discuss the factors that affect a citizen's choice of whether or not to vote.

    1.   List and explain three major reasons why people might vote.

        1.

        2.

        3.

2.   What is the major provision of the 1993 Motor Voter Act?

3.   List and explain six demographic factors that are related to voter turnout.

   1.

   2.

   3.

   4.

   5.

   6.

Objective 4: Explain how Americans vote and what factors influence how they vote.

   1.   What is meant by the "mandate theory of elections"?

   2.   How has the influence of party identification on voting changed since the 1950s?

   3.   What are the three most important dimensions of candidate image?

      1.

      2.

      3.

   4.   What are the four conditions necessary for true policy voting to take place?

      1.

      2.

3.

4.

Objective 5: Explain how the electoral college works and what biases it can introduce.

    1.   Briefly explain how the electoral college works.

    2.   What are the two reasons why the electoral college is important to presidential elections?

        1.

        2.

Objective 6: Understand how elections affect democracy, public policy, and the scope of government.

    1.   What are the two tasks that elections accomplish, according to democratic theory?

        1.

        2.

    2.   According to the text, what is the clearest way in which elections broadly affect public policy?

    3.   What is retrospective voting?

KEY TERMS

Identify and describe:

legitimacy

referendum

initiative petition

suffrage

political efficacy

civic duty

voter registration

Motor Voter Act

mandate theory of elections

policy voting

electoral college

retrospective voting

Compare and contrast:

initiative petition and referendum

suffrage and voter registration

voter registration and Motor Voter Act

policy differences and civic duty

mandate theory of elections and policy voting

Name that term:

1.   This term is used to describe elections that are almost universally accepted as a fair and free method to select political leaders.

   _____

2.   This enables voters in 23 states to put proposed legislation on the ballot.

   _____

3.   This varies among the states and tends to dampen voter turnout.

   _____

4.   This reflects the belief that one's vote can make a difference.

   _____

5.   Politicians are more attracted to this idea than are political scientists.

   _____

6.   This unique American institution was created by the Constitution.

   _____

7.   This is when voters essentially ask the simple question, "What have you done for me lately?"

_____

USING YOUR UNDERSTANDING

1.   The text points out that the United States has one of the lowest voter turnout rates among all democratic nations. Examine the reasons why voter turnout is so low and outline a comprehensive plan to increase voter turnout in the United States. What policies need to be changed to accomplish this? How might incentives be used to get people to vote? You might want to look at voting laws in other countries with high turnout rates to get ideas. Also include an examination of the Motor Voter Act. Speculate on how the Motor Voter Act might increase participation. What are the main criticisms of the Motor Voter Act? Comment on how your suggestions might be implemented.

2.   Find out about electoral turnout in your state for the 2004 and 2008 elections. How did the participation rates for various population groups (based on race, income, region, etc.) differ? Compare your state's voting rate to the national turnout rate and to that of other states. How well does your state fare? See if you can identify some of the demographic features of your state that might help explain its rate of turnout, such as its size, urbanization, or population composition. How did participation rates differ between 2004 and 2008 and why? How might the voter registration system in your state affect turnout? Briefly describe what you found and suggest ways to improve electoral participation.

MULTIPLE CHOICE QUESTIONS

Circle the correct answer:

1. Which of the following functions do elections LEAST serve?
    a. Selecting public officials
    b. Making and coordinating public policy
    c. Providing regular access to political power
    d. Providing legitimacy to the political system
    e. Connecting citizens to government officials

2. Daniel Smith argues that initiatives typically stem from
    a. broad public demand for the policy.
    b. the actions of a dedicated policy entrepreneur.
    c. the natural emergence of policy issues.
    d. responsive elected officials, working in a coalition.
    e. None of the above

3. Of the following, which is the most direct form of democracy?
   a. Initiative
   b. Referendum
   c. Direct primary
   d. Presidential election
   e. Recall

4. The election of 1800 was
   a. decided by the direct vote of the people.
   b. decided by the Electoral College.
   c. decided by the House of Representatives.
   d. overturned by the Supreme Court.
   e. decided by the full Congress.

5. What was the focus of the election of 1896?
   a. Economics
   b. Slavery
   c. The religious beliefs of Jefferson
   d. World War I
   e. The Great Depression

6. All of the following factors helped catapult Barack Obama to victory in the 2008 presidential election EXCEPT
   a. His perceived experience in foreign policy issues.
   b. The credit crisis that rocked the financial markets in late September.
   c. The intense focus on the economy during the campaign.
   d. The perception that vice presidential candidate Sarah Palin was not qualified to assume the presidency.
   e. The ability of Obama to link McCain to President George W. Bush.

7. Which of the following is TRUE about American elections over the past 100 years?
   a. The suffrage has broadened, and the turnout has increased.
   b. The suffrage has broadened, and the turnout has decreased.
   c. The suffrage has narrowed, and the turnout has increased.
   d. The suffrage has narrowed, and the turnout has decreased.
   e. Suffrage has broadened, but there has been no change in turnout.

8. Which of the following statements about voting is FALSE?
   a. In many cases, your vote will not make a difference to the outcome of the election.
   b. It might not be rational to spend time becoming informed, deciding who to vote for, and turning out on Election Day.
   c. The costs of voting frequently outweigh the benefits of voting.
   d. If there is little difference in the policy positions of the candidates, it is not rational to vote.
   e. None of the above

9. What new way to register to vote was implemented with the passage of the Motor Voter Act?
    a. By checking a box on your driver's license application or renewal form.
    b. After you take driver's education classes.
    c. When you buy or lease a car, by checking off a voter registration form.
    d. In an approved drive-through motor vehicles' bureau.
    e. By filling out a form that is driven to your house.

10. Political efficacy refers to the belief that
    a. the costs of voting outweigh the benefits.
    b. significant policy differences exist between the parties.
    c. one should always support democratic government.
    d. ordinary people can influence the government.
    e. government is very inefficient and needs to be streamlined.

11. Which of the following countries has the lowest voter turnout rate?
    a. Australia
    b. United States
    c. Italy
    d. France
    e. Bulgaria

12. Which of the following characteristics would make one more likely to vote in an election?
    a. Having a college degree
    b. Being a young adult
    c. Having a low income
    d. Being a college student
    e. Being a welfare recipient

13. The mandate theory of elections is the idea that
    a. a candidate must get at least sixty percent of the vote to win.
    b. a candidate must get a majority of the votes cast (fifty percent plus one) in order to take office.
    c. the election winner has authorization from the voters to carry out his or her promised policies.
    d. in order to improve turnout rates in the United States, voting must be made a legal requirement of all citizens, with the failure to vote resulting in a small fine.
    e. a candidate must get at least 75 percent of the vote to win.

14. Which of these is the least important dimension of a candidate's image?
    a. Intelligence
    b. Integrity
    c. Reliability
    d. Competence
    e. Experience

15. Research on voting behavior has shown that
    a. policy voting has become somewhat easier than in the past.
    b. a candidate's image is not as important today as it was in the past.
    c. Americans tend to identify with the underdog.
    d. party identification has become more important in voting decisions.
    e. policy voting has become harder than in the past.

16. Studies have shown that during the 1960s and 1970s,
    a. voting according to political party identification increased.
    b. Democrats voted along party lines more than Republicans.
    c. the hold of the parties on voters eroded substantially.
    d. political party identification no longer affected voting behavior.
    e. large numbers of people who had been eligible to vote but never voted surged into the electorate.

17. The "electors" in the Electoral College are
    a. the members of Congress from each state, who vote strictly according to who won the majority of their state's votes.
    b. the members of the House from each state, who vote strictly according to who won the majority of their district's votes.
    c. selected by state parties, usually as a reward for faithful service to the party over the years.
    d. a bipartisan group of political scientists, public officials, jurists, and other respected individuals chosen by the governor of each state.
    e. selected by state legislatures well in advance of the presidential election, and each elector votes his or her own conscience as to who would be the best president.

18. Retrospective voting refers to voting for
    a. a candidate who promises to continue policies that have made you feel better off.
    b. a candidate because of his or her past stands on the issues.
    c. the same party and candidates election after election.
    d. different parties and candidates election after election.
    e. candidates for nostalgic reasons because they promise to return the country to some golden age in its past.

19. While the threat of electoral punishment constrains policymakers, it also helps to increase generalized support for
    a. the private sector.
    b. individualistic, rather than, collective policy solutions.
    c. government and its powers.
    d. incumbents who have done a good job.
    e. unelected government officials in the bureaucracy.

20. Individuals who believe that they can influence government are also more likely to believe
    a. that government should have more power.
    b. that government should be cut back.
    c. that the president should have more power.
    d. that the courts should be a much smaller part of the governmental system.
    e. that elections should be held more often.

TRUE/FALSE QUESTIONS

Circle the correct answer:

1. California's Proposition 13 is an example of an initiative petition. T / F

2. Nearly 80 percent of the voting eligible population voted in the election of 1896. T / F

3. Barack Obama was relatively unknown when he announced his presidential candidacy in 2007 and had virtually no national constituency. T / F

4. Rational people might decide that the costs of voting outweigh the benefits. T / F

5. The Motor Voter Act made voter registration easier. T / F

6. Less than 30 percent of the population votes. T / F

7. Single people are more likely to vote than are married people. T / F

8. It is possible to manipulate a candidate's appearance in a way that affect's voters. T / F

9. State parties are responsible for choosing their slate of electors. T / F

10. The president and vice president are selected by the American people. T / F

SHORT ANSWER/SHORT ESSAY QUESTIONS

1. Explain the difference between an initiative petition and a referendum?

2. Why, according to Anthony Downs, would an individual decide that it was rational to vote?

3. Explain and evaluate the mandate theory of elections.

4. Compare and contrast voting behavior between 1960 and 2008, paying particular attention to the role of religion, race, gender, age, and education.

5. Why have young people been among the strongest supporters of third party candidates?

ESSAY QUESTIONS

1. Why is electoral legitimacy such an important aspect of America's political system? Is this sense of legitimacy deserved, in your opinion? If our elections are accepted as legitimate, why don't more people vote? Explain.

2. Briefly describe the major issues and events of the elections of 1800, 1896, and 2008. How engaged was the American public in each of these elections? How might differences in turnout across these elections be explained?

3. How does the Electoral College system work? Do you prefer it to direct popular election? Who serves in this college? Describe the outcome of the 2000 presidential campaign. Who objected? Did it threaten the legitimacy of our political system?

4. What are the two major tasks accomplished by elections according to democratic theory? Why is it often difficult for voters to vote based on a candidate's public policy preferences? Does this weaken democracy? Explain.

5. What are the pros and cons of registering and voting by email? Should we move to some form of online or email based voting? Why or why not?

CHAPTER 11

INTEREST GROUPS

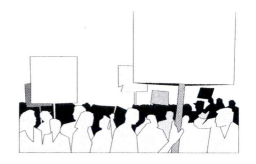

CHAPTER OUTLINE

I.   Introduction (pp. 331–332)
   A.   The worst and oldest stereotype of a lobbyist is of someone who bribes a lawmaker.
   B.   An incredible array of interest make their voices heard in Washington.
   C.   Although turnout in elections has declined since 1960, participation in interest groups has mushroomed.

II.   The Role of Interest Groups (p. 333)
   A.   An **interest group** is an organization of people with similar policy goals who enter the political process to try to achieve those aims.
   B.   Interest groups are often policy specialists, whereas parties are policy generalists.

III.   Theories of Interest Group Politics (pp. 333–336)
   A.   Pluralism and Group Theory
      1.   **Pluralist theory** argues that interest group activity brings representation to all.
      2.   The group theory of politics contains several arguments.
         a.   Groups provide a key link between people and government.
         b.   Groups compete.
         c.   No one group is likely to become too dominant.
         d.   Groups usually play by the "rules of the game."
         e.   Groups weak in one resource can use another.
   B.   Elites and the Denial of Pluralism
      1.   **Elite theory** argues that a few groups, primarily the wealthy, have most of the power.
      2.   Groups are extremely unequal in power.
      3.   Awesome power is controlled by the largest corporations.
      4.   The power of a few is fortified by a system of interlocking directorates.
      5.   Corporate elites prevail when it comes to the big decisions.
   C.   Hyperpluralism and Interest Group Liberalism
      1.   **Hyperpluralist theory** asserts that too many groups are getting too much of what they want, resulting in a government policy that is often contradictory and lacking in direction.
      2.   The phrase "interest group liberalism" refers to government's excessive deference to groups.
         a.   Groups have become too powerful in the political process as government tries to aid every conceivable interest.
         b.   Interest group liberalism is aggravated by numerous **subgovernments.**

173

        c.   Trying to please every group results in contradictory and confusing policy.

IV.   What Makes an Interest Group Successful? (pp. 336–341)

    A.   The Surprising Ineffectiveness of Large Groups

        1.   A **potential group** is composed of all people who might be group members because they share some common interest.

        2.   An **actual group** is composed of those in the potential group who choose to join.

        3.   A **collective good** is something of value that cannot be withheld from a potential group member.

        4.   The **free-rider problem** occurs when members of the potential group share in benefits that members of the actual group work to secure.

        5.   **Olson's law of large groups** states that the larger the group, the further it will fall short of providing an optimal amount of a collective good.

        6.   **Selective benefits** are goods that a group can restrict to those who pay their yearly dues.

    B.   Intensity

        1.   Intensity is a psychological advantage that can be enjoyed by small and large groups alike.

        2.   A **single-issue group** is a group that has a narrow interest, dislikes compromise, and single-mindedly pursues its goal.

    C.   Financial Resources

V.   The Interest Group Explosion (pp. 341–342)

    A.   The number of interest groups in the United States has been increasingly rapidly over the past several decades.

    B.   Technology has contributed to the growth in the number of interest groups.

VI.   How Groups Try To Shape Policy (pp. 342–348)

    A.   Lobbying

        1.   **Lobbying** is a communication, by someone other than a citizen acting on his or her own behalf, directed to a governmental decision-maker with the hope of influencing his or her decision.

        2.   Lobbyists can help a member of Congress.
            They are an important source of information.
            They can help politicians with political strategy.
            They can help formulate campaign strategy.
            They are a source of ideas and innovations.

    B.   Electioneering

        1.   **Electioneering** consists of aiding candidates financially and getting group members out to support them.

        2.   **Political Action Committees (PACs)** provide a means for groups to participate in electioneering.

C. Litigation
1. ***Amicus curiae* briefs** consist of written arguments submitted to the courts in support of one side of a case.
2. **Class action lawsuits** enable a group of similarly situated plaintiffs to combine similar grievances into a single suit.
D. Going Public
1. Interest groups appeal to the public for support.

VII. Types of Interest Groups (pp. 348–355)
A. Economic Interests
1. Labor
a. The **union shop** requires new employees to join the union representing them.
b. **Right-to-work laws** outlaw union membership as a condition of employment.
2. Business
B. Environmental Interests
C. Equality Interests
D. Consumers and Public Interest Lobbies
1. **Public interest lobbies** are organizations that seek a collective good.
2. The consumer movement was spurred by the efforts of Ralph Nader.

VIII. Understanding Interest Groups (pp. 355–356)
A. Interest Groups and Democracy
B. Interest Groups and the Scope of Government

IX. Summary (p. 357)

LEARNING OBJECTIVES

After studying Chapter 11, you should be able to:

1. Define interest groups and distinguish them from political parties.

2. Compare and contrast the pluralist, elite, and hyperpluralist theories of interest groups.

3. Explain what makes an interest group successful and why small groups have an advantage over large groups.

4. Identify and describe the strategies that groups use to shape public policy.

5. Describe some of the many types of groups in the American political system.

6. Evaluate interest groups in terms of their influence on democracy and the scope of government.

The following exercises will help you meet these objectives:

Objective 1: Define interest groups and distinguish them from political parties.

1.   Provide a definition of the term "interest group."

2.   Name two factors that distinguish interest groups from political parties.

    1.

    2.

Objective 2: Compare and contrast the pluralist, elite, and hyperpluralist theories of interest groups.

1.   Complete the following table on the theories of interest group politics.

Theory	Definition	Role of Groups	Who Holds Power	Group Impact on Public Policy
Pluralist Theory				
Elite Theory				
Hyper-pluralist Theory				

2.   List five essential arguments of the group theory of politics.

　　　1.

　　　2.

　　　3.

　　　4.

　　　5.

3.   List four major points made by the elitist view of the interest group system.

　　　1.

　　　2.

　　　3.

　　　4.

4.   List the three major points of the hyperpluralist position on group politics.

　　　1.

　　　2.

　　　3.

Objective 3: Explain what makes a group successful and why small groups have an advantage over large groups.

    1.   What is the difference between a potential group and an actual group?

    2.   What is Olson's law of large groups?

    3.   Define the term single-issue group and give an example.

Objective 4: Identify and describe the strategies that groups use to shape public policy.

    1.   List the four general strategies used by interest groups to shape public policy.

        1.

        2.

        3.

        4.

    2.   What are the two basic types of lobbyists?

        1.

        2.

3.   List four important ways lobbyists can help a member of Congress.

        1.

        2.

        3.

        4.

4.   What are the five most common answers from PAC directors as to why they give money to certain candidates?

        1.

        2.

        3.

        4.

        5.

5.   What is an *amicus curiae* brief?

Objective 5: Describe some of the many types of groups in the American political system.

        1.   What was the main purpose of the Taft-Hartley Act?

2.   List three issues that trade and product associations seek when lobbying Capitol Hill.

       1.

       2.

       3.

3.   List three items environmental groups have promoted and three items they have opposed.

       Promoted:

       1.

       2.

       3.

       Opposed:

       1.

       2.

       3.

4.   Name two important organizations involved in promoting equality and summarize their major goals.

       1.

       2.

5.   What is meant by a public interest lobby?

Objective 6: Evaluate interest groups in terms of their influence on democracy and the scope of government.

    1.   Summarize the pluralist, elitist, and hyperpluralist perspectives on interest groups and democracy.

        1. Pluralist:

        2. Elitist:

        3. Hyperpluralist:

    2.   How do interest groups affect the scope of government?

KEY TERMS

Identify and describe:

interest group

pluralist theory

elite theory

hyperpluralist theory

subgovernments

potential group

actual group

collective good

free-rider problem

Olson's law of large groups

selective benefits

single-issue group

lobbying

electioneering

political action committees (PACs)

amicus curiae briefs

class action lawsuits

union shop

right-to-work laws

public interest lobbies

Compare and contrast:

pluralist theory, elite theory, and hyperpluralist theory

hyperpluralist theory and subgovernments

potential group and actual group

collective good and free-rider problem

Olson's law of large groups and selective benefits

lobbying and electioneering

electioneering and political action committees

amicus curiae briefs and class action lawsuits

union shop and right-to-work laws

Name that term:

1. This is an organization of people with similar policy goals entering the political process to try to achieve those goals.

   _____

2. These are also known as iron triangles.

   _____

3. There are usually more members in this group than in the actual group.

   _____

4. This occurs when it is easier to not join a group because you will receive the benefits anyway.

   _____

5. This states that, "the larger the group, the further it will fall short of providing an optimal amount of a collective good."

   _____

6. People in this group tend to dislike compromise and single-mindedly pursue their goal.

   _____

7. In recent years, these have provided a means for groups to participate in electioneering more than ever before.

   _____

8. This enables a group of similarly situated plaintiffs to combine similar grievances into a single suit.

   _____

9. These organizations seek a collective good that will not selectively benefit the membership of the organization.

   _____

USING YOUR UNDERSTANDING

1. Investigate an interest group about which you are curious. Contact the group to see if they can provide information on the group and its policy goals. Find out how the group's actual membership compares to its potential membership. Try to identify the strategies that the group uses in efforts to achieve its policy goals. Briefly describe what you found in terms of how well the group is achieving its goals and forging a link between people and policy.

2. Using newspapers or newsmagazines, collect some current examples of group involvement in the policy process. Try to find examples of various types of groups — groups in different policy arenas, public interest lobbies, and single-issue groups. Analyze each example in terms of the policymaking area in which group activity was focused (e.g., electoral, legislative, administrative, or judicial), strategies used by the group to affect policy, and the degree to which the group was successful in achieving its policy goals. Discuss whether or not your findings support the interpretation of groups provided by pluralist theory, elite theory, and hyperpluralist theory.

MULTIPLE CHOICE QUESTIONS

Circle the correct answer:

1. An organization of people with similar policy goals entering the political process to try to achieve those aims is called

    a. a political party.
    b. a political action committee.
    c. an interest group.
    d. a collective.
    e. a political corporation.

2. The successes of civil rights and women's rights groups in redirecting the course of public policy, once they were organized, is pointed to as evidence to support the _____ theory that American politics is open and not a problem.

    a. pluralist
    b. hyperpluralist
    c. elite
    d. hyperelitist
    e. free market

3. _____ theorists are impressed by how insignificant most organized interest groups are.

    a. Pluralist
    b. Hyperpluralist
    c. Elitist
    d. Pluralist and hyperpluralist
    e. Deconstruction

4. Interest group liberalism is promoted through networks of

    a. ideologically liberal interest groups and not conservative groups.
    b. one group winning and another losing in the competition for government action or funding.
    c. subgovernments.
    d. hyperpluralists.
    e. All of the above

5. The idea that too many groups are getting too much of what they want is associated with

    a. elite theory.
    b. pluralist theory.
    c. hyperpluralist theory.
    d. democratic theory.
    e. proliferation theory.

6. Which of the following ideas is NOT associated with hyperpluralism?

    a. Groups have become too powerful in the political process.
    b. Interest group liberalism is aggravated by numerous subgovernments.
    c. Trying to please every group results in contradictory and confusing policy.
    d. Political power is highly concentrated.
    e. The dominance of an economic elite.

7. E. E. Schattsneider's remark that "pressure politics is essentially the politics of small groups...pressure tactics are not remarkably successful in mobilizing general interests," suggests that

    a. small groups have organizational advantage.
    b. large groups have organizational advantage.
    c. interest groups have organizational advantage over elites.
    d. elites have organizational advantage over interest groups.
    e. Both b and c

8. According to Olson's law of large groups,
   a. the larger the group, the further it will fall short of providing an optimal amount of a collective good.
   b. the smaller the group, the further it will fall short of providing an optimal amount of a collective good.
   c. the more levels of authority within a group, the more faith its members will have in it.
   d. the more levels of authority within a group, the less faith its members will have in it.
   e. the larger the group, the more likely it is to win.

9. Which of the following groups has the largest potential membership?
   a. National Association for the Advancement of Colored People
   b. National Organization for Women
   c. American Medical Association
   d. Air Transport Association of America
   e. American Political Science Association

10. An example of a collective good is
    a. food.
    b. employment.
    c. clean air.
    d. housing.
    e. All of the above

11. Selective benefits refer to
    a. goods that the government distributes to interest groups.
    b. goods that interest groups distribute to the government
    c. goods that a group can restrict to those who pay membership dues or otherwise join an organization.
    d. goods that interest groups distribute to the wider society.
    e. goods, such as membership fees, that individual members distribute to interest groups.

12. _____ is a communication by someone other than a citizen acting on his or her own behalf, directed to a government decision maker, particularly in the legislative and executive branch, with the hope of influencing his or her decision.
    a. Electioneering
    b. An *amicus curiae* brief
    c. Lobbying
    d. Litigation
    e. Campaigning

13. The text identifies two types of lobbyists,
    a. full-time employees and consultants.
    b. policy experts and legal specialists.
    c. attorneys and non-attorneys.
    d. those based in Washington, D.C., and those based elsewhere.
    e. "old school" and "modern style" lobbyists.

14. Groups that engage in electioneering
    a. seek to mobilize group members in support of a candidate.
    b. aid candidates financially.
    c. Create an iron triangle.
    d. All of the above
    e. Both a and b

15. Most PAC money goes overwhelmingly to incumbents because incumbents
    a. need more money due to the restraints of being in office.
    b. have already been "bought off" by interest groups.
    c. have already become friends and supporters of lobbyists.
    d. are the most likely to be able to return the investment.
    e. have the need for large amounts of money to maintain themselves in power.

16. In 1977, flight attendants won a(n) _____ against the airline industry's regulation that all stewardesses had to be unmarried.
    a. *amicus curiae* brief
    b. writ of habeas corpus
    c. bill of attainder
    d. class action lawsuit
    e. administrative appeal

17. Which of the following statements about interest groups going public is FALSE?
    a. Interest groups carefully cultivate their public images.
    b. Interest groups market not only their stand on issues but their reputations as well.
    c. More and more organizations have launched expensive public relations efforts.
    d. The public relations of most groups tend to be characterized by hard sell and bias.
    e. Both a and c

18. Which of the following methods for influencing members of Congress is NOT legal?
    a. Lobbyists can give information to members of Congress.
    b. Lobbyists can help politicians with political strategy for getting legislation through.
    c. Lobbyists can help formulate campaign strategies and get the group's members behind a politician's reelection campaign.
    d. Lobbyists can be a source of ideas and innovation.
    e. All of the answers above are ways that lobbyists can legally influence members of Congress.

19. The Taft-Hartley Act of 1947
    a. banned soft money in campaigns.
    b. permitted states to adopt right-to-work laws.
    c. dealt a severe blow to the labor movement.
    d. reenergized the labor movement.
    e. Both b and c

20. Environmental groups have been most successful at
    a. stopping strip mining.
    b. halting the trans-Alaskan pipeline.
    c. thwarting the expansion of the nuclear power industry.
    d. stopping the development of commercial supersonic aircraft.
    e. protecting the reefer toad and other endangered species.

TRUE/FALSE QUESTIONS

Circle the correct answer:

1. A key difference between interest groups and political parties is that interest groups are policy generalists. T / F

2. A central assumption in pluralist theory is that free and open competition prevents any single group from becoming too dominant. T / F

3. The goal of a subgoverment is to protect self-interest. T / F

4. People who might be interest group members because they share some common interest are called a potential group. T / F

5. Between 1959 and 1995, the number and diversity of interest groups has declined. T / F

6. Free-riding is an increasingly popular litigation strategy used by interest groups. T / F

7. *Amicus curiae* brief are briefs submitted by a "friend of the court," for the purpose of influencing the court's decisions. T / F

8. The union shop is a provision found in some collective bargaining agreements that requires all employees of a business to join the union as a condition of employment. T / F

9. The National Organization for Women is an example of a consumer lobby. T / F

10. Interest group politics has the effect of reducing the scope of government. T / F

SHORT ANSWER/SHORT ESSAY QUESTIONS

1. Compare and contrast how a pluralist, elitist, and hyperpluralist would describe the most significant features of the interest group system today.

2. What are subgovernments? Why are they important?

3. What is a selective benefit? Provide examples of selective benefits and their use in the interest group system.

4. What is lobbying?

5. What does it mean when interest groups "go public"? Why is "going public" a strategy that interest groups pursue?

ESSAY QUESTIONS

1. Define interest groups. What do Americans generally feel about interest groups? What are some of the common characteristics of groups today? How do interest groups in the United States differ from groups in other democracies?

2. What is Olson's law of large groups, and how does it pertain to the power of various interest groups in American politics? How does the free-rider problem fit into Olson's scheme? Does Olson's law seem correct to you? Explain.

3. How can interest groups use litigation to achieve their goals? Why has litigation been a particularly powerful tool for environmental groups? Is this an outlet that ought to be encouraged within our system? Explain.

4. What was Madison's solution to the problem of factions? Was Madison's solution adequate? Why or why not?

5. Evaluate the extent to which the U.S. political system provides for the representation of all groups seeking to influence policymaking.

CHAPTER 12

Congress

CHAPTER OUTLINE

I. Politics in Action: Governing in Congress (pp. 363–364)
   - A. Congress is the central policymaking branch and the principal representative branch.
   - B. Congress's tasks become more difficult each year.

II. The Representatives and Senators (pp. 364–367)
   - A. The Job
   - B. The Members
   - C. Why Aren't There More Women in Congress?

III. Congressional Elections (pp. 367–374)
   - A. Who Wins Elections?
     1. **Incumbents** are individuals who already hold office.
     2. Incumbents usually win.
   - B. The Advantages of Incumbents
     1. Advertising
     2. Credit Claiming
        a. **Casework** is helping constituents as individuals.
        b. The **pork barrel** is the mighty list of federal projects, grants, and contracts available to cities, businesses, colleges, and institutions.
     3. Position-Taking
     4. Weak Opponents
     5. Campaign Spending
   - C. The Role of Party Identification
   - D. Defeating Incumbents
   - E. Open Seats
   - F. Stability and Change

IV. How Congress Is Organized to Make Policy (pp. 374–385)
   - A. American Bicameralism
     1. A **bicameral legislature** is a legislature divided into two houses.
     2. The House
        a. The House is more institutionalized and less anarchic than the Senate.
        b. The **House Rules Committee** reviews most bills coming from a House committee before they go to the full House.
     3. The Senate
        a. The Senate is less disciplined and centralized than the House.

   b. **Filibusters** allow unlimited debate in the Senate until a vote for cloture halts a filibuster.

B. Congressional Leadership

 1. The House

   a. The **Speaker of the House** is the most important leadership position in the House.

   b. The **majority leader** is responsible for scheduling bills and rounding up votes on behalf of the party.

   c. The party **whips** carry the word to party troops and help round up votes on behalf of the party.

   d. The **minority leader** is responsible for party cohesion among the minority party members.

 2. The Senate

   a. The vice president of the United States is the president of the Senate.

   b. Power is widely dispersed in the Senate.

 3. Congressional Leadership in Perspective

C. The Committees and Subcommittees

 1. Types of committees

   a. **Standing committees** are formed to handle bills in different policy areas.

   b. **Joint committees** exist in a few policy areas and are composed of both House and Senate members.

   c. **Conference committees** are formed when the Senate and House pass a particular bill in different forms.

   d. **Select committees** are appointed for a specific purpose.

 2. The Committees at Work: Legislation and Oversight

   a. All bills go though a committee that has considerable power over the fate of the bill.

   b. **Legislative oversight** is the process of monitoring the bureaucracy and its administration of policy, usually handled through hearings.

 3. Getting on a Committee

 4. Getting Ahead on the Committee: Chairs and the Seniority System

   a. **Committee chairs** are the most important influencers of the committee agenda.

   b. The **seniority system** is the general rule for selecting chairs, but there are exceptions.

D. Caucuses: The Informal Organization of Congress

 1. A **caucus** is a grouping of members of Congress who share some interest or characteristic.

 2. The explosion of caucuses has made the representation of interests in Congress a more direct process.

E. Congressional Staff

 1. Personal Staff

 2. Committee Staff

LEARNING OBJECTIVES

After studying Chapter 12, you should be able to:

1. Describe the characteristics of our senators and representatives, and the nature of their jobs.

2. Explain what factors have the greatest influence in congressional elections.

3. Explain the structure of power and leadership in the United States Congress, and the role of committees.

4. Identify what members of Congress do and discuss the congressional process and the many influences on legislative decision making.

5. Evaluate Congress in terms of American democracy and the scope of government.

The following exercises will help you meet these objectives:

Objective 1: Describe the characteristics of our senators and representatives, and the nature of their jobs.

    1.   List seven perks members of Congress receive.

            1.

            2.

            3.

            4.

            5.

            6.

            7.

    2.   Describe a "typical" member of Congress in terms of the following categories.

            Sex:

            Race:

            Age:

            Religion:

            Prior Occupation:

            Wealth:

    3.   What is the difference between descriptive and substantive representation?

            Descriptive:

            Substantive:

4.   Give two reasons why women are less likely to run for Congress than men.

        1.

        2.

Objective 2:   Explain what factors have the greatest influence in congressional elections.

        1.   List and explain five advantages incumbents have over their opponents in congressional elections.

                1.

                2.

                3.

                4.

                5.

        2.   What is the difference between casework and pork barrel?

                Casework:

                Pork barrel:

        3.   What are the main criticisms of political action committees?

        4.   List and explain three ways that an incumbent might be defeated.

                1.
                2.
                3.

5. List three criticisms of term limitations.

1.

2.

3.

Objective 3: Explain the structure of power and leadership in the United States Congress, and the role of committees.

1. What are the main functions of the House Rules Committee?

2. List four formal powers of the Speaker of the House.

1.

2.

3.

4.

3. List the four types of congressional committees.

1.

2.

3.

4.

4. What is legislative oversight?

5. How does the seniority system work?

6. What is the difference between the personal staff and the committee staff?

7. List three congressional staff agencies.

   1.

   2.

   3.

Objective 4: Identify what members of Congress do and discuss the congressional process and the many influences on legislative decision making.

   1. Draw a diagram of how a bill becomes a law.

   2. List the ten times a president must usually win in order to hope for final passage of his or her proposed legislation.

      1.

      2.

      3.

      4.

      5.

6.

7.

8.

9.

10.

3.   Give two reasons why the congressional parties have become more ideologically polarized.

1.

2.

4.   What is the difference between trustees, instructed delegates, and politicos?

Trustees:

Instructed Delegates:

Politicos:

5.   List three ways Congress can frustrate the activities of lobbyists.

1.

2.

3.

Objective 5: Evaluate Congress in terms of American democracy and the scope of government.

1. Present the arguments of supporters and critics on the effectiveness of Congress.

   Supporters:

   Critics:

2. How does the organization of Congress contribute to the expanding scope of government?

KEY TERMS

Identify and describe:

incumbents

casework

pork barrel

bicameral legislature

House Rules Committee

filibuster

Speaker of the House

majority leader

whips

minority leader

standing committees

joint committees

conference committees

select committees

legislative oversight

committee chairs

seniority system

caucus

bill

Compare and contrast:

casework and pork barrel

majority leader, minority leader, and whips

standing committees and select committees

joint committees and conference committees

committee chairs and seniority system

Name that term:

1. They usually win congressional elections.

    _____

2. This describes the two house structure of Congress.

    _____

3. This is unlimited debate in the U.S. Senate.

    _____

4. This group reviews most of the bills coming from a House committee before they go to the full House.

    _____

5. He or she exercises substantial control over which bills get assigned to which committees in the House.

    _____

6.   This monitoring process is handled mainly through congressional hearings.

     _____

7.   This is a grouping of members of Congress sharing some interest.

     _____

8.   This is a proposed law, drafted in precise, legal language.

     _____

USING YOUR UNDERSTANDING

1.   Investigate one or more of the members of Congress from your state or congressional district. Find out about their membership on congressional committees and their leadership positions. Also find out whether or not one of your members might be considered a policy entrepreneur and why. See how well your representatives are doing in the media, and whether or not they have achieved a reputation for servicing their constituency and representing it adequately in Washington. Do your representatives tend to act as trustees, delegates, or politicos on particular issues? Profile your representatives or senators in terms of how well they seem to be performing their many duties.

2.   Study the legislative history of a particular law in a particular policy area. Trace the law from its original sources to its enactment. Try to find out when and where the bill originated, where its support came from (the president, interest groups, etc.), how it was altered by congressional committees, who voted for it, and whether or not the president actually signed it into law. Assess how long the process took from beginning to end and how much the law changed during the process. How did the final product compare with the original intent? Evaluate the legislative process in terms of this particular law and your perspective on how the system works.

MULTIPLE CHOICE QUESTIONS

Circle the correct answer:

1. The United States House of Representatives has _____ members.
   a. 638
   b. 100
   c. 435
   d. 80
   e. 535

2. The Constitution specifies that members of the House must be _____ years of age; senators must be_____ years of age.
   a. 25; 35
   b. 35; 45
   c. 18; 25
   d. 30; 50
   e. 25; 30

3. Descriptive representation refers to
   a. representing the interests of groups.
   b. serving constituents through pork barrel projects.
   c. representing constituents by mirroring their personal, politically relevant characteristics.
   d. living in the geographical area of one's constituents.
   e. All of the above

4. Which of the following statements about Political Action Committees (PACs) is FALSE?
   a. PACs contribute about one-fourth of the funds raised by candidates for Congress.
   b. PACs sometimes make contributions after an election.
   c. Challengers receive more PAC money than incumbents.
   d. PACs make contributions to candidates because they want access to policymakers.
   e. None of the above

5. Which of the following is NOT one of the three primary activities that members of Congress engage in to increase the probability of their reelection?
   a. Advertising
   b. Credit claiming
   c. Position taking
   d. Oversight
   e. None of the above; oversight is a form of position taking.

6. Members of Congress use their virtually unlimited franking privileges to
    a. pay staff salaries.
    b. travel to their home states and districts.
    c. hire interns.
    d. communicate with constituents.
    e. get research services from the Library of Congress.

7. Federal grants and contracts that members of Congress try to obtain for their constituents are collectively referred to as
    a. pork barrel.
    b. casework.
    c. public service.
    d. perquisites.
    e. affirmative action.

8. In *U.S. Term Limits, Inc. et. al. v. Thonrton et. al.,* the Supreme Court ruled that
    a. state-imposed term limits were constitutional.
    b. state-imposed term limits were unconstitutional.
    c. states were required to limit the terms of members of Congress.
    d. state-imposed term limits were constitutional, but only if they permitted members of Congress to serve at least three consecutive terms.
    e. state-imposed term limits were constitutional, but only if they permitted members of Congress to serve at least four consecutive terms.

9. A bicameral legislature is one that
    a. uses committees.
    b. has two houses.
    c. is elected.
    d. holds biannual sessions.
    e. is reelected every two years.

10. Articles of impeachment must be passed by
    a. either the House or the Senate.
    b. both the House and the Senate.
    c. the Senate.
    d. the House.
    e. the Supreme Court.

11. Setting the legislative agenda in the Senate is the responsibility of
    a. the Rules committee.
    b. the president of the Senate.
    c. party leaders.
    d. the minority leader.
    e. the Speaker.

12. What is the vice president's only constitutionally defined job?
    a. President of the Senate
    b. Majority leader
    c. Party whip
    d. Minority leader
    e. Speaker of the House

13. Which of the following is an example of a House standing committee?
    a. Agriculture
    b. Armed Services
    c. Judiciary
    d. Ways and Means
    e. All of the above

14. Members of Congress seek committees that will help them achieve each of the following goals EXCEPT
    a. reelection.
    b. influence in Congress.
    c. a salary increase.
    d. opportunities to make policy in areas they think are important.
    e. opportunities to make policy in areas important to their constituents.

15. Congressional reforms of the 1970s
    a. professionalized the operation of Congress and made it much more efficient.
    b. decentralized power and democratized Congress.
    c. were aimed at rooting out scandal and corruption.
    d. ended the two-party monopoly of Congress and brought new parties into Congress.
    e. All of the above

16. Personal staff help members of Congress with
    a. constituent problems.
    b. drafting legislation.
    c. negotiating agreements.
    d. All of the above
    e. None of the above

17. The Government Accountability Office (GAO)
    a. performs oversight functions by reviewing the activities of the executive branch to ensure it is complying with congressional intent.
    b. sets government standards for accounting, provides legal opinions, and settles claims against the government.
    c. analyzes the president's budget and makes economic projections about the performance of the economy.
    d. Both a and b
    e. All of the above

18. Successful presidential leadership of Congress requires
    a. Congress and the president to belong to the same political party.
    b. the president to act as a facilitator, working at the margins of coalition building.
    c. a powerful president able to convince members of Congress to follow his policy program.
    d. presidents to successfully lobby members of Congress to vote for the president's program.
    e. strict control over the president's party members.

19. When voting on labor issues,
    a. Democrats lean toward the side of unions.
    b. Republicans lean toward the side of unions.
    c. Democrats lean toward the side of business.
    d. Republicans lean toward the side of business.
    e. Both a and d

20. The English politician and philosopher Edmund Burke favored the concept of legislators as _____, using their best judgment to make policy in the interests of the people.
    a. constituent robots
    b. trustees
    c. instructed delegates
    d. politicos
    e. judges

TRUE/FALSE QUESTIONS

Circle the correct answer:

1. The typical member of the House of Representatives serves on six committees and subcommittees; the typical senator is a member of ten committees. T / F

2. There are 535 members of Congress. T / F

3. House incumbents tend to be more vulnerable in election contests than Senate incumbents. T / F

4. Helping a constituent obtain a Social Security check is a form of casework. T / F

5. The House of Representatives is more institutionalized, centralized, and hierarchical than the Senate. T / F

6. The Rules Committee is unique to the House. T / F

7. The most powerful leader in Congress is the Speaker of the House. T / F

8. Select committees have membership drawn from both houses of Congress. T / F

9. Oversight does not give Congress any real power to pressure agencies to comply with their wishes. T / F

10. According to John Kingdon, no single influence is important enough to determine a congressperson's votes. T / F

SHORT ANSWER/SHORT ESSAY QUESTIONS

1. What is the dominant prior occupation for members of Congress?

2. Compare and contrast casework and pork barrel.

3. What is a filibuster, and how is it used?

4. How does Congress perform its oversight function?

5. What is the difference between the role of legislators as trustees, instructed delegates, and politicos?

ESSAY QUESTIONS

1. In what ways is the constitutional design of the House and the Senate linked to the different operations of each chamber?

2. Comment on the representativeness of Congress. Are the members of Congress truly representative of the American people and the overall needs of the nation? What effect do PACs and interest groups have on the representativeness of Congress?

3. How do committees exercise power over the legislative process? Do they have too much power? Not enough?

4. How can the president influence congressional action? Do you think the president is too powerful or not powerful enough in dealing with Congress? Explain.

5. How important is party membership to a senator or member of the House in casting a vote? Are votes on some issues more or less likely to follow party lines? What other factors influence how an individual legislator casts a vote?

CHAPTER 13

The Presidency

CHAPTER OUTLINE

I. Introduction (399–400)
   A. Two fundamental questions concerning the president revolve around presidential power and the relationship with the public.
   B. Presidential power is the power to persuade.
   C. Presidents must have highly developed political skills.

II. The Presidents (pp. 400–406)
   A. Great Expectations
   B. Who They Are
   C. How They Got There
      1. Elections: The Typical Road to the White House
         a. The **Twenty-second Amendment** limits presidents to two terms.
         b. Only 13 presidents have served two or more terms.
      2. Succession and Impeachment
         a. **Impeachment** is the political equivalent of an indictment in criminal law.
         b. The House Judiciary Committee voted to recommend Richard Nixon's impeachment as a result of the **Watergate** scandal.
         c. The **Twenty-fifth Amendment** permits the vice president to become acting president if the president is disabled.

III. Presidential Powers (pp. 406–408)
   A. Constitutional Powers
   B. The Expansion of Power
   C. Perspectives on Presidential Power

IV. Running the Government: The Chief Executive (pp. 408–415)
   A. The Vice President
   B. The **Cabinet** consists of the heads of the executive departments.
   C. The Executive Office
      1. The **National Security Council (NSC)** links the president's key foreign and military policy advisors.
      2. The **Council of Economic Advisors (CEA)** advises the president on economic policy.
      3. The **Office of Management and Budget (OMB)** prepares the president's budget.
   D. The White House Staff
   E. The First Lady

V.   Presidential Leadership of Congress: The Politics of Shared Powers (pp. 415–422)
 A.   Chief Legislator
  1.   The Constitution gives the president power to **veto** congressional legislation.
  2.   A **pocket veto** occurs if Congress adjourns within ten days after submitting a bill and the president fails to sign it.
 B.   Party Leadership
  1.   The Bonds of Party
  2.   Slippage in Party Support
  3.   Leading the Party
   a.   **Presidential coattails** occur when voters cast their ballots for congressional candidates of the president's party because those candidates support the president.
   b.   The president's party typically loses seats in midterm elections.
 C.   Public Support
  1.   Public Approval
  2.   Mandates
 D.   Legislative Skills

VI.   The President and National Security Policy (pp. 422–427)
 A.   Chief Diplomat
  1.   The president alone extends diplomatic recognition to foreign governments.
  2.   The president has sole power to negotiate treaties.
  3.   Presidents can negotiate *executive agreements* with heads of foreign governments.
 B.   Commander in Chief
 C.   War Powers
  1.   The **War Powers Resolution** mandated the withdrawal of forces after 60 days unless Congress declared war or granted an extension.
  2.   The use of the War Powers Resolution may constitute a **legislative veto** violating the doctrine of separation of powers.
 D.   Crisis Manager
  1.   A **crisis** is a sudden, unpredictable, and potentially dangerous event.
  2.   Presidents can instantly monitor events almost anywhere and act quickly.
 E.   Working with Congress

VII.   Power from the People: The Public Presidency (pp. 427–432)
 A.   Going Public
 B.   Presidential Approval
 C.   Policy Support
 D.   Mobilizing the Public

VIII.   The President and the Press (pp. 432–435)
 A.   Presidents and the press tend to be in conflict.
 B.   The president's *press secretary* serves as a conduit of information from the White House to the press.

      C.   The best known direct interaction between the president and the press is the presidential press conference.

      D.   Most of the news coverage of the White House focuses on the president's personal and official activities.

      E.   News coverage of the presidency often tends to emphasize the negative.

IX.   Understanding the American Presidency (pp. 435–436)
      A.   The Presidency and Democracy
      B.   The Presidency and the Scope of Government

X.   Summary (p. 436)

LEARNING OBJECTIVES

After studying Chapter 13, you should be able to:

1.   Describe the American presidents—who they are, how they got there, and what they do.

2.   List the constitutional powers of the president and explain how these powers have expanded.

3.   Explain how the office of the presidency is organized to make policy.

4.   Discuss the relationship between the president and Congress and the ways in which the president is able to lead Congress.

5.   Explain the role of the president in developing national security policy.

6.   Discuss the importance of public opinion to the president and his ability to obtain the support of the public.

7.   Examine the relationship between the president and the media.

8.   Understand the place of the presidency in American democracy and the effect the presidency has had on the scope of government.

The following exercises will help you meet these objectives:

Objective 1: Describe the American presidents—who they are, how they got there, and what they do.

1. What are the two contradictory expectations that Americans have about the presidency?

    1.

    2.

2. Make a list of the ten presidents you believe to have been the best and briefly explain why.

    1.

    2.

    3.

    4.

    5.

    6.

    7.

    8.

    9.

    10.

3. Outline the procedure for removing a president from office.

Objective 2: List the constitutional powers of the president and explain how these powers have expanded.

    1.   Look at Table 13.3 on page 406 and choose one constitutional power of the president from each category that you believe to be the most important.

        1.

        2.

        3.

        4.

    2.   Describe two ways in which the power of the president has expanded from its constitutional base.

        1.

        2.

Objective 3: Explain how the office of the presidency is organized to make policy.

    1.   List three recent vice presidents who have played a prominent role in the administration.

        1.

        2.

        3.

    2.   What is the cabinet and what does it do?

3. List and explain the function of three major policymaking bodies of the Executive Office.

   1.

   2.

   3.

4. What is the difference between a hierarchical organization and a wheel-and-spokes system of White House management?

   Hierarchical:

   Wheel-and-spokes:

5. Make a list of four First Ladies and the way each influenced the presidency.

   1.

   2.

   3.

   4.

Objective 4: Discuss the relationship between the president and Congress and the ways in which the president is able to lead Congress.

   1. List the three options the president has once Congress passes a bill.

      1.

2.

3.

2.   What is the difference between a veto, a pocket veto, and a line-item veto?

Veto:

Pocket Veto:

Line-Item Veto:

3.   Explain the term "presidential coattails."

4.   What are the two indicators of public support for the president?

1.

2.

5.   What is meant by the president's "honeymoon" period?

Objective 5: Explain the role of the president in developing national security policy.

1.   What is an executive agreement and how does it differ from a treaty?

2.   What are the main provisions of the War Powers Resolution?

3. Why is the president more equipped to handle a crisis than Congress?

4. What are the "two presidencies"?

1.

2.

Objective 6: Discuss the importance of public opinion to the president and his or her ability to obtain the support of the public.

1. What is the difference between the president as head of state and head of government?

Head of State:

Head of Government:

2. Rank the past ten presidents in terms of their ability to garner public support.

1.

2.

3.

4.

5.

6.

7.

8.

9.

10.

Objective 7: Examine the relationship between the president and the media.

1.   What is the role of the president's press secretary?

2.   In what way(s) are the press biased in their coverage of the president?

Objective 8: Understand the place of the presidency in American democracy and the effect the presidency has had on the scope of government.

1.   In what way(s) is the institution of the presidency undemocratic?

2.   How does the presidency increase and decrease the scope of government?

KEY TERMS

Identify and describe:

Twenty-second Amendment

Impeachment

Watergate

Twenty-fifth Amendment

cabinet

National Security Council (NSC)

Council of Economic Advisors (CEA)

Office of Management and Budget (OMB)

veto

pocket veto

presidential coattails

War Powers Resolution

legislative veto

crisis

Compare and contrast:

impeachment and Watergate

Twenty-second Amendment and Twenty-fifth Amendment

National Security Council, Council of Economic Advisors, and Office of Management and Budget

veto, pocket veto, and legislative veto

War Powers Resolution and legislative veto

Name that term:

1.   It limits the president to two terms of office.

   _____

2.   Because of this scandal, the House Judiciary Committee voted to recommend the impeachment of President Nixon.

   _____

3.   Although not in the Constitution, every president has had one.

   _____

4.   This links the president's key foreign and military advisors.

   _____

5.   A two-thirds vote in each house of Congress can override it.

   _____

6.   Few congressional races are actually determined by this factor today.

   _____

7.   This is a sudden, unpredictable, and potentially dangerous event.

   _____

USING YOUR UNDERSTANDING

1. Compare and contrast the Clinton presidency with the Bush presidency in terms of the principal roles the president plays. Identify particular policies in which the president is involved as head of state, commander in chief, chief legislator, and so on. You may want to collect newspaper or news magazine items that illustrate contemporary policy problems that both presidents faced. Pay special attention to presidential roles with respect to specific policy areas and national security.

2. All presidents seem to want to hold a prominent place in history. People are sometimes asked to identify the "top presidents" in our nation's history. Make a list of those presidents that you believe played prominent roles, for better or worse. You may even wish to rank them. Justify your choices by making a statement or two about each president's success or notoriety in one of the presidential roles, in policymaking achievements in domestic or foreign policy, in relations with Congress, and/or in terms of his image of power. Compare your choices with those of your colleagues. On the basis of your assessment, briefly describe what you believe to be the factors that help ensure that a president will have a prominent place in history.

MULTIPLE CHOICE QUESTIONS

Circle the correct answer:

1. Richard Neustadt has argued that presidential power is the power to
    a. instruct.
    b. command.
    c. educate.
    d. control.
    e. persuade.

2. How many presidents were political scientists?
    a. About half of them
    b. One
    c. All but one of them
    d. Two
    e. All of them

3. _____ of the 43 presidents have served two or more full terms in the White House.
    a. Five
    b. Ten
    c. Thirteen
    d. Twenty
    e. Thirty

4. Once the House votes for impeachment, the president
   a. must leave office.
   b. is fined or sentenced to prison.
   c. is tried by the Supreme Court.
   d. is tried by the Senate.
   e. must be indicted by a grand jury before being removed from office.

5. According to the Twenty-fifth Amendment, in the event of a vacancy in the vice presidency,
   a. the Electoral College elects a new vice president.
   b. the Speaker of the House is automatically the new vice president.
   c. the office remains vacant until a subsequent national election takes place.
   d. the Congress picks a new vice president from a list of five names submitted by the president.
   e. the president nominates a replacement, who must be confirmed by both houses of Congress.

6. The order of succession to the presidency, should the president be unable to fulfill his or her duties is
   a. vice president, president pro tempore of the Senate, Speaker of the House, cabinet members in order that their department was created.
   b. vice president, Speaker of the House, president pro tempore of the Senate, chief justice of the Supreme Court, cabinet members in order that their department was created.
   c. vice president, Speaker of the House, president pro tempore of the Senate, cabinet members in the order that their department was created.
   d. vice president, chief justice of Supreme Court, president pro tempore of the Senate, Speaker of the House.
   e. vice president, Speaker of the House, president pro tempore, cabinet members in the order that their department was created.

7. The presidential cabinet
   a. is the electronically locked vault where the president keeps his top secret papers.
   b. is given tremendous power under the Constitution.
   c. includes, by law, a minimum of two sitting members of Congress at all times.
   d. consists of the head of each executive department, plus any additional government officials the president designates.
   e. can veto actions by the president.

8. Cabinet-level executive departments are created by
   a. Congress.
   b. the Constitution.
   c. the president.
   d. rarely held national referendums.
   e. All of the above

9. The budgetary implications of the president's budget are provided to the president by the
    a. Executive Budget Office.
    b. Department of the Treasury.
    c. Council of Economic Advisors.
    d. Internal Revenue Service.
    e. Office of Management and Budget.

10. Which of the following was created in 1947 to coordinate the president's foreign and military policy advisers?
    a. Department of State
    b. Department of Defense
    c. National Security Council
    d. Department of Homeland Security
    e. Office of Management and Budget

11. Which president did *not* have a hierarchical, but rather, a wheel-and-spokes form of organization to his White House staff?
    a. John F. Kennedy
    b. Franklin D. Roosevelt
    c. Woodrow Wilson
    d. Richard Nixon
    e. Jimmy Carter

12. The Brownlow Committee's argument that presidential assistants should have a "passion for anonymity," meant that
    a. presidential assistants should be unknown and unfamiliar individuals.
    b. presidential assistants should be undaunted by the prospects of being relatively unknown and hidden from the president.
    c. presidents should select individuals who they do not know to work in the White House.
    d. All of the above
    e. None of the above

13. A pocket veto is the situation in which the president
    a. vetoes particular items in a spending bill.
    b. lets a bill die by neither signing nor vetoing it after Congress has adjourned.
    c. rejects a Congressional override.
    d. lets a bill become law by neither vetoing nor signing it.
    e. sends a law back to Congress with the reasons for rejecting it.

14. The Constitution gives the president the power to influence the legislative process through his responsibility to
    a. make laws by decree without the consent of Congress in some situations.
    b. direct the business of Congress and initiate impeachment.
    c. report on the state of the union and veto acts of Congress.
    d. recommend legislation and make appointments.
    e. manage the economy, lead the party, and deal with national crises.

15. What are the president's most useful resources?
    a. Party leadership, public support, and their own legislative skills
    b. Tenure in office, party leadership, and public support
    c. Tenure in office, proven mandates, and public support
    d. Tenure in office, mandates, and their own legislative skills
    e. Congressional support, party leadership, and tenure in office

16. In midterm elections, the
    a. president's coattails are the strongest.
    b. president's party typically gains seats.
    c. president almost always wins reelection; a president who does not is the exception.
    d. president usually does not become involved.
    e. president's party typically loses seats.

17. John Kindgon's study of the policymaking process concluded that
    a. no other actor in the political system has the capability of the president to set agendas.
    b. no other actor in the political system has the capability of Congress to set agendas.
    c. no other actor in the political system has the capability of the Supreme Court to set agendas.
    d. no other actor in the political system has the capability of the media to set agendas.
    e. no other actor in the political system has the capability of the public to set agendas.

18. The War Powers Resolution
    a. prohibited the president from committing American troops without congressional approval.
    b. established the chain of command of the armed forces in the event the president is incapacitated.
    c. gave the president the formal power to declare war in the case of nuclear attack.
    d. mandated the withdrawal of forces after 60 days unless Congress declared war or granted an extension.
    e. established the code protocols that launch nuclear missiles in order to prevent accidental or unauthorized missile launches.

19. Who was considered the first "television president"?
    a. FDR
    b. JFK
    c. Richard Nixon
    d. Ronald Reagan
    e. Bill Clinton

20. Which of the following conclusions can be drawn from **Figure 13.3?**
    a. Public opinion tends to be more favorable at the beginning of a president's term.
    b. Public opinion tends to more favorable at the end of a president's term.
    c. George W. Bush enjoyed some of the highest and some of the lowest public approval ratings among all presidents since Eisenhower.
    d. On average, a majority of Americans approve of the president's handling of his job.
    e. A, c, and d

TRUE/FALSE QUESTIONS

Circle the correct answer:

1. George W. Bush was elected in 2000 without a plurality of the popular vote. T / F

2. Most presidents have served two full terms in office. T / F

3. The Twenty-fifth Amendment permits the vice president to become acting president if the vice president and the president's cabinet determine that the president is disabled or if the president declares his own disability. T / F

4. For more than 10 percent of American history, the presidency has been occupied by individuals who were not elected to the office. T / F

5. Bill Clinton was impeached. T / F

6. The National Security Council is formally composed of the president, the vice president, and the secretaries of state and defense. T / F

7. The Constitution creates no role for the First Lady. T / F

8. President Clinton rarely involved himself in policy detail. T / F

9. Since the passage of the War Powers Resolution, declarations of war have been much more frequent. T / F

10. Presidents frequently fail to garner widespread public support. T / F

SHORT ANSWER/SHORT ESSAY QUESTIONS

1. What are the qualifications for the presidency as specified in the Constitution?

2. Describe and explain the significance of the Watergate scandal.

3. What role does the vice president play? Give examples.

4. When can a president claim a mandate? What is the importance of a mandate?

5. What is the relationship between the president and the press?

ESSAY QUESTIONS

1. Explain why, as Richard Neustadt argued, presidential power is the power to persuade, rather than to command.

2. Compare and contrast the constitutional powers of the president with the informal expansion of presidential power.

3. Describe the process by which a president can veto a bill. What recourse does Congress have to respond to a veto, and how often is this recourse successful? Would you favor a line-item veto for the president? Why, or why not?

4. Why is the president given the power as the nation's chief diplomat and the commander in chief of the armed forces? What checks does Congress have on the president's national security prerogatives? Are these sufficient? Explain.

5. How does the contemporary presidency differ from that envisioned by the Founders? Has the modern presidency grown too powerful? Ought we be concerned?

CHAPTER 14

THE CONGRESS, THE PRESIDENT, AND THE BUDGET:
THE POLITICS OF TAXING AND SPENDING

CHAPTER OUTLINE

I. Politics in Action: The Politics of Budgeting (pp. 441–443)
   A. Central to public policy are the questions of who bears the burdens of paying for government and who receives the benefits.
   B. A **budget** is a policy document allocating burdens (taxes) and benefits (expenditures).
   C. A budget **deficit** occurs when **expenditures** exceed **revenues** in a fiscal year.

II. Sources of Federal Revenue (pp. 443–450)
   A. Income Tax
      1. Individuals are required to pay the government a portion of the money they earn, called an **income tax.**
      2. The **Sixteenth Amendment** permitted Congress to levy an income tax.
   B. Social Insurance Taxes
   C. Borrowing
      1. The **federal debt** is all of the money borrowed over the years that is still outstanding.
      2. Government borrowing may crowd out private borrowers from the loan marketplace.
      3. The federal government docs not have a capital budget.
   D. Taxes and Public Policy
      1. **Tax expenditures** are revenue losses attributable to provisions of the federal tax laws.
      2. Tax expenditures may be seen as loopholes or choices that support a worthy social activity.
      3. Tax reduction has frequently been called for.
      4. Tax reform has simplified taxes and made them more equitable.

III. Federal Expenditures (pp. 450–457)
   A. Big Governments, Big Budgets
   B. The Rise and Decline of the National Security State
   C. The Rise of the Social Service State
      1. The **Social Security Act** intended to provide a minimal level of sustenance to older Americans.
      2. **Medicare** provides both hospital and physician coverage to the elderly.
   D. Incrementalism
      1. **Incrementalism** means that the best predictor of this year's budget is last year's budget plus a little bit more.

2. The budgetary process is affected by groups with interests in taxes and expenditures.
E. "Uncontrollable" Expenditures
1. **Uncontrollable expenditures** result from policies that make some group automatically eligible for some benefit.
2. **Entitlements** are policies in which Congress has obligated itself to pay X level of benefits to Y number of recipients each year.

IV. The Budgetary Process (pp. 457–464)
A. Budgetary Politics
1. Stakes and Strategies

2. The Players
a. The interest groups.
b. The agencies.
c. The Office of Management and Budget (OMB).
d. The president.
e. The Tax Committees in Congress.
(1) **House Ways and Means Committee.**
(2) **Senate Finance Committee.**
f. The Budget Committees and the Congressional Budget Office.
g. The subject-matter committees.
h. The Appropriations Committees and their subcommittees.
i. The Congress as a whole.
j. The Government Accountability Office (GAO).
B. The President's Budget
C. Congress and the Budget
1. Reforming the Process
a. The **Congressional Budget and Impoundment Act of 1974**
(1) A fixed budget calendar.
(2) A budget committee in each house.
(3) The **Congressional Budget Office (CBO).**
b. A **budget resolution** is supposed to set limits on expenditures based on revenue projections.
c. Budget **reconciliation** revises program authorizations to achieve required savings.
d. An **authorization bill** is an act of Congress that establishes a discretionary government program or an entitlement.
e. An **appropriations bill** must be passed to actually fund programs established by authorization bills.

2. Evaluating the 1974 Reforms
a. **Continuing resolutions** are laws that allow agencies to spend at the previous year's level.
b. The 1974 reforms have helped Congress view the entire budget early in the process.

3.   More Reforms
    a.   The Gramm-Rudman-Hollings Act (1985) mandated maximum allowable deficit levels for each year until the budget was to be balanced in 1993.
    b.   In 1990 Congress switched from a focus on controlling the size of the deficit to controlling increases in spending.
    c.   Republican and Democratic efforts to balance the budget.

V.   Understanding Budgeting (pp. 464–466)
    A.   Democracy and Budgeting
    B.   The Budget and the Scope of Government

VI.   Summary (pp. 466–467)

LEARNING OBJECTIVES

After studying Chapter 14, you should be able to:

1.   Describe the major sources of federal revenues.

2.   Understand the nature of the tax system in America.

3.   Explain the nature of federal expenditures and why so much of the budget is uncontrollable.

4.   Discuss how the budgetary process works, who is involved, and the politics of budgetary reform.

5.   Understand how budgeting affects democracy and the scope of government in America.

The following exercises will help you meet these objectives:

Objective 1: Describe the major sources of federal revenues.

1.   List four sources of federal revenues.

    1.

    2.

    3.

    4.

2.　　How does the federal government borrow money?

3.　　What is a capital budget?

Objective 2:　Understand the nature of the tax system in America.

1.　　Define tax expenditures and give three examples.

　　Definition:

　　Examples:

　　　　1.

　　　　2.

　　　　3.

2.　　What were the three major reforms of the Tax Reform Act of 1986?

　　1.

　　2.

　　3.

Objective 3: Explain the nature of federal expenditures and why so much of the budget is uncontrollable.

1. Name the two conditions associated with government growth in America.

   1.

   2.

2. What is meant by the phrase "military industrial complex"?

3. Explain how Social Security is a kind of intergenerational contract.

4. List four features of incremental budgeting.

   1.

   2.

   3.

   4.

5. Explain how entitlements are "uncontrollable expenditures."

Objective 4: Discuss how the budgetary process works, who is involved, and the politics of budgetary reform.

1.   How might each of the following political actors have a stake in the federal budget?

Mayors:

Defense contractors:

Scientists:

Bureaucratic agencies:

Members of Congress:

Presidents:

Farmers:

2.   List the ten main actors in the budgetary process.

1.

2.

3.

4.

5.

6.

7.

8.

9.

10.

3. Explain the three main provisions of the Congressional Budget and Impoundment Control Act of 1974.

1.

2.

3.

4. What is a budget resolution?

5. Explain the two ways in which laws are changed to meet the budget resolution.

1.

2.

6. What was the Gramm-Rudman-Hollings Act and why did it fail?

Objective 5: Understand how budgeting affects democracy and the scope of government in America.

1. List three possible explanations for the substantial growth of government in twentieth-century democracies.

1.

2.

3.

2.   How could the budgetary process limit government?

KEY TERMS

Identify and describe:

budget

deficit

expenditures

revenues

income tax

Sixteenth Amendment

federal debt

tax expenditures

Social Security Act

Medicare

incrementalism

uncontrollable expenditures

entitlements

House Ways and Means Committee

Senate Finance Committee

Congressional Budget and Impoundment Control Act of 1974

Congressional Budget Office (CBO)

budget resolution

reconciliation

authorization bill

appropriations bill

continuing resolutions

Compare and contrast:

budget and deficit

expenditures and revenues

income tax and Sixteenth Amendment

income tax and tax expenditures

Social Security Act and Medicare

uncontrollable expenditures and entitlements

House Ways and Means Committee and Senate Finance Committee

reconciliation and authorization bill

Name that term:

1.   This policy document allocates burdens and benefits.

      _____

2.   This is all of the money borrowed over the years and still outstanding.

      _____

3.   This was intended to provide a minimal level of sustenance to older Americans.

      _____

4.   These revenue losses are attributable to provisions of the federal tax laws that allow a special exemption, exclusion, or deduction.

      _____

5.   This policy suggests that the best predictor of this year's budget is last year's budget, plus a little bit more.

      _____

6.   These result from policies that make some group automatically eligible for some benefit.

      _____

7.   This agency advises Congress on the probable consequences of its budget decisions.

      _____

8.   This occurs in Congress every April.

      _____

9.   This is an act of Congress that actually funds programs within limits established by authorization bills.

      _____

10.   These allow agencies to spend at the previous year's level.

      _____

USING YOUR UNDERSTANDING

1.   Take a look at a recent edition of the *United States Budget in Brief.* Identify expenditure categories that relate to specific policy arenas, such as equality, the economy, social welfare, technology, and national security. Create your own policy arenas using broad or specific categories. Briefly describe what you found in terms of the policy priorities represented by the budget. Evaluate the budget according to where you believe your tax dollars should be spent.

2.   This chapter has emphasized the budget of the United States government. Locate a budget document for your state or community. These should be available in the Government Documents section of your school library, through state and local government offices, or on the Internet. Assess the sources of revenues on which this unit of government depends and the types of expenditures it makes in various policy areas. Take note of whether or not the budget represents a deficit (expenditures exceeding revenues) or a surplus (revenues exceeding expenditures), and the magnitude of the amount. Compare the major features of this budget to those of the budget of the United States. Investigate the politics of the budgetary process at the state or local level and compare what you find to the national level. Alternatively you could examine a budget of another Western democracy and compare it to that of the United States using these same guidelines.

MULTIPLE CHOICE QUESTIONS

Circle the correct answer:

1.   No government policy affects as many Americans as
    a.   tax policy.
    b.   defense policy.
    c.   social welfare policy.
    d.   foreign policy.
    e.   housing policy.

2.   All of the following are examples of an excise tax EXCEPT
    a.   The gas tax
    b.   Sales tax paid on the purchase of a new coat
    c.   Social Security taxes
    d.   All of these are excise taxes.
    e.   None of these are excise taxes.

3. In *Pollock v. Farmer's Loan and Trust Co.* (1895), the Supreme Court ruled that
    a. the income tax was constitutional.
    b. the national sales tax was unconstitutional.
    c. banks and corporations must pay higher taxes.
    d. the income tax was unconstitutional.
    e. business income taxes were unconstitutional but individual income taxes were constitutional.

4. A tax can be considered progressive if
    a. it pays for programs people desire.
    b. the rate of tax revenues increases annually.
    c. the distribution of taxes falls equally on individuals in all income brackets.
    d. those with more taxable income pay higher rates of tax than those with less.
    e. those with less taxable income pay more taxes than those with more.

5. The main function of the Internal Revenue Service (IRS) is
    a. to collect social security taxes.
    b. to collect the federal income tax.
    c. to allocate tax funds to government programs.
    d. to provide oversight to the federal budget.
    e. to provide tax refunds.

6. Some economists are concerned about the national debt because they believe
    a. government borrowing encourages individuals to borrow more money.
    b. government competition for loans lowers interest rates.
    c. government borrowing may crowd out private borrowers.
    d. the more government borrows, the less likely banks will be to lend the government money.
    e. governments who gain revenue through borrowing are less accountable than those that gain revenue through taxes.

7. The ability of taxpayers to deduct charitable contributions from their income is an example of
    a. tax reductions.
    b. tax cuts.
    c. tax expenditures.
    d. tax shelters.
    e. tax evasion.

8. The tax cuts proposed by President Reagan and adopted by Congress in 1981 reduced Americans' taxes by
    a. 75 percent.
    b. 50 percent.
    c. 40 percent.
    d. 25 percent.
    e. 10 percent.

9. What phrase did President Eisenhower coin to capture the relationship between the military and the defense industry?
   a. The defense industrial complex
   b. The military industrial complex
   c. The defense industry monopoly
   d. Manufacturers of war
   e. The arms industry

10. The biggest expenditure in the federal budget today is
    a. foreign aid programs.
    b. welfare for the poor.
    c. interest on the debt.
    d. national defense.
    e. income security programs.

11. The Social Security Act, which established the Social Security system, was passed in
    a. 1935.
    b. 1913.
    c. 1895.
    d. 1962.
    e. 1950.

12. All of the following are examples of social programs supported by federal expenditures, EXCEPT
    a. food subsidies for the poor.
    b. funding for research and design of the Stealth Bomber.
    c. support for businesses run by minority entrepreneurs.
    d. guaranteed loans to college students.
    e. environmental education.

13. How much of the federal budget is estimated to be uncontrollable, unless Congress changes a law or existing benefits?
    a. Two-thirds
    b. One-half
    c. One-quarter
    d. One-fifth
    e. Three-quarters

14. The Office of Management and Budget is charged with
    a. developing appropriations bills for members of the House of Representatives.
    b. assisting the president in developing and carrying out the budget.
    c. collecting revenues and administering the federal income tax.
    d. holding public hearings on the federal budget.
    e. setting levels of spending on military and social programs.

15. Until Congress passed the Budget and Accounting Act of 1921,
    a. agencies of the executive branch sent their budget requests directly to the president, who alone had the authority to approve and fund the bureaucracy.
    b. agencies of the executive branch sent their budget requests to the secretary of the treasury, who forwarded them on to Congress, with the president playing little or no role in the entire process.
    c. there was no federal income tax in the United States.
    d. the United States had no formalized budget process.
    e. the federal budget had to be balanced, by law.

16. Auditing, monitoring, and evaluation of what agencies are doing with their budgets is the responsibility of
    a. the Congressional Budget Office.
    b. the Government Accountability Office.
    c. the Internal Revenue Service.
    d. the Treasury Department.
    e. the Federal Bureau of Investigation.

17. The president is required to propose an executive budget to Congress by
    a. Article I of the U.S. Constitution.
    b. tradition established by George Washington.
    c. the Budget and Accounting Act of 1921.
    d. the Sixteenth Amendment to the U.S. Constitution.
    e. the Office of Management and Budget.

18. In what part of the year is the next year's budget policy developed by the president?
    a. Spring
    b. Summer
    c. Fall
    d. Winter
    e. The president is always developing next year's budget

19. Budget _____ revises program authorizations to achieve required savings.
    a. impoundment
    b. realignment
    c. closure
    d. appropriations
    e. reconciliation

20. The idea that any new programs, or increased spending on existing programs, must be offset by either budget cuts or increased revenues is known as
    a. deficit spending.
    b. pay as you go.
    c. borrowing from Peter to pay Paul.
    d. pork barrel spending.
    e. sequestration.

TRUE/FALSE QUESTIONS

Circle the correct answer:

1. More federal revenue comes from corporate, rather than personal income taxes. T / F

2. Congress first adopted an income tax in order to pay for the Civil War. T / F

3. Corporations, like individuals, pay income taxes. T / F

4. A progressive tax is one that allows for the funding of new social programs. T / F

5. Foreign investors currently hold a majority of the federal government's public debt. T / F

6. The government encourages charitable donations through tax expenditures. T / F

7. The Reagan tax cuts benefited the wealthiest Americans more than the poorest. T / F

8. The Hope Credit is a tax credit that was created to make college education at least a bit more affordable.
   T / F

9. Medicare provides both hospital and physician coverage to the elderly. T / F

10. Uncontrollable expenditures result from constitutionally mandated funding requirements, like the military budget. T / F

SHORT ANSWER/SHORT ESSAY QUESTIONS

1. How is the Sixteenth Amendment related to the federal budgetary process?

2. What is the Social Security Act, and what is its importance to budgeting?

3. What changed as a result of the *Tax Reform Act of 1986*?

4. What is the military industrial complex, and how does it affect federal spending?

5. What did the Gramm-Rudman-Hollings Act try to do, and why did it fail to meet its goals?

ESSAY QUESTIONS

1. Where does the federal government's revenue come from and where does it go?

2. How does the federal government borrow money? What are the potential economic and political dangers associated with deficit spending and an increasing national debt?

3. Do you agree with President Carter's assessment that America's tax system is a "national disgrace"? Why or why not?

4. Compare the role of the president with the role of Congress in the budgetary process. Who do you believe has the greater influence and why?

5. Why is it so difficult to curb or roll back levels of federal spending?

CHAPTER 15

The Federal Bureaucracy

CHAPTER OUTLINE

I. Politics in Action: Regulating Food (pp. 471–472)
  A. Bureaucracies are central to our lives.
  B. Max Weber's conception of **bureaucracy**
    1. Bureaucracies have a hierarchical authority structure.
    2. Bureaucracies use task specialization.
    3. Bureaucracies develop extensive rules.
    4. Bureaucracies operate on the merit principle.
    5. Bureaucracies behave with impersonality.

II. The Bureaucrats (pp. 472–479)
  A. Some Bureaucratic Myths and Realities
    1. Americans dislike bureaucrats.
    2. Bureaucracies are growing bigger each year.
    3. Most federal bureaucrats work in Washington, DC.
    4. Bureaucracies are ineffective, inefficient, and always mired in red tape.
  B. Who They Are and How They Got There
    1. Civil Service: From Patronage to Protection
      a. **Patronage** is a hiring and promotion system based on knowing the right people.
      b. The **Pendleton Civil Service Act** created the federal civil service.
      c. All **civil service** systems are based on merit and the desire to create a nonpartisan government service.
      d. The **merit principle** uses entrance exams and promotion ratings to reward qualified individuals.
      e. The **Hatch Act** prohibits civil service employees from active participation in partisan politics while on duty.
      f. The **Office of Personnel Management (OPM)** is in charge of hiring for most federal agencies.
      g. Each civil service job is assigned a **GS (General Schedule) rating**.
      h. The very top of the civil service system is the **Senior Executive Service**.
  C. The Other Route to Federal Jobs: Recruiting from the Plum Book
    1. The plum book lists top federal jobs available for direct presidential appointment.
    2. The most important trait of presidential appointees is their transience.

III. How Bureaucracies Are Organized (pp. 479–483)
  A. Cabinet Departments
  B. Independent Regulatory Commissions
    1. Each **independent regulatory commission** has responsibility for some sector of the economy.
    2. Interest groups are closely involved with independent regulatory commissions.
  C. **Government Corporations**
    1. These organizations provide services that could be provided by the private sector.
    2. They and charge for their service, though usually at a reduced rate.
  D. The **independent executive agencies** are essentially all the rest of the government.

IV. Bureaucracies as Implementors (pp. 483–492)
  A. What Implementation Means
    1. **Policy implementation** is the stage of policymaking between the establishment of a policy and its consequences.
    2. Implementation is the continuation of policymaking by other means.
  B. Why the Best-Laid Plans Sometimes Flunk the Implementation Test
    1. Program Design
    2. Lack of Clarity
    3. Lack of Resources
    4. Administrative Routine
      a. **Standard operating procedures** (SOPs) help bureaucrats make everyday decisions.
      b. SOPs may become "red tape" and obstacles to action.
    5. Administrators' Dispositions
      a. **Administrative discretion** is the authority of administrative actors to select among various responses to a given problem.
      b. **Street-level bureaucrats** are in constant contact with the public and have considerable discretion.
    6. Fragmentation
  C. A Case Study: The Voting Rights Act of 1965

V. Privatization (p. 492)
  A. Private contractors have become a virtual fourth branch of government.
  B. The theory behind contracting for services is that competition in the private sector will result in better service at lower costs, although there is no evidence to prove this.
  C. Contracting also leads to less public scrutiny.

VI. Bureaucracies As Regulators (pp. 492–496)
  A. Regulation in the Economy and in Everyday Life
    1. Government **regulation** is the use of governmental authority to control or change some practice in the private sector.
    2. A Full Day of Regulation

B.   Regulation: How It Grew, How It Works
1.   In the **command-and-control policy**, the government tells business how to reach certain goals, checks that these commands are followed, and punishes offenders.
2.   An **incentive system** uses taxes and rewards to promote certain behavior.
C.   Toward **Deregulation**
1.   Regulation raises prices.
2.   Regulation hurts America's competitive position abroad.
3.   Regulation does not always work well.

VII.   Understanding Bureaucracies (pp. 497–503)
A.   Bureaucracy and Democracy
1.   Presidents Try to Control the Bureaucracy
a.   They appoint the right people to head the agency.
b.   They issue **executive orders**.
c.   They alter an agency's budget.
d.   They reorganize an agency.
2.   Congress Tries to Control the Bureaucracy
a.   They influence the appointment of agency heads.
b.   They alter an agency's budget.
c.   They hold hearings.
d.   They rewrite the legislation or make it more detailed.
3.   Iron Triangles and Issue Networks
a.   When agencies, groups, and committees all depend on one another and are in close, frequent contact, they form what are sometimes called **iron triangles**, or subgovernments.
b.   The system of subgovernments is now overlaid with an amorphous system of *issue networks*.
B.   Bureaucracy and the Scope of Government

VIII.   Summary (p. 503)

LEARNING OBJECTIVES

After studying Chapter 15, you should be able to:

1.   Describe the bureaucrats—who they are, how they got there, and what they do.

2.   Discuss how the federal bureaucracy is organized.

3.   Explain how bureaucracies function as implementors of public policy and how privatization has impacted their role.

4.   Explain how bureaucracies function as regulators.

5.   Evaluate the problem of controlling bureaucracies in a democratic government and the ways bureaucracies affect the scope of government.

The following exercises will help you meet these objectives:

Objective 1: Describe the bureaucrats—who they are, how they got there, and what they do.

List five elements of the Weberian model of bureaucracy.

1.

2.

3.

4.

5.

2. List four prevalent myths about bureaucracy.

1.

2.

3.

4.

3. What is the difference between patronage and the merit principle?

4. What is the purpose of the Hatch Act?

5. What are some of the common characteristics of plum book appointees?

Objective 2: Discuss how the federal bureaucracy is organized.

1. What are the four basic types of agencies in the federal executive branch?

1.

2.

3.

4.

2. Explain the relationship between interest groups and independent regulatory commissions.

3. In what two ways are government corporations like private corporations and different from other parts of the government?

   1.

   2.

4. What are the three biggest independent executive agencies?

   1.

   2.

   3.

Objective 3: Explain how bureaucracies function as implementors of public policy and how privatization has impacted their role.

1. What are the three minimum elements of implementation?

   1.

   2.

   3.

2. List six reasons why policy implementation might fail.

   1.

   2.

   3.

4.

5.

6.

3.   What are three advantages of using standard operating procedures?

   1.

   2.

   3.

4.   What is administrative discretion? Give an example.

5.   Give an example of bureaucratic fragmentation.

6.   Explain two criticisms of government use of private contractors for services.

   1.

   2.

Objective 4: Explain how bureaucracies function as regulators.

1.   What was the significance of *Munn v. Illinois* (1877)?

2.	List three elements common to all regulation.

	1.

	2.

	3.

3.	What is the difference between command-and-control policy and incentive system?

	Command-and-Control:

	Incentive:

4.	List three criticisms of regulation.

	1.

	2.

	3.

Objective 5: Evaluate the problem of controlling bureaucracies in a democratic government and
	the ways bureaucracies affect the scope of government.

	1.	List four methods in which the president can control the bureaucracy.

		1.

		2.

		3.

		4.

2. List four methods in which Congress can control the bureaucracy.

   1.

   2.

   3.

   4.

3. Explain the difference between an iron triangle and an issue network.

   Iron Triangle:

   Issue Network:

4. What effect does bureaucracy have on the scope of government?

KEY TERMS

Identify and describe:

bureaucracy

patronage

Pendleton Civil Service Act

civil service

merit principle

Hatch Act

Office of Personnel Management (OPM)

GS (General Schedule) rating

Senior Executive Service

independent regulatory commission

government corporations

independent executive agencies

policy implementation

standard operating procedures

administrative discretion

street-level bureaucrats

regulation

deregulation

command-and-control policy

incentive system

executive orders

iron triangles

Compare and contrast:

patronage and merit principle

Pendleton Civil Service Act and civil service

civil service and merit principle

GS (General Schedule) rating and Senior Executive Service

independent regulatory commissions, government corporations, and independent executive agencies

standard operating procedures and administrative discretion

administrative discretion and street-level bureaucrats

regulation and deregulation

command-and-control policy and incentive system

Name that term:

1.   This law created the federal civil service.

      _____

2.   This law limits the political activity of government employees.

      _____

3.   This agency is in charge of hiring for most federal agencies.

      _____

4.   The Federal Trade Commission is an example of this.

      _____

5.   The U.S. Postal Service is an example of this.

      _____

6.   This is needed because most policies are not self-executing.

      _____

7.   Examples of these might include a police officer or a welfare worker.

      _____

8.	Presidents sometime use these to control the bureaucracy.

	_____

9.	These are also known as subgovernments.

	_____

USING YOUR UNDERSTANDING

1.	The organization of the federal government is very complex; policy responsibilities are delegated among many different agencies and offices. Take a look at the simplified organization chart of the bureaucracy. (See for example, Figure 15.3, p. 480.) Based on what you know about the particular responsibilities of these many offices, try to categorize them according to different policy arenas such as the economy, social welfare, equality issues, environment, technology, or national security. Keep in mind that these policy arenas encompass many different types of policies. Take note of any agencies that fall within one or more of the policy groups. Briefly describe what you found in terms of the relative organizational emphasis on each of the policy arenas.

2.	Regulations affect many different aspects of our everyday lives. (See the section, "A Full Day of Regulation," p. 493.) Keep a record of your regulated day from the time you wake up to the time you go to bed, recording which aspects of your life are regulated and what federal agency is doing the regulation. After your record is complete, make an overall assessment of the degree to which federal regulation affects you. Based on your assessment, consider whether or not the costs of regulation exceed the benefits it provides you. Also consider whether or not any of the regulations you recorded are unnecessary or could be handled to your satisfaction by some other method or by a private, rather than governmental, means.

MULTIPLE CHOICE QUESTIONS

Circle the correct answer:

1.	Which of the following is TRUE about the federal bureaucracy?
	a.	Most federal bureaucrats work in Washington, D.C.
	b.	The state and local governments have far more employees than the federal bureaucracy.
	c.	The size of the federal bureaucracy has grown dramatically over the past twenty years.
	d.	Most Americans are dissatisfied with their encounters with bureaucrats.
	e.	all of the above

2. The classic conception of a bureaucracy was advanced by _____, who argued that the bureaucracy was a "rational" way for a modern society to conduct its business.
   a. Max Weber
   b. Thomas Jefferson
   c. John Locke
   d. Charles L. Schultze
   e. James Madison

3. There are roughly _____ civilian federal government employees.
   a. 500,000
   b. 1 million
   c. 2.7 million
   d. 19.6 million
   e. 40 million

4. _____ is a hiring and promotion system based on knowing the right people, working in an election campaign, making large political donations, and/or having the right connections to win jobs with the government.
   a. The patronage system
   b. The federal civil service
   c. The bureaucracy
   d. The golden gate
   e. Administrative discretion

5. The Pendleton Act established the
   a. patronage system.
   b. federal civil service.
   c. Office of Management and Budget.
   d. plum book.
   e. Interstate Commerce Commission.

6. Once hired into the federal bureaucracy, a person is assigned a _____ rating, which determines one's salary range.
   a. Federal Register
   b. Weber
   c. General Schedule
   d. step ladder
   e. plum book

7. The rationale for the civil service rests on the
   a. goal of centralizing government employment at the federal level.
   b. desire to create a nonpartisan government service and promotion on the basis of merit.
   c. General Schedule rating system for patronage appointees.
   d. need to separate military institutions from civilian institutions to prevent undue military influence.
   e. need for job replacements when a new party comes to power.

8. The plum book lists
    a. all federal contracts available for bid.
    b. top federal jobs available by presidential appointment.
    c. all civil service jobs above GS 12.
    d. job openings in the prestigious Office of Personnel Management.
    e. appeals filed with the Merit Systems Protection Board.

9. Which of the following is a cabinet department?
    a. Department of State
    b. Department of Homeland Security
    c. Department of Education
    d. All of the above.
    e. None of the above.

10. Government corporations
    a. typically charge for their services at reduced rates.
    b. are independent regulatory agencies.
    c. provide services that cannot be provided by private businesses.
    d. tend to be controlled by interest groups.
    e. are always formed from "sick" industries.

11. Which of the following is NOT involved in implementation?
    a. Creating new agencies or assigning new responsibilities to existing agencies.
    b. Translating policy goals into operational rule and development of guidelines for programs.
    c. Coordinating resources and personnel to achieve intended goals.
    d. Passing legislation.
    e. None of the above.

12. Standard operating procedures accomplish all of the following EXCEPT
    a. bring uniformity to complex organizations.
    b. save time.
    c. make personnel interchangeable.
    d. reduce red tape.
    e. treat citizens equally, regardless of class or race.

13. What factor(s) work(s) against reorganizing the government to address the problems of fragmentation?
    a. The decentralization of power
    b. Hyperpluralism
    c. Elite theory
    d. All of the above.
    e. Both a and b.

14. The Supreme Court case of *Munn v. Illinois* (1877)
    a. declared that regulation was not within the realm of state powers.
    b. first established the right to own property as one of the rights of the Bill of Rights.
    c. set the precedent for deregulation.
    d. upheld the right of government to regulate the business operations of a firm.
    e. upheld the constitutionality of the Interstate Commerce Commission.

15. Deregulation has resulted, at least in part, in each of the following EXCEPT
    a. environmental damage.
    b. the proliferation of government agencies.
    c. competitive airline fares.
    d. an expensive bailout of the savings and loan industry.
    e. less government oversight in some key areas.

16. The typical system of regulation in which government tells business how to reach certain goals, checks that these commands are followed, and punishes offenders is known as
    a. the incentive system.
    b. command-and-control policy.
    c. deregulation.
    d. the merit system.
    e. patronage.

17. As the oversight powers of Congress in regard to the bureaucracy have become more vigorous,
    a. Congress is increasingly the policy-implementation branch of government.
    b. it has become easier to rein in the bureaucracy.
    c. they have also become more fragmented.
    d. "iron triangles" have weakened considerably.
    e. the amount of government corruption has decreased dramatically.

18. A subcommittee on aging, senior citizens interest groups, and the Social Security Administration are likely to
    a. disagree on the need for more Social Security benefits.
    b. agree on the need for more Social Security benefits.
    c. agree on the need to eliminate Social Security benefits.
    d. Dominate Social Security policymaking.
    e. B and d.

19. Subgovernments promote
    a. centralization of authority.
    b. strong executive branch control of policymaking.
    c. the control of the bureaucracy by Congress.
    d. decentralized and fragmented policymaking.
    e. presidential control of bureaucratic discretion.

20. A group of participants in bureaucratic policymaking with technical policy expertise and intellectual and emotional commitment to the issue is called
    a. a government corporation.
    b. an "iron triangle."
    c. a subgovernment.
    d. an issue network.
    e. a vested cohort.

TRUE/FALSE QUESTIONS

Circle the correct answer:

1. Each bureaucratic agency is created by Congress, which sets its budget and writes the basic policies it is to administer. T / F

2. Scholars have demonstrated that government bureaucracies are more efficient and effective than private bureaucracies. T / F

3. The merit principle determines entrance and promotion on the basis of "who you know." T / F

4. The Pendleton Civil Service Act of 1883 created the federal civil service. T / F

5. The Hatch Act of 1940 prohibits civil service employees from active participation in partisan politics. T / F

6. The government established Amtrak as the government corporation providing passenger railroad service when the private passenger railroads became a sick industry some years ago. T / F

7. Policy implementation is the stage of policymaking between the establishment of a policy and the consequences of the policy for the people it affects. T / F

8. One of the staunchest supporters of deregulation was President Ronald Reagan. T / F

9. Because the voters do not elect civil servants, bureaucracies cannot respond to or represent the public's interests. T / F

10. Mutually dependent relationships between bureaucratic agencies, interest groups, and congressional committees are known as iron triangles. T / F

SHORT ANSWER/SHORT ESSAY QUESTIONS

1. Explain Max Weber's classic conception of bureaucracy.

2. How and under what circumstances was the civil service created?

3. What is the difference between administrative discretion and standard operating procedures?

4. What is the plum book, and what is its role in staffing the federal bureaucracy? How do its offices differ from those staffed through the civil service? How do the people who serve in plum book jobs differ from civil service employees? Explain.

5. What is deregulation? Who are its proponents and why do they favor deregulation?

ESSAY QUESTIONS

1. Evaluate the size of the American bureaucracy. Is the bureaucracy too big or too small?

2. What is an independent regulatory agency, and what does it do? Briefly name two or three examples of such agencies. How do they differ from cabinet departments in terms of presidential control? How do they differ from government corporations? Are these differences appropriate? Explain.

3. Describe the purpose of the Voting Rights Act of 1965. What factors made it a successful case of implementation? Why are laws and regulations seldom this successful? Explain.

4. What methods are at the disposal of presidents and Congress to control the bureaucracy? Which are most widely used? How effective are they? Do you think these controls are sufficient? Explain.

5. What is an "iron triangle," and what is its significance in American government? Give an example. Are these natural groupings, which should be encouraged or at least tolerated, or are they fundamentally dangerous to a democracy? Explain.

CHAPTER 16

THE FEDERAL COURTS

CHAPTER OUTLINE

I. Politics in Action: Appealing to the Supreme Court (pp. 509–510)
    A. The Supreme Court has considerable power.
    B. The Supreme Court makes only the tiniest fraction of American judicial policy.

II. The Nature of the Judicial System (pp. 510–513)
    A. Introduction
        1. In criminal law cases, an individual is charged by the government with violating a specific law.
        2. Civil law involves no charge of criminality, but concerns a dispute between two parties.
    B. Participants in the Judicial System
        1. Litigants
            a. Every case is a dispute between a plaintiff and a defendant.
            b. **Standing to sue** means that litigants must have serious interest in a case.
            c. **Class action suits** permit a small number of people to sue on behalf of all other people similarly situated.
            d. **Justiciable disputes** are issues that are capable of being settled by legal methods.
        2. Groups sometimes try to influence courts by using particular cases and litigants and *amicus curiae* briefs.
        3. Attorneys

III. The Structure of the Federal Judicial System (pp. 513–518)
    A. Introduction
        1. Congress has created *constitutional courts* (lower federal courts) and *legislative courts* (courts for specialized purposes).
        2. Courts with **original jurisdiction** are those in which a case is heard first, usually in a trial.
        3. Courts with **appellate jurisdiction** hear cases brought to them on appeal from a lower court.
    B. District Courts
        1. The entry point for most litigation in the federal courts is one of the 91 **district courts.**
        2. Most of the cases handled in the district courts are routine.
    C. Courts of Appeal
        1. The U.S. **courts of appeal** are appellate courts empowered to review all final decisions of district courts.

2. The courts of appeal focus on correcting errors of procedure and law that occurred in the original proceedings of legal cases.
D. The Supreme Court
1. The pinnacle of the American judicial system is the U.S. **Supreme Court.**
2. Almost all of the business of the Court comes from the appellate process.

IV. The Politics of Judicial Selection (pp. 518–522)
A. The Lower Courts
1. According to **senatorial courtesy,** nominations for lower court positions are not confirmed when opposed by a senator of the president's party from the state in which the nominee is to serve.
2. The president usually has more influence in the selection of judges to the federal courts of appeal than to the federal district courts.
B. The Supreme Court
1. Nominations to the Court may be a president's most important legacy to the nation.
2. The president operates under fewer constraints in nominating members to the Supreme Court.
3. Nominations may run in to trouble at the end of a president's term or when the president's party is in the minority in the Senate.

V. The Background of Judges and Justices (pp. 522–526)
A. Judges serving on the federal district and circuit courts are all lawyers and overwhelmingly white males.
B. Supreme Court justices are an elite group.
C. Ideology is important in the selection of judges and justices.

VI. The Courts as Policymakers (pp. 526–533)
A. Accepting Cases
1. The most common way for the Court to put a case on its docket is by issuing to a lower federal or state court a *writ of certiorari,* a formal document that calls up a case.
2. The **solicitor general** is in charge of the appellate court litigation of the federal government.
B. Making Decisions
1. *Amicus curiae* ("friend of the court") briefs are briefs from parties who are interested in the outcome of the case but are not formal litigants.
2. An **opinion** is a statement of the legal reasoning behind the decision.
3. The vast majority of cases reaching the courts are settled on the principle of *stare decisis*, meaning that an earlier decision should hold for the case being considered.
4. All courts rely heavily upon **precedent**, the way similar cases were handled in the past, as a guide to current decisions.
5. **Original intent** holds that judges and justices should determine the intent of the framers of the Constitution regarding a particular matter and decide cases in line with that intent.

C.   Implementing Court Decisions
      1.   **Judicial implementation** refers to how and whether court decisions are translated into actual policy, affecting the behavior of others.
      2.   Implementation of court decisions involves interpreting, implementing, and consumer populations.

VII.   The Courts and the Policy Agenda (pp. 533–537)
      A.   A Historical Review
            1.   John Marshall and the Growth of Judicial Review
                  a.   In *Marbury v. Madison* (1803), Chief Justice Marshall established the power of **judicial review,** the power of the courts to hold acts of Congress, and by implication the executive, in violation of the Constitution.
            2.   The "Nine Old Men"
            3.   The Warren Court
            4.   The Burger Court
                  a.   The Burger Court was more conservative than the liberal Warren Court.
                  b.   In *United States v. Nixon* (1974), the Burger Court ordered President Nixon to turn over White House tapes to the courts.
            5.   The Rehnquist Court

VIII.   Understanding the Courts (pp. 537–541)
      A.   The Courts and Democracy
      B.   What Courts Should Do: The Scope of Judicial Power
            1.   **Judicial restraint** is when judges adhere closely to precedent and play minimal policymaking roles.
            2.   **Judicial activism** is when judges make bolder policy decisions, even charting new constitutional ground.
            3.   The doctrine of **political questions** is a means to avoid deciding some cases, principally those regarding conflicts between the president and Congress.
            4.   If an issue is one of **statutory construction,** in which a court interprets an act of Congress, the legislature routinely passes legislation that clarifies existing laws.

IX.   Summary (pp. 541–542)

LEARNING   OBJECTIVES

After studying Chapter 16, you should be able to:

1.   Understand the nature of the judicial system.

2.   Explain the organization of courts in the United States and the nature of their jurisdiction.

3.   Describe the role of judges in the judicial process, as well as their backgrounds and how they were selected.

4.   Discuss Supreme Court policymaking and judicial implementation.

5.   Explain the role of the courts in shaping the policy agenda in America.

6.   Evaluate how the courts operate in a democratic system and how their activities affect the scope of government.

The following exercises will help you meet these objectives:

Objective 1:   Understand the nature of the judicial system.

1.   Explain the difference between criminal law and civil law.

Criminal Law:

Civil Law:

2.   List three regular participants in the judicial system other than judges.

1.

2.

3.

3.   What are justiciable disputes?

Objective 2: Explain the organization of courts in the United States and the nature of their jurisdiction.

1. What are the differences between constitutional courts and legislative courts?

    Constitutional Courts:

    Legislative Courts:

2. Complete the following table on the structure of the federal judicial system.

Court	Number of Courts	Number of Judges	Jurisdiction	Policy Implications
District Court				
Court of Appeal				
Supreme Court				

3. What is the role of a U.S. attorney?

Objective 3: Describe the role of judges in the judicial process, as well as their backgrounds and how they were selected.

1. Explain the practice of senatorial courtesy.

2. Name three conditions under which nominations to the Supreme Court are more likely to run into trouble.

    1.

    2.

    3.

3.   Present a demographic profile of the "typical" federal judge.

4.   List six criteria that have been important in choosing Supreme Court justices over the years.

     1.

     2.

     3.

     4.

     5.

     6.

Objective 4: Discuss Supreme Court policymaking and judicial implementation.

     1.   What are the four key functions of the solicitor general?

          1.

          2.

          3.

          4.

     2.   What are the functions of *amicus curiae* briefs?

     3.   What are the differences between a majority opinion, a dissenting opinion, and a concurring opinion?

     Majority Opinion:

     Dissenting Opinion:

Concurring Opinion:

4.   What is the difference between *stare decisis* and precedent?

        Stare Decisis:

        Precedent:

5.   List and explain the three elements of judicial implementation according to Charles Johnson and Bradley Canon.

        1.

        2.

        3.

Objective 5: Explain the role of the courts in shaping the policy agenda in America.

      1.   Explain the principle of judicial review.

2. Complete the following table on public policy and the Supreme Court.

Court	Basic Ideology	Judicial Restraint or Judicial Activism	Key Cases
Warren Court			
Burger Court			
Rehnquist Court			

Objective 6: Evaluate how the courts operate in a democratic system and how their activities affect the scope of government.

1. In what ways might it be said that courts are not a very democratic institution?

2. Explain the difference between judicial activism and judicial restraint.

Judicial Activism:

Judicial Restraint:

3.   Define the terms "political question" and "statutory construction" as they apply to the Supreme Court and give an example of each.

Term	Definition	Example
Political Question		
Statutory Construction		

KEY TERMS

Identify and describe:

standing to sue

class action suits

justiciable disputes

amicus curiae briefs

original jurisdiction

appellate jurisdiction

district courts

courts of appeal

Supreme Court

senatorial courtesy

solicitor general

opinion

stare decisis

precedent

judicial implementation

original intent

Marbury v. Madison

judicial review

United States v. Nixon

judicial restraint

judicial activism

political questions

statutory construction

Compare and contrast:

standing to sue and class action suits

original jurisdiction and appellate jurisdiction

district courts, courts of appeal, and Supreme Court

stare decisis and precedent

Marbury v. Madison and judicial review

judicial restraint and judicial activism

political questions and statutory construction

Name that term:

1.   These are capable of being settled by legal methods.

    _____

2.   This is a way of disposing of state-level federal judicial nominations.

    _____

3.   This office represents the government before the Supreme Court.

    _____

4.   Interested parties who are not litigants submit these.

    _____

5.   This is a statement of the legal reasoning behind a Supreme Court decision.

    _____

6.   This determines how and whether court decisions are translated into policy.

    _____

7.   This is sometimes referred to as strict constructionism.

    _____

8.   This Supreme Court case hastened the resignation of a president.

    _____

9.   This doctrine is used to avoid deciding some cases.

    _____

USING YOUR UNDERSTANDING

1. Investigate the composition of the current Supreme Court in terms of the different types of individuals that are found there. Find out who appointed them, their political party affiliations, their ages, their ethnicities, their religions, their home states, their previous occupations, and other such defining characteristics. Then see if you can find out how the different justices voted on some recent court cases having to do with public policy issues. Try to develop a profile of the Supreme Court in which you relate the characteristics of its members to their voting behaviors. Briefly discuss the implications of a justice's background for the way he or she behaves on the bench.

2. Conduct a study of judicial selection by comparing the two Supreme Court nominations from the Clinton administration (Ruth Bader Ginsburg and Stephen G. Breyer) with the two nominations from the George W. Bush administration (Samuel A. Alito and John G. Roberts). How do Bush's choices differ from Clinton's choices? How did the nominations differ? What were the most important factors influencing the presidents' choices? Who else was considered as a potential nominee by each president, and why were the successful candidates chosen instead of any of the others? How did the public react to the nominations? How did the Senate react to the nominations? Compare the confirmation hearings of the nominees. How did they differ and how were they similar? Evaluate the judicial selection process for Supreme Court justices in light of these cases. Is the process fair? How might the process be improved?

MULTIPLE CHOICE QUESTIONS

Circle the correct answer:

1. One of the differences between criminal law and civil law is that in civil law
    a. there is no charge that a law has been violated.
    b. there is no jury.
    c. the case cannot be appealed.
    d. the government cannot be one of the litigants.
    e. common law takes precedent over statutory law.

2. Standing to sue is determined by
    a. the judiciary committee of Congress.
    b. whether or not the case involves a class action suit.
    c. the solicitor general's office.
    d. whether or not the litigants have a serious interest in a case.
    e. a court-appointed jury.

3. One constraint on federal courts is that they may decide only
    a. statutory law.
    b. appellate cases.
    c. justiciable disputes.
    d. constitutional issues.
    e. interstate conflicts.

4. The Tax Court, Court of Military Appeals, Court of Claims, and Court of International Trade are examples of
    a. Legislative courts
    b. Appellate courts
    c. Supreme courts
    d. Independent regulatory commissions
    e. Courts of appeal

5. _____ courts are the only federal courts in which trials are held and in which juries may be impaneled.
    a. District
    b. Appellate
    c. Supreme
    d. Legislative
    e. Specialized

6. For handling cases at the courts of appeal level, the United States is divided into _____ judicial circuits, including one for the District of Columbia.
    a. 55
    b. 26
    c. 12
    d. 51
    e. 91

7. Which of the following statements about the Supreme Court is FALSE?
    a. Congress has altered the size of the Supreme Court many times.
    b. The Constitution sets the number of Supreme Court justices at nine.
    c. In 1866, Congress reduced the size of the Court from 10 to seven so that Andrew Johnson could not nominate new justices to fill vacancies.
    d. Congress increased the size of the Court to nine during President Grant's administration because it was confident that he would nominate judges that Congress approved of.
    e. All of the above are false.

8. The customary manner in which the Senate disposes of federal judicial nominations in one state is through
    a. the seniority system.
    b. senatorial courtesy.
    c. majority vote, usually along party lines.
    d. judicial review.
    e. state's review.

9. Usually more than 90 percent of presidents' judicial nominations are members of
    a. the Department of Justice.
    b. law school faculties.
    c. state legislatures.
    d. their own party.
    e. Congress.

10. A *writ of certiorari*
    a. means that judges have decided a case on the basis of precedent.
    b. frees a detained person whom a court has found is being held in violation of due process.
    c. is used by the Supreme Court to call up a case.
    d. is the official record of a court's decision, stating the facts of the case and the rationale for the decision.
    e. is used to move a case from a court of original jurisdiction to a federal district court.

11. A *per curiam* decision is a
    a. decision without explanation.
    b. decision by the court not to hear a case.
    c. written opinion of a case.
    d. decision that can be used as a precedent.
    e. court decision of narrow scope that can be issued by a single judge in limited circumstances.

12. Original intent suggests
    a. the Constitution should be interpreted according to the intent of the Framers.
    b. the decision must stand.
    c. the content of an opinion is as important as the decision.
    d. all Supreme Court nominees must not be opposed.
    e. plaintiffs must have a serous interest in a case.

13. Judicial review means
    a. the right of the Congress to determine whether a decision of the Supreme Court is or is not Constitutional.
    b. the power to remove Supreme Court justices from the bench if deemed unfit to retain office.
    c. the right of the president to determine whether a decision of the Supreme Court is or is not constitutional.
    d. the right of the courts to determine the constitutionality of acts of the legislature and/or the executive.
    e. the solicitor general's oversight of the courts to make sure that rulings are uniform nationwide and that procedural due process is being followed by all courts.

14. The Rehnquist Court
    a. slowly chipped away at liberal decisions.
    b. was deeply divided between liberals and conservatives, and personality conflicts have added to a court in turmoil.
    c. created a revolution in constitutional law.
    d. was a disappointment to conservatives.
    e. went further to shape public policy than the Warren Court.

15. In *Federalist*, No. 78, Hamilton argued that the judiciary would
    a. be the most dangerous branch.
    b. be the least dangerous branch.
    c. control the purpose.
    d. control the sword.
    e. both c and d.

16. Advocates of _____ emphasize that the courts may alleviate pressing needs, especially of those who are weak politically or economically, left unmet by the majoritarian political process.
    a. judicial activism
    b. the jurisprudence of original intent
    c. judicial restraint
    d. judicial implementation
    e. judicial review

17. As a means to avoid deciding some cases, the federal courts have developed a doctrine of
    a. judicial precedent.
    b. strict constructionism.
    c. statutory construction.
    d. judicial activism.
    e. political questions.

18. Cases that involve statutory construction
    a. can be overturned by Congress by clarifying an existing law.
    b. must be decided according to a strict construction of the Constitution.
    c. are usually precedent setting.
    d. involve policy issues.
    e. can only be changed through a constitutional amendment.

19. Which of the following resulted from the 2004 Supreme Court ruling that the Guantanamo Bay naval base fell within the jurisdiction of U.S. law and therefore the habeas corpus statute applies?
    a. Congress moved to impeach justices from the Supreme Court.
    b. Congress altered the federal courts, stripping them from hearing habeas corpus petitions from the detainees.
    c. The Bush Administration selected a different naval base to replace Guantanamo Bay.
    d. Congress began the work of amending the Constitution.
    e. All of the above.

20. Approximately how many state and local laws has the Supreme Court found unconstitutional?
    a. Fewer than 200
    b. 1,100
    c. 5,000
    d. 10,000
    e. 20,000

TRUE/FALSE QUESTIONS

Circle the correct answer:

1. *Amicus curiae* briefs are legal briefs submitted by "friends of the court." T / F

2. Original jurisdiction refers to the jurisdiction of courts that hear cases brought to them on appeal from lower courts. T / F

3. Most civil and criminal cases begin and end in the state courts. T / F

4. Only members of the Supreme Court are called justices; all others are called judges. T / F

5. The current chief justice of the U.S. Supreme Court is John Roberts. T / F

6. The vast majority of cases reaching the federal courts are settled on the basis of *stare decisis*. T / F

7. *Marbury v. Madison* was the first case that struck down a legislative act in the United States. T / F

8. *Bush v. Gore* (2000) represents a high point in judicial restraint. T / F

9. The Warren Court was an especially active court. T / F

10. When the court interprets an act of Congress, one response on the part of Congress is to pass legislation that clarifies the existing law, in effect overturning the court. T / F

SHORT ANSWER/SHORT ESSAY QUESTIONS

1. Describe the typical participants and types of cases involved in the judicial system.

2. What is the difference between Constitutional courts and legislative courts?

3. Compare and contrast the Supreme Court with lower federal courts in terms of how judges are chosen, how cases are chosen, and who hears cases before the court.

4. What is the principle of *stare decisis* and why and how is its use connected to the legitimacy of the courts?

5. Compare and contrast the principles of judicial restraint and judicial activism.

ESSAY QUESTIONS

1. Discuss three decisions of the Supreme Court and explain how they have affected the extent to which our political system is democratic.

2. How are nominees to the federal district courts selected? Who has veto power over the selections, and what is this called? Who checks the background of nominees to these courts? Is the entire selection process sensible? Explain.

3. What kinds of cases are accepted for review by the Supreme Court, and how does the process usually work? Why are the Court's rulings so significant? Explain.

4. How do court decisions become public policy? What is involved in judicial implementation? Use examples to illustrate the potential problems of implementing court decisions.

5. What is the proper role of a Supreme Court justice? How ought to justices apply their personal preferences, partisanship, and political ideology to their work, if at all? It is reasonable to expect justices to put aside their personalities and human qualities when approaching the Constitution?

CHAPTER 17

Economic Policymaking

CHAPTER OUTLINE

I.   Introduction (pp. 547–548)
      A.   Capitalism is an economic system in which individuals and corporations own the principal means of production.
      B.   A mixed economy is a system in which the government, while not commanding the economy, is still deeply involved in economic decisions.
      C.   Multinational corporations, businesses with vast holdings in many countries, dominate the world's economy.

II.   Government, Politics, and the Economy (pp. 549–554)
      A.   Economic Policy at Work: Wal-Mart
            1.   Government Regulation and Business Practices
                  a.   The main government regulatory agency responsible for the regulation of business practices is the Securities and Exchange Commission (SEC).
                  b.   Minimum wage is the legal minimum hourly wage for large employers.
                  c.   A labor union is a workers' organization for bargaining with an employer.
                  d.   Collective bargaining consists of negotiations between representatives of labor unions and management to determine pay and acceptable working conditions.
            2.   Wal-Mart and the World Economy
      B.   "It's the Economy, Stupid": Voters, Politicians, and Economic Policy
            1.   Economic conditions are the best single predictors of voters' evaluation of the president.
            2.   Democrats stress the importance of employment; Republicans stress the importance of inflation.
      C.   Two Major Worries: Unemployment and Inflation
            1.   The unemployment rate has a direct affect on government and politics.
            2.   The Consumer Price Index (CPI) measures inflation (the rise in prices for consumer goods).

III. Policies for Controlling the Economy (pp. 554–557)
      A.   Laissez-faire is the principle that government should not meddle with the economy.
      B.   Monetary Policy and "The Fed"
            1.   Monetary policy is the manipulation of the supply of money and credit in private hands.

2.   Monetarism holds that the supply of money is the key to the nation's economic health.

3.   The main agency for making monetary policy is the Board of Governors of the Federal Reserve System.

C.   Fiscal Policy of Presidents and Parties

    1.   Fiscal policy describes the impact of the federal budget on the economy.

    2.   Keynesian economic theory holds that government spending can help the economy weather its normal ups and downs.

    3.   Supply-side economics argues that the key task for government economic policy is to stimulate the supply of goods, not their demand.

IV.   Why it is Hard to Control the Economy (pp. 557–558)

A.   Instruments for controlling the economy are difficult to use.

B.   Economic policies take a long time to implement.

C.   Most of the budget expenditures are uncontrollable.

D.   The private sector dominates the economy.

V.   Politics, Policy, and the International Economy (pp. 558–560)

A.   Most emerging economies want to follow an economic policy of protectionism.

B.   The World Trade Organization (WTO) is an international organization that regulates international trade.

C.   The loss of American jobs overseas has become an important political issue.

VI.   Arenas of Economic Policymaking (pp. 560–562)

A.   Business and Public Policy

    1.   Corporate Corruption and Concentration

        a.   Antitrust policy ensures competition and prevents monopoly.

    2.   Regulating and Benefiting Business

B.   Consumer Policy: The Rise of the Consumer Lobby

    1.   The Food and Drug Administration (FDA) has broad regulatory powers over the manufacturing, contents, marketing, and labeling of food and drugs.

    2.   The Federal Trade Commission (FTC) has become a defender of consumer interests in truth in advertising.

C.   Labor and Government

    1.   The National Labor Relations Act guarantees workers the right of collective bargaining.

    2.   The Taft-Hartley Act continued to guarantee collective bargaining, but prohibited unfair practices by unions as well.

    3.   Section 14B of Taft-Hartley permitted right-to-work laws that forbid labor contracts from requiring workers to join unions to hold their jobs.

VII.   Understanding Economic Policymaking (pp. 563–564)

A.   Democracy and Economic Policymaking

B.   Economic Policymaking and the Scope of Government

VIII.   Summary (p. 564)

LEARNING OBJECTIVES

After studying Chapter 17, you should be able to:

1. Understand the relationship between politics and the economy.

2. Describe the policies and programs that policymakers use to affect the state of the economy.

3. Explain why it is hard to control both the domestic and international economy.

4. Discuss the major issues and policy directions that have been pursued in the areas of business, consumer, and labor policy.

5. Understand the relationship between democracy, the scope of government, and economic policymaking in the United States.

The following exercises will help you meet these objectives:

Objective 1: Understand the relationship between politics and the economy.

1. Briefly explain how Wal-Mart can be used to illustrate each of the following concepts:

    Inflation:

    Securities and Exchange Commission:

    Labor union:

    Collective bargaining:

    Occupational Health and Safety Administration:

    Globalization:

2. Explain the basic difference between the Republican Party and the Democratic Party in terms of their approaches to economic policies.

Republicans:

Democrats:

3. Briefly explain how the unemployment rate is measured.

4. What is the Consumer Price Index (CPI) and why is it important?

Objective 2: Describe the instruments and programs that policymakers use to affect the state of the economy.

1. Explain how the Fed works to affect the supply of money and credit.

2. What is fiscal policy?

3. Explain the basic differences between Keynesian economic theory and supply-side economics.

Keynesian Theory:

Supply-Side Economics:

Objective 3: Explain why it is hard to control both the domestic and international economy.

1.   What is the "political business cycle"?

2.   Explain how the American capitalist system imposes restraints on controlling the economy.

3.   What are the major arguments for and against the World Trade Organization?

Objective 4: Discuss the major issues and policy directions that have been pursued in the areas of business, consumer, and labor policy.

1.   Complete the following table listing one major congressional act and one major governmental policy for each of the arenas of economic policymaking discussed in the text.

Arena	Major Congressional Act	Major Government Policy
Business		
Consumers		
Labor		

2.   List four ways in which the government benefits business.

1.

2.

3.

4.

3.   How do the Food and Drug Administration (FDA) and the Federal Trade Commission (FTC) benefit consumers?

FDA:

FTC:

4.   What were the main provisions of the National Labor Relations Act and the Taft-Hartley Act?

National Labor Relations Act:

Taft-Hartley Act:

Objective 5: Understand the relationship between democracy, the scope of government, and economic policymaking in the United States.

1.   What does the conflict about free trade in 2008 tell us about democracy and economic policymaking?

2. What is the main difference between liberal and conservative views of the scope of government in economic policymaking?

Liberals:

Conservatives:

KEY TERMS

Identify and describe:

capitalism

mixed economy

multinational corporations

Securities and Exchange Commission

minimum wage

labor union

collective bargaining

unemployment rate

inflation

Consumer Price Index (CPI)

Laissez-faire

monetary policy

monetarism

Federal Reserve System

fiscal policy

Keynesian economic theory

supply-side economics

protectionism

World Trade Organization (WTO)

antitrust policy

Food and Drug Administration (FDA)

National Labor Relations Act

Compare and contrast:

capitalism and mixed economy

labor union and collective bargaining

inflation and Consumer Price Index (CPI)

laissez-faire, monetarism, and Keynesian economic theory

monetary policy and fiscal policy

Keynesian economic theory and supply-side economics

protectionism and World Trade Organization (WTO)

National Labor Relations Act and collective bargaining

Name that term:

1. Some of these have annual budgets exceeding those of foreign countries.

   _____

2. This agency was created during the New Deal to regulate stock fraud.

   _____

3. Today this amounts to $6.55 per hour.

   _____

4. This is the percentage of Americans actively seeking employment but unable to find work.

   _____

5. It regulates the lending practices of banks.

   _____

6. This economic theory was popularized by President Reagan.

   _____

7. This is used to ensure competition and prevent monopoly.

   _____

8. This agency is responsible for ascertaining the safety and effectiveness of new drugs before approving them for marketing in the United States.

   _____

USING YOUR UNDERSTANDING

1. Find copies of the government's objective indicators of economic conditions—the unemployment and inflation rates—for some recent years. Government Internet sources would be a good place to start. Try your hand at plotting these indicators on a graph. Then try to locate an indicator of the importance of these issues on the public agenda, as measured by public opinion about the seriousness of these economic problems. Plot this indicator along with

the objective indicators you found. If a national election occurred during the time frame you are considering, draw a line representing when the election occurred. Briefly describe what you found in terms of the relationship between the government's measurement of economic problems and their place on the public's agenda. If applicable, describe the apparent impact of the election on the indicators you plotted.

2. Using newspapers, newsmagazines and/or the Internet, collect some current examples of economic policymaking in the United States. Try to find items that illustrate the different tools that policymakers use to try to control the economy and the different sectors of the economy that they seek to control. Consider the impact of the political party in power on current economic policymaking and whether or not it is consistent with what would be expected. Describe what you found in terms of the direction and impact of contemporary policies in the economic arena.

MULTIPLE CHOICE QUESTIONS

Circle the correct answer:

1. One of the responsibilities of the National Bureau of Economic Research is
   a. To set the exchange rate for U.S. currency.
   b. To regulate trade.
   c. To oversee the implementation of tax policy.
   d. To declare the U.S. economy is in recession.
   e. All of these are responsibilities of the National Bureau of Economic Research.

2. When the economy experiences two consecutive quarters of negative growth, it is said to be in
   a. A hard time.
   b. A great depression.
   c. A modest downturn.
   d. A cycle of decline.
   e. A recession.

3. Thomas Jefferson's economic ideas ultimately lost out to Alexander Hamilton's because Jefferson
   a. Supported slavery.
   b. Favored farmers and small towns.
   c. Advocated five-year plans to promote industrial growth.
   d. Sought to equalize wealth.
   e. Advocated a national income tax.

4. Why has globalization added income to the average U.S. family?
   a. Because it has allowed them to purchase cheaper products.
   b. Because illegal immigrants work for lower wages.
   c. Because stores like Wal-Mart have fought against labor unions.
   d. Because it has increased the amount companies are willing to pay employees.
   e. Because it has allowed the average family to travel the world in search of bargains.

5. The issue most stressed by Democrats is
   a. High tax rates.
   b. Employment.
   c. Inflation.
   d. Home ownership.
   e. Free trade.

6. The percentage of Americans seeking work, but who are unable to find it is known as
   a. The rate of discouraged workers.
   b. Inflation.
   c. Stagflation.
   d. The unemployment rate.
   e. The underemployment rate.

7. Why isn't unemployment among younger workers an important campaign issue?
   a. Because younger people are less likely to be unemployed than older people.
   b. Because younger people do not participate as regularly in elections as older people.
   c. Because younger voters are all in college and high school.
   d. Because younger workers are ineligible for unemployment insurance.
   e. Because it is easier for younger workers to find new jobs.

8. The rise in the price for consumer goods is known as
   a. Deflation.
   b. Stagflation.
   c. Inflation.
   d. Conflagration.
   e. Stagnation.

9. One reason for inflation in the cost of food is
   a. America's obesity problem.
   b. The increased use of "biofuels"
   c. Collusion on the part of large food growers.
   d. Union demands for increased wages and benefits.
   e. The end of price controls for key food items.

10. The Federal Reserve System is governed by
    a. A seven member Board of Governors appointed by the president and confirmed by the Senate.
    b. The director of the Internal Revenue Service.
    c. The president's Council of Economic Advisors.
    d. The Secretary of the Treasury.
    e. The Secretary of Commerce.

11. Which of the following statements about the tools government has to manage the economy is accurate?
    a. The ability to manipulate the supply of credit in private hands is the most important tool the government has.
    b. Monetary policy is the most important tool the government has.
    c. The most important tool government has is its control over the money supply.
    d. None of the above.
    e. All of the above.

12. An example of the use of monetary policy is
    a. Instituting a freeze on prices.
    b. Subsidizing farmers.
    c. Making low interest, long term loans to college students.
    d. Requiring banks to keep more money on reserve.
    e. All of the above.

13. Taxing, spending, and borrowing decisions by Congress and the president are known collectively as
    a. Supply-side economics
    b. Monetary policy
    c. Budgetary policy
    d. Fiscal policy
    e. Econometrics

14. Since the New Deal
    a. Policymakers have made it part of their regular business to seek to control the economy.
    b. The federal government has become less involved in economic policy.
    c. The principle of laissez-faire has dominated economic policy.
    d. Economic issues have become less politicized.
    e. Keynesian economics has replaced supply-side theory in American fiscal policy.

15. An example of a Keynesian economic policy is:
    a. Allowing the free market to determine economic health.
    b. Creating more money to help pay for deficits.
    c. Borrowing funds to cover the federal deficit.
    d. Creating government jobs to ease unemployment.
    e. Deregulating commerce and industry.

16. One of the major causes of the Great Depression was
    a. The promotion of international trade epitomized by the formation of the World Trade Organization.
    b. The New Deal economic policies of President Franklin Roosevelt.
    c. The 20 percent hike in tariffs known as the Smoot-Hawley tariff.
    d. The tax cuts advocated by President Reagan.
    e. Strikes waged by labor unions for higher wages and benefits.

17. Antitrust legislation is designed to
    a. Promote union rights.
    b. Prevent foreign investors from owning U.S. corporations.
    c. Stop the growth of multinational corporations like Wal-Mart.
    d. Ensure competition and prevent monopolies.
    e. Foster industrial growth through tariffs designed to keep out foreign goods.

18. The major change in government policy toward labor took place during
    a. World War I
    b. The New Deal
    c. The Progressive Era
    d. The 1960s
    e. The late 1890s.

19. The National Labor Relations Act was passed in order to
    a. Assure workers the right to join and form unions.
    b. Limit the power and influence of labor unions.
    c. Prohibit corporate monopolies.
    d. Determine a national minimum wage.
    e. Prevent unions from forming in the public sector.

20. Legislation that forbids labor contracts from requiring workers to join unions in order to hold their jobs is known as
    a. Unfair labor practice legislation.
    b. Right-to-work laws.
    c. Right-to-choose laws.
    d. Right-to-unionize laws.
    e. Fair share laws.

TRUE/FALSE QUESTIONS

Circle the correct answer:

1. Part of the economic slowdown that hit the United States in 2008 is the result of a significant increase in the cost of oil. T / F

2. The father of the American economy is Thomas Jefferson. T / F

3. The Securities and Exchange Commission is responsible for the regulation of business practices and stock fraud. T / F

4. "Pocketbook voting" is something done by unsophisticated voters. T / F

5. "Discouraged workers" is a term that captures how many Americans are unsatisfied with their current jobs and are searching for new positions. T / F

6. The Consumer Price Index measures changes in the cost of buying a fixed basket of goods. T / F

7. The Federal Reserve System has had limited ability to prevent economic swings because of how politicized the system has become. T / F

8. The major economic hero of the Republican Party is Ronald Reagan. T / F

9. Critics claim that China's human rights abuses allow factory owners to keep labor costs artificially low. T / F

10. Throughout most of the nineteenth century, the federal government allied with business elites to squelch labor unions. T / F

SHORT ANSWER/SHORT ESSAY QUESTIONS

1. Explain the arguments in favor of and opposed to the stimulus package promoted by President Bush and passed by the Congress in 2008.

2. Why are companies like Wal-Mart partly to blame for the decline of labor unions' political and economic power?

3. Explain how the New Deal policies of President Franklin Roosevelt represent an example of Keynesian economic theory put into practice.

4. Explain how the federal government has sought to prevent monopolies and promote competition.

5. What is meant by democratic control over economic policymaking?

ESSAY QUESTIONS

1. How has globalization transformed the American economy, and how has the American public reacted to these changes? Subsequently, how have American politicians and political parties responded to globalization?

2. Compare and contrast the role for government in shaping economic policy offered by Democrats and Republicans. Citing specific examples, how have candidates from each party successfully campaigned on their economic policies?

3. Explain how monetary policy is made in the United States? Why was the decision made to place the Federal Reserve System beyond the control of the president and Congress?

4. Explain what is meant by protectionism. Why have individuals and politicians supported protectionist policies in the past? Is protectionism still a viable policy option for American politicians? Why or why not?

5. Should American politicians and citizens understand the rise of China as a threat to America's economic well-being, or as a benefit?

CHAPTER 18

Social Welfare Policymaking

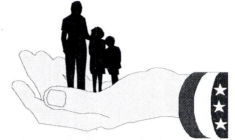

CHAPTER OUTLINE

I.   Politics in Action: The Family and Social Policy (pp. 569–570)
        A.   Social welfare policies involve the vast range of public policies that support individuals and families.
        B.   Debates about social policy are debates about social responsibility.

II.   What is Social Policy and Why is it so Controversial? (pp. 570–572)
        A.   **Social welfare policies** are the programs through which government provides support and assistance to specific groups of people.
        B.   **Entitlement programs** consist of government benefits that certain qualified individuals are entitled to by law, regardless of need.
        C.   **Means-tested programs** are benefits provided only to people with specific needs.

III.   Income, Poverty, and Public Policy (pp. 572–577)
        A.   Who's Getting What?
                1.   **Income distribution** describes the share of national income earned by various groups in the United States.
                2.   **Income** is the amount of money collected between any two points in time.
                3.   **Wealth** is the value of one's assets.
        B.   Who's Poor in America?
                1.   The **poverty line** takes into account what a family would need to spend to maintain an "austere" standard of living.
                2.   Poverty may be more extensive than the poverty line suggests.
                3.   Because of the high incidence of poverty among unmarried mothers and their children, experts on poverty often describe the problem today as the **feminization of poverty.**
        C.   What Part Does Government Play?
                1.   Taxation
                        a.   A **progressive tax** takes a bigger bite from the incomes of the rich than the poor.
                        b.   A **proportional tax** takes the same percentage from everyone.
                        c.   A **regressive tax** takes a higher percentage from the lower income levels than from the rich.
                        d.   Through the **Earned Income Tax Credit** (EITC), the poorest of the poor receive a check from Washington instead of sending one.
                2.   Government Expenditures
                        a.   **Transfer payments** transfer money from the general treasury to those in specific need.
                        b.   Social Security and Medicare are the most costly social welfare programs.

IV. Helping the Poor? Social Policy and Poverty (pp. 577–579)
  A. "Welfare" as We Knew It
    1. The **Social Security Act of 1935** brought together scattered, uneven state programs under a single federal umbrella.
    2. President Johnson's Great Society expanded welfare programs.
    3. President Reagan limited social welfare spending.
  B. Ending Welfare as We Knew It: The Welfare Reforms of 1996
    1. The **Personal Responsibility and Work Opportunity Reconciliation Act** (PRWORA) gave each state a fixed amount of money, required welfare recipients to work, and placed a time limit on welfare.
    2. **Temporary Assistance to Needy Families** (TANF) replaced AFDC as the means-tested aid to the poor.

V. Immigration and Social Policy (pp. 579–583)
  A. **Immigration** is the movement of people to another country with the intention of remaining there.
  B. Immigration Policy and Politics: Old and New
  C. Immigration and Policy: Washington and the States
    1. The **Simpson-Mazzoli Act** provided amnesty to many immigrants and toughened border controls.
    2. Different state policies reflect the fact that states are hit harder than the federal government by the costs of illegal immigrants.

VI. Living on Borrowed Time: Social Security (pp. 584–587)
  A. The New Deal, the Elderly, and the Growth of Social Security
    1. Social Security is the most expensive public policy in the United States.
    2. Both employee and employer contributions are paid into the **Social Security Trust Fund.**
    3. Currently, the Trust Fund receives more money than it pays out, but this will soon change.
  B. How George W. Bush Tried and Failed to Reform Social Security
    1. Bush proposed diverting a small portion of Social Security contributions to private retirement funds.
    2. Democrats argued privatization would hasten the bankruptcy of Social Security.

VII. Social Welfare Policy Elsewhere (pp. 587–588)
  A. Most industrial nations are more generous with social policy benefits than the United States.
  B. European nations tend to support greater governmental responsibility for poverty.
  C. Europeans pay high taxes for social welfare policies.

VII. Understanding Social Welfare Policy (pp. 588–589)
  A. Social Welfare Policy and the Scope of Government
  B. Democracy and Social Welfare

VIII. Summary (p. 589)

LEARNING OBJECTIVES

After studying Chapter 18, you should be able to:

1. Understand the debate over social welfare policy in the United States and why it is so controversial.

2. Discuss the nature of wealth and poverty and how public policy affects income in the United States.

3. Explain the evolution of social welfare programs in the United States.

4. Discuss the issues surrounding the immigration debate including how it relates to social policy and how the federal government and state governments have responded.

5. Understand the debate concerning the future of social welfare policy and Social Security.

6. Explain how social welfare policy in other countries differs from that in the United States.

7. Understand the place for social welfare policies in a democracy and how they contribute to the scope of government.

The following exercises will help you meet these objectives:

Objective 1: Understand the debate over social welfare policy in the United States.

1. Define "social welfare policies."

2. What is the difference between entitlement programs and means-tested programs?
   Entitlement Programs:

   Means-Tested Programs:

Objective 2: Discuss the nature of wealth and poverty and how public policy affects income in the United States.

1.   What is the difference between income and wealth?

     Income:

     Wealth:

2.   How does the U.S. Bureau of the Census define poverty?

3.   What are the three types of taxes? How can each affect citizens' incomes?

     1.

     2.

     3.

4.   What is meant by a transfer payment? Give an example.

5.   Make a list of three entitlement programs and three means-tested programs.

Entitlement Programs	Means-Tested Programs

Objective 3:   Explain the evolution of social welfare programs in the United States.

1.   Complete the following table by briefly summarizing the major emphasis of social welfare and listing a major social welfare act during the New Deal (Roosevelt), Great Society (Johnson), Reagan, and Clinton eras.

Era	Social Welfare Emphasis	Social Welfare Act/Program
New Deal		
Great Society		
Reagan Years		
Clinton Years		

2.   List the three major provisions of the Personal Responsibility and Work Opportunity Reconciliation Act (PRWORA).

1.

2.

3.

Objective 4: Discuss the issues surrounding the immigration debate including how it relates to social policy and how the federal government and state governments have responded.

1. List three myths about immigrants and immigration.

1.

2.

3.

2. List the three main provisions of the Simpson-Mazzoli Act.

    1.

    2.

    3.

3.   Briefly explain how each of the following states have dealt with their immigration policy.

    California:

    Oklahoma:

    Texas:

    Arizona:

Objective 5: Understand the debate concerning the future of social welfare policy and Social Security.

    1.   Briefly explain the major problem facing the Social Security program today.

    2.   Explain how the Social Security Trust Fund works.

    3.   What are the major arguments for and against the privatization of Social Security?

Objective 6: Explain how social welfare policy in other countries differs from that in the United States.

    1.   List three ways in which social welfare in the United States differs from programs most western European countries.

        1.

        2.

        3.

Objective 7: Understand the place for social welfare policies in a democracy and how they contribute to the scope of government.

    1.   In what ways has social welfare policy increased the scope of government?

    2.   What are the differences between the poor and the elderly in terms of their ability to influence social welfare policy?

        Poor:

        Elderly:

KEY TERMS

Identify and describe:

    social welfare policies

    entitlement programs

means-tested programs

income distribution

income

wealth

poverty line

feminization of poverty

progressive tax

proportional tax

regressive tax

Earned Income Tax Credit

transfer payments

Social Security Act of 1935

Personal Responsibility and Work Opportunity Reconciliation Act

Temporary Assistance for Needy Families

immigration

Simpson-Mazzoli Act

Social Security Trust Fund

Compare and contrast:

social welfare policies and transfer payments

entitlement programs and means-tested programs

income and wealth

progressive tax, proportional tax, and regressive tax

Personal Responsibility and Work Opportunity Reconciliation Act and Temporary Assistance for Needy Families

immigration and Simpson-Mazzoli Act

Name that term:

1.	This is the share of national income earned by various groups in the United States.

	_____

2.	This is a measure that takes into account what a family would need to spend to maintain an "austere" standard of living.

	_____

3.	This is the increasing concentration of poverty among women.

	_____

4.	When the rich pay five percent of their income in taxes while the poor pay 50 percent of theirs, it is an example of this.

	_____

5.	This is a negative income tax.

	_____

6.	These benefits are paid either in cash or in kind.

	_____

7.	This act created an entitlement program for the aged and a national program to assist the poor.

	_____

8.	This is the new name for public assistance to needy families.

	_____

9.	Both employee and employer contributions are paid into this.

	_____

USING YOUR UNDERSTANDING

1. Look for various ways in which income is distributed in the United States. For example, you may want to find out how income differs among various regions, states, cities, age groups, races, and genders. Illustrate differences between groups using bar or pie charts. You may also want to examine how income has changed over time in the categories you use. Try to explain why incomes are higher for one group and not another. Identify public policies, such as taxes, that affect the incomes of the different groups.

2. Develop a comparison between a social welfare policy in the United States and that of another western democracy. For example, Medicare and Medicaid could be compared with the National Health Service in the United Kingdom. Briefly describe the history of each policy. Examine the issues or controversies associated with the policy today. Find out how much the policy costs and what benefits are bestowed, both in their entirety and on a per capita basis. Find out how the policy is paid for through taxes. Who are the primary recipients of the benefits? Consider whether one system has any advantages over the other.

MULTIPLE CHOICE QUESTIONS

Circle the correct answer:

1. Approximately _____ percent of all mothers have never been married.
   a. 5
   b. 10
   c. 15
   d. 30
   e. 40

2. About _____ of all money for social programs goes to universally available benefit programs, including Social Security and Medicare?
   a. one-tenth
   b. one-quarter
   c. one-third
   d. one-half
   e. five-sixths

3. _____ refer(s) to the "shares" of the national income earned by various groups.
   a. Entitlements
   b. Income distribution
   c. Wealth
   d. Taxable income
   e. Profits

4. The top one percent of wealth-holders currently possess about _____ of all American wealth.
   a. 1 percent
   b. One-tenth
   c. one-quarter
   d. one-third
   e. one-half

5. Compared to the general population, poverty is more common among all of the following EXCEPT
   a. African Americans and Hispanics.
   b. the elderly.
   c. children.
   d. inner city residents.
   e. Asian Americans.

6. To count the poor, the United States Bureau of the Census has established the _____, which takes into account what a family would need to spend to maintain an "austere" standard of living.
   a. culture of poverty
   b. urban underclass
   c. poverty line
   d. relative deprivation index
   e. poverty index

7. Which of the following statements about poverty is FALSE?
   a. Poverty is equally distributed among all ethnic groups.
   b. There is a higher concentration of poverty among unmarried women.
   c. Around half of all Americans have experienced living in poverty in the past year.
   d. The official poverty count underestimates the seriousness of poverty.
   e. The poverty line counts the number of poor people.

8. A tax in which government takes 20 percent of the income of both rich and poor families in taxes is a(n)_____ tax.
   a. progressive
   b. flat
   c. proportional
   d. regressive
   e. binary

9. Federal taxes are
   a. progressive
   b. regressive
   c. proportional
   d. uniform
   e. binary

10. Benefits given by the government directly to individuals are known as
    a. tax cuts
    b. transfer payments
    c. tax rebates
    d. federal refunds
    e. federal exchanges

11. Medicaid provides
    a. hospital care for the retired and disabled people covered by Social Security.
    b. medical insurance to those over 65 and disabled.
    c. medical and hospital aid to the poor on the basis of need through federally assisted state health programs.
    d. cash payments to aged, blind, or disabled people whose income is below a certain amount.
    e. hospital care for people covered by Social Security.

12. The Social Security Act of 1935
    a. brought government into the equation of the obligations of one generation to another.
    b. substantially freed adults from the obligation of caring for both their children and parents.
    c. provided free medical care for all citizens over the age of 65 until it was repealed by the Republican congress of 1953.
    d. freed American citizens from the obligation of supporting the poor.
    e. substantially freed children and adults from paying their parents' medical expenses.

13. Food stamps and low-interest college loans are examples of
    a. In-kind benefits
    b. Transfer payments
    c. Federal refunds
    d. All of the above.
    e. Both a and b.

14. Prior to the twentieth century, family welfare was considered
    a. a private concern.
    b. a government burden.
    c. too expensive.
    d. impossible for small governments to manage.
    e. the responsibility of the church.

15. Charles Murray's study of the programs of the Great Society argued all of the following EXCEPT
    a. a key problem all along was inadequate funding to see the antipoverty programs through.
    b. public policies discouraged the poor from solving their own problems.
    c. the programs actually made it profitable to be poor and victimized.
    d. many of the programs not only failed to halt the spread of poverty, they actually made matters worse.
    e. many of the programs actually increased poverty in the U.S.

16. Supplementary Security Income (SSI) is a means-tested program for
    a. the unemployed.
    b. elderly Americans who have not yet reached retirement age.
    c. elderly, blind, or disabled people whose income is below a certain amount.
    d. women, infants, and children.
    e. workers who have been laid off and cannot work.

17. Today's Social Security payment is approximately ___ percent of the average worker's wages.
    a. 10
    b. 15
    c. 36
    d. 46
    e. 56

18. Which of the following statements regarding immigration is FALSE?
    a. For the first 100 years of U.S. history, there was no immigration policy.
    b. The Fourteenth Amendment clearly recognized that immigrants could become citizens.
    c. The U.S. did not require passports until 1918.
    d. Restrictive immigration laws were first implemented in 1924.
    e. Few immigrants took advantage of the provisions of the Simpson-Mazzoli Act.

19. The average monthly Social Security check is
    a. $500
    b. $900
    c. $1500
    d. $2500
    e. $3500

20. Compared to the U.S., European countries provide their citizens with more generous _____ benefits.
    a. health care
    b. child care
    c. parental leave
    d. benefits to the elderly
    e. all of the above

TRUE/FALSE QUESTIONS

Circle the correct answer:

1. Only about 5 percent of Americans live in a traditional family, with a working father and a nonworking mother. T / F

2. The greatest percentage of all money for social programs goes to means-tested programs. T / F

3. Social insurance in the U.S. has waned, while employers are doing less for their workers. T / F

4. The 1980s and 1990s have been a period where the "rich get richer, and the poor get poorer." T / F

5. More than half of the people in the United States live below the poverty line. T / F

6. White Americans have a one in 10 chance of being poor. T / F

7. Charging millionaires 50 percent in taxes and the poor 5 percent in taxes is a form of progressive taxation. T / F

8. Unemployment insurance is a form of "in-kind" benefits. T / F

9. The goal of the 1996 welfare reform was to reduce poverty. T / F

10. The number of Social Security recipients is growing rapidly, while the number of Social Security contributors is growing only slowly. T / F

SHORT ANSWER/SHORT ESSAY QUESTIONS

1. What is the difference between income and wealth? Give an example of each.

2. Explain the difference between progressive, proportional, and regressive taxes.

3. What was Charles Murray's main argument concerning the American social welfare system?

4. What is the Simpson-Mazzoli Act and how was it significant in the social policy area of immigration?

5. Describe how the United States social welfare system has evolved over the past century. How does our system differ from those in other countries?

ESSAY QUESTIONS

1. Compare and contrast entitlement and means-tested social welfare programs in the United States. Which one is more costly? Popular? Why?

2. Describe the difference between the deserving poor and undeserving poor. How does this perception affect Americans' attitudes toward entitlement programs and means-tested programs? Are some groups truly deserving while others are undeserving?

3. Do you favor a more progressive federal income tax? Why or why not? Should the rich pay a greater proportion of their income in taxes than do the poor?

4. How did President George W. Bush connect promoting marriage to welfare reform? Do you agree or disagree with the principle of permitting states to use federal dollars marked for social welfare policy to promote marriage and traditional two-parent, heterosexual marriages?

5. What is the place of social welfare in a democracy? What competing demands on democratic government does social welfare policy create, what groups are involved in the process, and how do these groups interact? What effect does social welfare policy have on the scope of government?

CHAPTER 19

Policymaking for Health Care and the Environment

CHAPTER OUTLINE

I. Politics in Action: Health Care Crisis in the Medical Capital of the World (pp. 595–596)
    A. Health care and the environment both involve life-and-death decisions.
    B. Health care and the environment both involve sophisticated technologies.
    C. Health care and the environment both involve high costs.

II. Health Care Policy (pp. 596–606)
    A. The Health of Americans and the Cost of Health Care in America
        1. The United States does not rank as high as many countries in life expectancy and infant mortality.
        2. American health care costs are both staggering and soaring.
    B. Uneven Coverage, Uneven Care
        1. Health Insurance
            a. Health insurance is closely tied to age and race.
        2. Managed Care
            a. **Health Maintenance Organizations (HMO)** provide all or most of a person's health care for a yearly fee.
    C. The Role of Government in Health Care
        1. Much medical research is financed through the National Institutes of Health (NIH).
        2. **National health insurance** is a proposal for a compulsory insurance program to finance all Americans' medical care.
        3. **Medicare** is part of the Social Security system and covers more than 38 million people.
        4. **Medicaid** is a program designed to provide health care for the poor.
    D. Policymaking for Health Care
        1. The Politics of Health Care
            a. Many interests are involved in health care policies (elderly, workers, business, and insurance companies).
        2. Two Presidents, Two Parties, Two Health Care Plans
    E. Health Policy: The Issues Ahead

III. Environmental Policy (pp. 606–609)
    A. Environmental Policies in America
        1. The **Environmental Protection Agency (EPA)** is the nation's largest federal regulatory agency.

2.	Clean Air
   a.	The **Clean Air Act of 1970** charges the Department of Transportation with the responsibility of reducing automobile emissions.
3.	Clean Water
   a.	The **Water Pollution Control Act of 1972** is designed to control pollution in the nation's lakes and rivers.
4.	Wilderness Preservation.
5.	Endangered Species
   a.	The **Endangered Species Act of 1973** created an endangered species protection program in the U.S. Fish and Wildlife Service.
6.	Toxic Wastes
   a.	The **Superfund** was created to clean up toxic wastes by taxing chemical products.

III.	Energy Policy (pp. 609–613)
   A.	Energy Sources and Energy Politics
      1.	Coal
      2.	Oil
      3.	Nuclear
   B.	The Global Warming Debate: Beyond Kyoto?
      1.	**Global warming,** a slow rise in the atmospheric temperature of the earth, results primarily from the burning of fossil fuels.
      2.	The United States did not sign the Kyoto Treaty to reduce greenhouse gases.
V.	Groups, Energy, and the Environment (pp. 613–614)

VI.	Understanding Health Care and Environmental Policy (pp. 614–615)
   A.	Democracy, Health Care, and Environmental Policy
   B.	The Scope of Government and Health Care and Environmental Policy

VII.	Summary (pp. 615–616)

LEARNING OBJECTIVES

After studying Chapter 19, you should be able to:

1.	Explain the nature of health care and health care policy in the United States.

2.	Discuss the issues surrounding the environment and the programs and policies to deal with them.

3.	Understand the issues surrounding energy policy and global warming.

4.	Understand the relationship between health and environmental policy and democracy and the scope of government.

The following exercises will help you meet these objectives:

Objective 1: Explain the nature of health care and health care policy in the United States.

    1.   How do life expectancy and infant mortality rates in the United States compare with those of other nations?

          Life Expectancy:

          Infant Mortality:

    2.   What is "defensive medicine"?

    3.   In what ways is access to health insurance unequal in the United States?

    4.   What are some of the advantages and disadvantages of managed care?

    5.   What is the difference between Medicare and Medicaid?

          Medicare:

          Medicaid:

6.   List and explain the involvement of three interest groups in health care policy.

        1.

        2.

        3.

7.   How did President George W. Bush's health care reform proposals differ from President Clinton's?

8.   Explain the major issues involved in the controversy over stem cell research.

Objective 2: Discuss the issues surrounding the environment and the programs and policies to deal with them.

        1.   What is the mission of the Environmental Protection Agency?

        2.   List the main provisions of the Clean Air Act of 1970, the Water Pollution Control Act of 1972, the Endangered Species Act of 1973, and the Superfund.

        Clean Air Act:

        Water Pollution Control Act:
        Endangered Species Act:

        Superfund:

Objective 3: Understand the issues surrounding energy policy and global warming.

1.   What are the four most important sources of energy in the United States?

    1.

    2.

    3.

    4.

2.   What are the main problems for each of the following energy sources?

    Coal:

    Petroleum:

    Nuclear:

3.   What are the main arguments against the 1997 treaty on global warming?

4.   What has been the primary argument of opponents of strict environmental laws?

Objective 4: Understand the relationship between health and environmental policy and democracy and the scope of government.

1.   Why are individual citizens rarely involved in policymaking for technological issues?

2.   How have technological issues affected the scope of government?

KEY TERMS

Identify and describe:

health maintenance organizations (HMOs)

national health insurance

Medicare

Medicaid

Environmental Protection Agency (EPA)

Clean Air Act of 1970

Water Pollution Control Act of 1972

Endangered Species Act of 1973

Superfund

global warming

Compare and contrast:

health maintenance organizations and national health insurance

national health insurance and Medicare

Medicare and Medicaid

Clean Air Act of 1970 and Water Pollution Control Act of 1972

Name that term:

1. This popular managed care system is designed to keep health care costs down.

   _____

2. This is our largest federal regulatory agency.

   _____

3. This law that requires the government to actively protect each of hundreds of species listed as endangered.

   _____

4. It is funded through taxes on chemical products.

   _____

5. This results primarily from the burning of fossil fuels—mainly coal and oil.

   _____

USING YOUR UNDERSTANDING

1. Drawing from newspapers, newsmagazines, or the Internet, find some current cases where public policy may be affected in the areas of health, energy, and/or the environment. High-tech medicine and medical research may evoke ethical, policy, or legal questions concerning life itself. The need for cheap and abundant energy may pose a threat to the environment. Make a list of the issues involved in each case and how it was resolved. Identify the tradeoffs involved and who would benefit and suffer from the different policy options available. Who are the individuals and groups, in and out of government, most involved in the issue and how much influence do they have on policy decisions? Consider how your examples reflect the current agenda in each policy area.

2. Every project utilizing federal funds is required to submit to the government an environmental impact statement. Analyze an environmental impact statement and report on its contents. It may be particularly useful to examine an EIS on an energy project, such as a power plant. Pay particular attention to the numerous types of environmental impacts predicted by the statement. Compare the amount of attention paid to physiographic, biological, social, and economic impacts, and evaluate the sophistication of the analysis. Analyze the comment section of the statement and determine who commented on the proposal, what they said, and whether their views were incorporated into the body of the report. Identify the groups in favor of the project and those who opposed it. Find out whether the proposed project or policy was actually implemented.

MULTIPLE CHOICE QUESTIONS

Circle the correct answer:

1. ____ percent of the American population is uninsured.
   a. Ten
   b. Fifteen
   c. Twenty-five
   d. Thirty
   e. Forty

2. The health care system in the United States is driven by the
   a. market.
   b. notion that health care is a basic right of citizenship.
   c. understanding that health care is an entitlement.
   d. view that health care is a responsibility.
   e. government.

3. In 1970, we spent approximately ____ percent of our GDP on health care; today we spend about ___ percent of our GDP on health care.
    a. 5; 10
    b. 7; 15
    c. 10; 25
    d. 15; 15
    e. 2; 5

4. Which of the following countries does NOT provide universal health care for its citizens?
    a. Canada
    b. Germany
    c. Japan
    d. Great Britain
    e. None of the above

5. _____ is part of the Social Security system and covers 40 million American seniors with hospitalization insurance and other optional health insurance.
    a. Medicaid
    b. Medicare
    c. The National Institutes of Health
    d. The Superfund
    e. The United States Health Service

6. Laurence J. Kotlikoff estimates that the U.S. owes _____ for its three major entitlement programs, Social Security, Medicare, and Medicaid.
    a. $700,000
    b. $7,000,000
    c. $7 billion
    d. $7 trillion
    e. $70 trillion

7. The most common reason for losing health insurance is
    a. being poor
    b. losing or changing a job
    c. growing old
    d. having a child
    e. divorce

8. The Emergency Medical Treatment and Labor Act of 1986 was designed to
    a. Make it illegal for emergency rooms to turn away people without treatment.
    b. Stem the problem of "patient dumping."
    c. Prevent hospitals and emergency rooms from asking patients if they have health insurance.
    d. All of the above.
    e. Both a and b.

9. The National Institutes of Health
    a. administers the national health insurance system in the United States.
    b. provides funds for medical research in the United States.
    c. is the largest hospital and physicians interest group in the United States.
    d. administers the Medicare and Medicaid programs.
    e. is the federal agency that regulates private health insurance companies.

10. National, state, and local governments pay for ___ percent of the country's total health bill.
    a. 20
    b. 30
    c. 46
    d. 56
    e. 66

11. Which of the following statements is FALSE?
    a. Every other industrialized nation in the world, other than the U.S., has adopted some form of national health insurance.
    b. About two-thirds of Americans support the idea of universal health care event if it involves more taxes.
    c. Fifty-nine percent of "conservatives" support universal health care.
    d. The American Medical Association opposes universal health care.
    e. Many American businesses are at a competitive disadvantage in the global economy because they carry hefty health care costs for their employees.

12. The public assistance program designed to provide health care for poor Americans is
    a. Medicaid
    b. Medicare
    c. Social Security
    d. CHIPs
    e. TANF

13. Which aspect of health care costs has increased the fastest?
    a. emergency room care
    b. prescription drugs
    c. prenatal care
    d. outpatient surgery
    e. treatment for drug and alcohol abuse

14. The enforcement of the Clean Air Act and other antipollution legislation is administered by what regulatory body?
    a. Department of Interior
    b. Environmental Protection Agency
    c. Department of Justice
    d. Occupational Safety and Health Administration
    e. Federal Pollution Board

15. Being on the endangered species list requires that
    a. both federal and state governments enact policies to protect the habitat of the species.
    b. the federal government alone must enact policies to protect the habitat of the species.
    c. state governments allow taxes to be raise to protect the habitat of the species.
    d. all habitats where the species may possibly reside be declared national parks.
    e. the Sierra Club raise funds to help protect the habitat of the species.

16. To successfully dispose of nuclear waste, it must be isolated from the environment for _____ years.
    a. 10
    b. 100
    c. 1,000
    d. 5,000
    e. 10,000

17. The Superfund is paid for by
    a. a voluntary check-off system on federal income tax forms.
    b. taxes on chemical products.
    c. a special tax on automobiles, trucks, snowmobiles, and motorized farm vehicles.
    d. the federal gasoline tax.
    e. aviation fuel taxes.

18. The United States has about ___ percent of the world's oil but uses ____ of it.
    a. 2; one-quarter
    b. 2; one-half
    c. 20; one-quarter
    d. 20; one-half
    e. 30; one-quarter

19. The Climate Stewardship Act
    a. would require large companies to reduce emissions to 1990 levels by 2020.
    b. was proposed by Senators John McCain and Joe Lieberman.
    c. is supported by a large majority of Americans.
    d. all of the above.
    e. none of the above.

20. Which of the following is TRUE of policymaking for technological issues?
    a. Individual citizens are unlikely to have the information or resources to participate meaningfully.
    b. It relies heavily on group representation.
    c. It has resulted in an increased scope of government, as government has headed the call for a greater role in high-tech issues.
    d. It is frequently very expensive.
    e. All of the above are true

TRUE/FALSE QUESTIONS

Circle the correct answer:

1. Although many nations consider health care a right, the United States does not. T / F

2. Americans are healthier and live longer than those who live in other democracies because Americans spend more for health care. T / F

3. Forty-six million Americans lack health insurance coverage. T / F

4. Access to health insurance in the U.S. is closely tied to race and income. T / F

5. Bill Clinton was the first president to propose a system of national health insurance. T / F

6. Medicare faces a more severe financial crisis than does Social Security. T / F

7. Nonrenewable resources are not replaced by nature once consumed. T / F

8. Eighty-seven percent of the nation's energy comes from coal, oil, and natural gas. T / F

9. President Clinton never submitted the Kyoto Treaty to the Senate for approval and in 2001 George W. Bush renounced it. T / F

10. Policy making for high-tech issues relies heavily on group representation. T / F

SHORT ANSWER/SHORT ESSAY QUESTIONS

1. What are some of the main causes for the increases in health care costs in the United States?

2. What is the purpose of Medicare? How does Medicare work? What challenges face Medicare in the future?

3. Explain President George W. Bush's approach to health care reform.

4. What were the main provisions of the Clean Air Act of 1970?

5. In what ways and how do high-tech issues limit public participation in democratic policymaking?

ESSAY QUESTIONS

1. Describe the health care system in the United States. How do the infant mortality rate, life expectancy, access to health care, and health care costs in the United States compare with other western industrialized countries?

2. Describe the development of health management organizations in the United States. What are the key characteristics of HMOs? What problems did they solve? What problems have they created?

3. What democratic concerns are raised by the limitations of health care in the United States? Do citizens need guaranteed health care in order to be considered "full citizens"? What is holding the U.S. from moving to a more universal system of health care—and what does this say about democratic policymaking.

4. What are the competing interests at stake in environmental policy? How can the government reconcile the need for environmental policy with other interests, such as economic competition, jobs, and finances?

5. What is the most significant environmental issue confronting the U.S.? What issue is most critical globally? Given this issue, what is the most appropriate policy solution? What do lessons from previous environmental policies (those involving, for example, clean air, clean water, endangered species, wilderness preservation, global warming) have to offer in the way of lessons for future change and reform?

CHAPTER 20

NATIONAL SECURITY POLICYMAKING

CHAPTER OUTLINE

I. Politics in Action: A New Threat (pp. 621–622)
    A. The role of national security is more important than ever.
    B. New and complex challenges have emerged to replace the conflict with communism.

II. American Foreign Policy: Instruments, Actors, and Policymakers (pp. 622–629)
    A. **Foreign policy** involves making choices about relations with the rest of the world.
    B. Instruments of Foreign Policy
        1. Military
        2. Economic
        3. Diplomacy
    C. Actors on the World Stage
        1. International Organizations
            a. Organizations such as the **United Nations (UN)** play an increasingly important role on the world stage.
        2. Regional Organizations
            a. Regional organizations have proliferated in the post-World War II era.
            b. The **North Atlantic Treaty Organization (NATO)** is a military alliance between the United States, Canada, and most of Western Europe.
            c. The **European Union (EU)** is an economic alliance of the major western European nations.
        3. Multinational Corporations
            a. These companies are sometimes more powerful than the governments under which they operate.
        4. Nongovernmental Organizations
        5. Individuals
    D. The Policymakers
        1. The President
        2. The Diplomats
            a. The **secretary of state** has traditionally been the key advisor to the president on foreign policy matters.
            b. Some recent presidents have established more personal systems for receiving foreign policy advice.
        3. The National Security Establishment
            a. The **secretary of defense** is the president's main civilian advisor on national defense matters.

     b. The commanding officers of each of the services, plus a chair, constitute the **Joint Chiefs of Staff.**

     c. The National Security Council (NSC) was formed to coordinate foreign and military policies.

     d. The **Central Intelligence Agency (CIA)** coordinates American information and data-gathering intelligence activities abroad.

   4. Congress

III. American Foreign Policy: An Overview (pp. 629–635)

  A. **Isolationism** was the foreign policy course followed throughout most of American history.

  B. The Cold War

   1. Containment Abroad and Anticommunism at Home

     a. The **containment doctrine** called for the United States to isolate the Soviet Union, contain its advances, and resist its encroachments.

     b. At the height of the **Cold War,** the United States and the Soviet Union were often on the brink of war.

     c. In the 1950s, the Soviet Union and the United States engaged in an **arms race.**

   2. The Vietnam War

  C. The Era of Détente

   1. **Détente** represented a slow transformation from conflict thinking to cooperative thinking in foreign policy strategy.

   2. One major initiative emerging from détente was the Strategic Arms Limitation Talks (SALT).

  D. The Reagan Rearmament

   1. President Reagan proposed the largest peacetime defense spending increase in American history.

   2. The **Strategic Defense Initiative** (SDI) was a plan for defense against missiles through a global umbrella in space.

  E. The Final Thaw in the Cold War

   1. The Cold War ended spontaneously.

IV. The War on Terrorism (pp. 635–637)

  A. Introduction

  B. Afghanistan and Iraq

   1. There is broad consensus that planning for postwar Iraq was poor.

   2. Many observers argue that relying primarily on the use of force to combat terrorism is responding to a tactic rather that to the forces that generate it.

V. Rethinking National Security Policy (pp. 637–637)

  A. Terrorism has forced America to reconsider basic tenets of its national security policy.

  B. The Bush administration national security doctrine moved toward a policy that supported preemptive strikes against terrorists and hostile states.

VI.   The Politics of Defense Policy (pp. 638–643)
     A.   Defense Spending
     B.   Personnel
     C.   Weapons
     D.   Reforming Defense Policy

VII.   The New Global Agenda (pp. 643–653)
     A.   The Changing Role of Military Power
          1.   Humanitarian Interventions
          2.   Economic Sanctions
     B.   Nuclear Proliferation
          1.   Policymakers are most concerned about countries that are actively developing nuclear weapons capability (North Korea and Iran).
          2.   Other nations have serious security concerns when faced with hostile neighbors possessing nuclear weapons.
     C.   The International Economy
          1.   Today's international economy is characterized by **interdependency.**
          2.   International Trade
               a.   The **tariff** is a special tax added to the cost of imported goods.
              b.   The North American Free Trade Agreement would eliminate most tariffs among North American countries.
              c.   The General Agreement on Tariffs and Trade is the mechanism by which most of the world's nations negotiate trade agreements.
          3.   Balance of Trade
               a.   **Balance of trade** is the ratio of what a country pays for imports to what it earns from exports.
              b.   Year after year, the American balance of trade has been negative.
          4.   Energy
               a.   The **Organization of Petroleum Exporting Countries (OPEC)** controls the price of oil and the amount that its members produce and sell to other nations.
          5.   Foreign Aid

VI.   Understanding National Security Policymaking (pp. 653–655)
     A.   National Security Policymaking and Democracy
     B.   National Security Policymaking and the Scope of Government

VII.   Summary (pp. 655–656)

LEARNING OBJECTIVES

After studying Chapter 20, you should be able to:

1. Identify the many actors involved in making and shaping American foreign policy and discuss the roles they play.

2. Describe how American foreign policy has changed since the end of World War II.

3. Discuss the politics of defense policy.

4. Examine the new issues on the global agenda, particularly those concerning the world economy, energy, and environment.

5. Understand the role of foreign and defense policymaking in a democracy and how foreign and defense policy affects the scope of government.

The following exercises will help you meet these goals:

Objective 1: Identify the many actors involved in making and shaping American foreign policy and discuss the roles they play.

1. What are the three types of tools that upon which foreign policies ultimately depend?

    1.

    2.

    3.

2. List five types of actors on the world scene and give an example of each.

    1.

    2.

    3.

    4.

    5.

3.   List some of the primary foreign policy functions of the president.

4.   What is the purpose of the National Security Council?

5.   Complete the following table on the major national security agencies. In the last
      column, comment on the agency's inclinations toward involvement in foreign
      ventures, giving an example when relevant.

Agency	Composition	Purpose	Comments
Joint Chiefs of Staff			
National Security Council			
Central Intelligence Agency			

Objective 2: Describe how American foreign policy has changed since the end of World War II.

1.	Complete the following timeline on the Cold War by indicating the event or events that occurred during the year or years listed.

	1946:

	1947:

	1948–1949:

	1949:

	1950–1953:

	1954:

	Mid-1960s:

	1972:

	1973:

	1979:

	1983:

	1989:

	1992:

2.	What types of foreign policies were followed during the era of détente?

3.	What was the purpose of the Strategic Defense Initiative (SDI)?

4.	According to George W. Bush, which states belong to the "axis of evil"?
	1.

	2.

	3.

5. What have been some of the major criticisms of the Bush administration's wars in Iraq and Afghanistan?

6. Briefly explained the Bush administration's national security strategy doctrine.

Objective 3: Discuss the politics of defense policy.

1. What is the "peace dividend"?

2. What is the triad of nuclear weapons upon which the United States relies for national defense?

1.

2.

3.

3. What were the main provisions of the Intermediate-range Nuclear Forces Treaty and the Strategic Arms Reduction Treaty?

Objective 4: Examine the new issues on the global agenda, particularly those concerning the world economy, energy, and environment.

1. Why isn't military power as important in foreign policy as it used to be?

2. Define "humanitarian interventions" and give three examples.

3.   Define the term "interdependency" as it relates to the international economy.

4.   What are the four major provisions of the General Agreement on Tariffs and Trade?

     1.

     2.

     3.

     4.

5.   List three consequences of a balance of trade deficit.

     1.

     2.

     3.

6.   What is the Organization of Petroleum Exporting Countries and why is it an important international actor?

7.   List four different types or forms of foreign aid.

1.

2.

3.

4.

Objective 5: Understand the role of foreign and defense policymaking in a democracy and how foreign and defense policy affects the scope of government.

1.   How might one argue that American foreign policymaking is a democratic process?

2.   How has foreign and defense policymaking contributed to the scope of government?

KEY TERMS

Identify and describe:

foreign policy

United Nations

North Atlantic Treaty Organization

European Union

secretary of state

secretary of defense

Joint Chiefs of Staff

Central Intelligence Agency

isolationism

containment doctrine

Cold War

arms race

détente

Strategic Defense Initiative

interdependency

tariff

balance of trade

Organization of Petroleum Exporting Countries

Compare and contrast:

foreign policy and isolationism

United Nations (UN), North Atlantic Treaty Organization (NATO), and European Union (EU)

secretary of state and secretary of defense

isolationism and interdependency

Cold War and détente

Organization of Petroleum Exporting Countries (OPEC) and interdependency

tariff and balance of trade

Name that term:

1. This regional organization involves the U.S. and most of Western Europe.

   _____

2. This major regional organization is based on an economic alliance.

   _____

3. These are the commanding officers of each of the armed services.

   _____

4. They have often been involved in other nations' internal affairs.

   _____

5. George F. Kennan proposed this to isolate the Soviet Union.

   _____

6. This eventually resulted in a situation of mutual assured destruction.

   _____

7. This is a change from conflict to cooperative thinking in foreign policy.

   _____

8. This was also known as "Star Wars."

   _____

USING YOUR UNDERSTANDING

1. Organize your colleagues to simulate a military or foreign policy decision-making situation. The situation may be a political or economic crisis, such as a terrorist attack, an oil embargo, or some other crisis. Alternatively, it may be an ongoing policy problem, such as global inequalities in human rights, inequalities in the distribution of the world's wealth, or the continued over-consumption of the world commons and pollution of the global environment. Different students should represent each of the key international actors concerned with the situation

and the policymaking actors responsible for addressing it. Representatives from nations other than the United States may also be present. Try to identify the major issues involved in the situation and the tradeoffs involved, keeping in mind that each of the actors on the stage has a different interest to protect. Collectively, try to come to agreement on a United States foreign policy that would contribute to a resolution of the situation.

2. Given the end of the Cold War, international relations and the global agenda are changing dramatically. Find examples, using newspapers, newsmagazines, and/or the Internet, that illustrate the changing global agenda. Include examples that stem from the decline of communism as well as the more traditional concerns about defense and military spending and the emerging agenda issues centering on terrorism, the economy, equality, energy, and environment. Identify those issues that seem to take a prominent position on the contemporary global agenda. At the same time, identify those issues that you see as important global concerns but that are not being given much attention. Assess the global agenda in terms of the relative importance of defense issues as compared to other policy issues and whether or not the agenda seems to be changing.

MULTIPLE CHOICE QUESTIONS

Circle the correct answer:

1. Foreign policy involves
   a. The way the U.S. government makes choices about relations with the rest of the world.
   b. The way foreign governments lobby U.S. government officials to obtain policies they favor.
   c. Only questions of war and peace.
   d. All of the above.
   e. None of the above.

2. Central America and the Caribbean
   a. Have been largely ignored by U.S. foreign policy.
   b. Have been the recipients of the most U.S. foreign aid.
   c. Are beyond the U.S.'s sphere of influence.
   d. Have historically been central regions for U.S. foreign policy.
   e. Are areas where the United States has never engaged in military conflict.

3. Economic tools of foreign policy include
   a. Trade regulations.
   b. Tariff policies.
   c. Monetary policies.
   d. None of the above.
   e. All of the above.

4. Which of the following statements most accurately captures international politics today?
    a. International politics has become simpler as there are now fewer countries in the world than there were prior to World War II.
    b. Foreign relations remain almost exclusively transactions among nations.
    c. Nations remain the main actors in international politics, but today there are a number of other actors that influence foreign relations.
    d. All of these statements are accurate.
    e. None of these statements are accurate.

5. The members of which international organization agree to renounce war and respect certain human rights and economic freedoms?
    a. The World Trade Organization
    b. The United Nations
    c. The League of Nations
    d. The European Union
    e. The North American Free Trade Agreement

6. To counter the NATO alliance, the Soviet Union spearheaded a regional alliance known as
    a. The Union of Soviet Socialist Republics.
    b. The Communist International.
    c. The Warsaw Pact.
    d. Stalin's Pact.
    e. Eastern Europe.

7. The role of chief diplomat in U.S. foreign policy is played by
    a. The president.
    b. The U.S. ambassador to the United Nations.
    c. The secretary of state
    d. The secretary of defense
    e. The chairmen of the Joint Chiefs of Staff

8. An example of a nongovernmental organization that promotes international human rights is
    a. Greenpeace.
    b. Amnesty International.
    c. The United Nations.
    d. The European Union.
    e. None of the above.

9. Foggy Bottom" refers to the
    a. State Department.
    b. Foreign Services.
    c. Joint Chiefs of Staff.
    d. Defense Department.
    e. Department of Homeland Security.

10. The first secretary of state was
    a. Alexander Hamilton.
    b. Thomas Jefferson.
    c. John Jay.
    d. John Adams.
    e. Benjamin Franklin.

11. The Iran-Contra affair involved
    a. A covert effort to support a domestic uprising against the regime in Iran.
    b. The covert sale of missiles to Iran in an effort to secure the release of American hostages held by Iranian-backed terrorists.
    c. The covert funneling of money to anticommunist rebels in Nicaragua.
    d. b and c only.
    e. All of the above.

12. The _____ was formed in 1947 to coordinate American foreign and military policies and advise the president.
    a. State Department.
    b. Department of Defense.
    c. Central Intelligence Agency.
    d. National Security Council.
    e. Joint Chiefs of Staff.

13. Military leaders who appear eager to use military force to project U.S. power are known as
    a. Warriors
    b. Doves
    c. Vultures
    d. Hawks
    e. Eagles

14. The overthrow of governments in Iran in 1953 and Guatemala in 1954 was partially orchestrated by
    a. The Joints Chiefs of Staff.
    b. The Federal Bureau of Investigation.
    c. The Secret Service.
    d. The Special Forces.
    e. The Central Intelligence Agency.

15. Which agency within the American intelligence community is responsible for electronic eavesdropping?
    a. The National Security Agency
    b. The National Security Council
    c. The National Reconnaissance Office
    d. The Central Intelligence Agency
    e. The Defense Intelligence Agency

16. One of the first results of the doctrine of containment put into practice was
    a. The Vietnam War.
    b. Summits with Soviet Leaders.
    c. The Korean War.
    d. The Cuban Missile Crisis.
    e. The secret bombing of Laos.

17. The North Atlantic Treaty Organization (NATO) was established in what year?
    a. 1948
    b. 1945
    c. 1949
    d. 1950
    e. 1953

18. Almost immediately following World War II, the United States entered into _____ with the Soviet Union.
    a. The Korean War
    b. The Cold War
    c. The lend lease plan
    d. A nuclear arms race
    e. Nuclear missile pacts

19. One of the few spots where violence and brutal government force crushed a prodemocracy reform movement in 1989 and allowed the communist government to endure was in
    a. Beijing.
    b. Prague.
    c. Moscow.
    d. East Berlin.
    e. Ho Chi Minh City.

20. The Strategic Arms Reduction Treaty was the first accord
    a. On nuclear weapons signed between the United States and the Soviet Union.
    b. To reduce current levels of nuclear weapons.
    c. Mandating the elimination of many long-range nuclear missiles.
    d. Cutting conventional arms in Europe.
    e. To be rejected by the United States Senate.

TRUE/FALSE QUESTIONS

Circle the correct answer:

1. The United States has employed force to influence actions most often in the Middle East. T / F

2. The United Nations Security Council is the seat of real power within the U.N. T / F

3. The U.N. voted to support the U.S. led invasion of Iraq in 2003. T / F

4. The State Department is the foreign policy arm of the U.S. government. T / F

5. George Patton and Curtis LeMay are military commanders known for their hawkish views of foreign policy. T / F

6. The Monroe Doctrine warned European countries to stay away from America's interests in the Middle East. T / F

7. Reagan's plan for a missile defense shield is more popularly known as "star wars." T / F

8. Some have argued that the changes to American foreign policy made under George W. Bush have squandered America's moral authority and diminished its global credibility. T / F

9. The overall liberal view of military spending can be summarized as: "too many guns, not enough butter." T / F

10. The collapse of apartheid in South Africa is partially explained by the success of economic sanctions. T / F

SHORT ANSWER/SHORT ESSAY QUESTIONS

1. What are the three types of tools used in making foreign policy?

2. Explain how the Korean War relates to the doctrine of containment.

3. Who are the Joint Chiefs of Staff, and what role do they perform?

4. How was Nixon's visit to China an example of détente?

5. What is meant by the term "soft power"? How can the United States use its "soft power" to pursue foreign policy goals?

ESSAY QUESTIONS

1. What are economic sanctions? What does it take for sanctions to be successful? Evaluate the arguments for and against the use of economic sanctions.

2. How has globalization and economic interdependence affected U.S. foreign policy?

3. Evaluate the arguments for and against humanitarian interventions.

4. Presidents have a disproportionate influence on shaping American foreign policy. Identify and discuss three presidents who are known for reshaping American foreign policy. Explain what specific policies they advocated, and how they differed from one another.

5. Should American foreign policy emphasize humility and caution, avoiding the role of "nation building," or should American foreign policy emphasize the spreading of American ideals and rebuilding failed states?

CHAPTER 21

THE NEW FACE OF STATE AND LOCAL GOVERNMENT

CHAPTER OUTLINE

I. Politics in Action: Subnational Governments and Homeland Security (pp. 661–664)
   A. State and local governments have traditionally been responsible for criminal justice policy.
   B. Since September 11, 2001 the national government has become more involved in criminal justice policy.
   C. **Subnational governments** are state and local governments.
   D. Subnational governments have been characterized by revitalization and diversity.

II. State Constitutions (pp. 664–666)
   A. State constitutions provide far more detail than the federal constitution.
   B. Amending State Constitutions

III. State Elections (pp. 666–673)
   A. Gubernatorial Elections
   B. State Legislative Elections
      1. Apportionment
      2. Partisan Competition, Legislative Turnover, and Term Limits
   C. The Changing Face of State-Elected Officials

IV. Governors and The Executive Branch (pp. 673–676)
   A. The Job of Governor
      1. Governors perform many roles.
      2. The **line-item veto** allows governors to veto only certain parts of a bill while allowing the rest of it to pass into law.
      3. Personal powers
   B. Other Executive Officers
      1. **Lieutenant governors** often preside over the state senate and are first in succession for governor.
      2. Other state executives may include attorney general, treasurer, secretary of state, auditor, comptroller, and various commissioners.

V. State Legislatures (pp. 676–679)
   A. Legislative professionalism reforms have improved the effectiveness of state legislatures.
   B. Some states have seen the beginning of a "de-professionalizing" trend.

VI.   State Court Systems (pp. 679–681)
A.   State Court Organization
B.   Selecting Judges
1.   In many states, voters elect judges for various courts.
2.   Many states follow a form of the **Merit Plan** that attempts to make appointments to the courts based upon merit.

VII.   Direct Democracy (pp. 682–684)
A.   **Direct democracy** is government controlled directly by citizens.
B.   Under the legislative **initiative**, the people directly author and vote on legislation.
C.   Under the **referendum**, the people can approve or reject measures submitted to them by the legislature.
D.   Under the **recall**, voters can gather enough signatures to call an election to decide whether a representative should continue in office.

VIII.   State and Local Government Relations (pp. 684–685)
A.   According to **Dillon's Rule**, local governments have only those powers that are explicitly given to them by the states.
B.   A **local charter** is the organizational statement and grant of authority from the state to a local government often used to give **home rule** to local governments.

IX.   Local Governments (pp. 685–692)
A.   Types of Local Government
1.   Counties
2.   Townships
3.   Municipalities
a.   Originally, many local communities operated under a form of direct democracy called the **town meeting.**
b.   Mayor-council government.
c.   Council-manager government: An appointed **city manager** carries out policy with the city bureaucracy.
d.   Commission government.
4.   School Districts
5.   Special Districts
B.   Fragmentation, Cooperation, and Competition
1.   Each governing body in a fragmented metropolis tends to look at problems from its own narrow, partial perspective.
2.   A **council of governments** (COG) consists of officials from various localities who meet to discuss mutual problems and plan joint action.

X.   State and Local Finance Policy (pp. 692–696)
A.   State revenues are derived primarily from taxes, intergovernmental aid, state insurance programs, and charges and fees.
B.   Half of state money is spent on state programs and 30 percent is given to local governments.

C. Local governments receive their revenues from taxes, user charges, and intergovernmental aid.

D. Local governments spend their money primarily on education, social services, and public safety.

XI. Understanding State and Local Governments (pp. 696–698)
   A. Democracy at the Subnational Level
   B. The Scope of Subnational Governments

XII. Summary (pp. 698–699)

LEARNING OBJECTIVES

After studying Chapter 21, you should be able to:

1. Describe the nature of state constitutions and how they differ from the U.S. Constitution.

2. Discuss the different types of state elections and how they differ from national elections.

3. Explain the function of state governors and the executive branch.

4. Understand the nature and function of state legislatures and how legislatures make policy.

5. Describe the structure of the state court systems.

6. Explain how direct democracy is used in the states.

7. Discuss the relationship between state and local governments.

8. Compare and contrast the different types of local government in the United States in terms of organization, functions, and policy roles.

9. Discuss the fiscal and budgetary policies of state and local governments.

10. Evaluate state and local government in the United States in terms of their contributions to democracy and the scope of government.

The following exercises will help you meet these objectives:

Objective 1: Describe the nature of state constitutions and how they differ from the U.S. Constitution.

    1.   Explain two important characteristics of subnational government.

          1.

          2.

    2.   What is the key difference between the federal and state constitutions?

    3.   Explain three methods used by states to amend their constitutions.

          1.

          2.

          3.

Objective 2: Discuss the different types of state elections and how they differ from national elections.

    1.   Explain the "presidentialization" of gubernatorial elections.

    2.   Explain the "congressionalization" of state legislative elections.

    3.   What are the major consequences of divided government in the states?

4. List and explain three things that tend to increase legislative partisanship and polarize legislative deliberations in the states.

   1.

   2.

   3.

Objective 3: Explain the function of state governors and the executive branch.

   1. Explain the two most important formal powers that governors have for controlling state government.

      1.

      2.

   2. What is the role played by most lieutenant governors?

   3. List four major executive positions elected in some states and explain the primary duties of each.

      1.

      2.

      3.

      4.

Objective 4: Understand the nature and function of state legislatures and how legislatures make policy.

1. List four functions performed by all state legislatures.

    1.

    2.

    3.

    4.

2. Explain the three legislative professionalism reforms.

    1.

    2.

    3.

3. Explain the "de-professionalizing" trend in some state legislatures.

Objective 5: Describe the structure of the state court systems.

1.   Complete the following table on the nature of state courts.

Court	Geographic Jurisdiction	Number of Presiding Judges	Types of Cases	Use of Jury
Trial Courts				
Intermediate Courts of Appeals				
Court of Last Resort				

2.   What is the Merit Plan?

Objective 6: Explain how direct democracy is used in the states.

1.   List and explain three procedures for direct democracy used in the states.

1.

2.

3.

2.   Give three examples of how initiatives have been used in the states.

     1.

     2.

     3.

Objective 7: Discuss the relationship between state and local governments.

1.   Explain Dillon's Rule.

2.   What are three ways in which local governments can influence their own destiny?

     1.

     2.

     3.

Objective 8: Compare and contrast the different types of local government in the United States in terms of organization, functions, and policy roles.

1.   What are the common functions of most counties?

2. List the three modern forms of municipal government and complete the following table explaining where executive and legislative power lies and naming at least one city as an example.

Government Form	Executive	Legislature	Example

3. Explain why regional cooperation at the local level is so difficult to achieve.

4. What is a council of government and what purpose does it serve?

Objective 9: Discuss the fiscal and budgetary policies of state and local governments.

1. List the three main sources of state revenues.

   1.

   2.

   3.

2.	List four main areas of state expenditures.

1.

2.

3.

4.

3.	List the three main sources of local revenues.

1.

2.

3.

4.	List the three main areas of local expenditures.

1.

2.

3.

Objective 10: Evaluate state and local government in the United States in terms of their contributions to democracy and the scope of government.

1.	Give four reasons state and local politics may fall short of the democratic ideal.

1.

2.

3.

4.

2. Explain two ways in which state and local governments have attempted to control spending, taxing, and employment growth.

1.

2.

KEY TERMS

Identify and describe:

subnational governments

line-item veto

lieutenant governor

Merit Plan

direct democracy

initiative

referendum

recall

Dillon's Rule

local charter

home rule

town meeting

city manager

council of governments

Compare and contrast:

direct democracy, initiative, referendum, and recall

Dillon's Rule and local charter

local charter and home rule

Name that term:

1. These are also known as state and local governments.

    _____

2. A governor has this power to veto part of a bill while leaving the rest intact.

    _____

3. This is the second-highest state executive officer.

    _____

4. Under this system, state judges are appointed from a list of persons recommended by the state bar or a committee of officials.

    _____

5. Under this system, all voting-age adults in a community gather once a year to make public policy.

    _____

6. This is the local government administrator who implements and administers council-manager government.

    _____

7. This organization of officials from various localities exists to discuss mutual problems and plan cooperative action.

    _____

USING YOUR UNDERSTANDING

1. Choose a state of interest to you, such as your home state or the state in which your college or university is situated. Compare the government of this state to the federal government on a number of dimensions including, but not necessarily limited to, constitutional arrangements, the structure and organization of government, the powers of the policymaking bodies, particularly the legislative and executive bodies, the judicial structure and the role of the courts, the budgetary process including how revenues are collected and spent, and the nature and extent of regulation, and bureaucratic involvement. You may wish to either write a comprehensive outline or use this exercise as the basis of a term paper.

2. Explore the issue of federalism by choosing a federal policy that is implemented by the states. Examples include various environmental regulations or social welfare policies. How do states implement these policies? Which state bureaucracies are involved and how? Does the state legislature get involved in the act? Are any local governments involved and, if so, how? What individuals have the most impact on implementing the policy and how? What are the financial arrangements? Who controls how the money is spent? Evaluate the implementation of the policy on the basis of the policy's intention. This exercise may be a case study of one state or a comparison of different states.

MULTIPLE CHOICE QUESTIONS

Circle the correct answer:

1. Another term for state and local governments is
   a. Federal governments
   b. Secondary governments
   c. Tertiary governments
   d. Subnational governments
   e. Subterranean governments

2. Most states allow for amending their constitutions, and this is usually accomplished through
   a. a simple majority vote of the legislature followed by the governor's signature.
   b. a two-thirds vote of the legislature followed by the governor's signature.
   c. a two-thirds vote of the legislature followed by a simple majority vote of state voters in the next election.
   d. a two-thirds vote of the legislature followed by ratification by three-fourths of the counties.
   e. a simple majority vote of the legislation followed by a simple majority vote of the state voters in the next election.

3. What does it mean when political scientists talk about the "presidentialization" of gubernatorial elections?
   a. Gubernatorial races have increasingly become focused on individual candidates rather than party affiliation.
   b. Gubernatorial races are now all timed to coincide with presidential elections.
   c. Governors are now becoming presidents.
   d. Running for governor has become nearly as expensive as running for president.
   e. In the past 20 years, presidents have not made a difference when they supported gubernatorial candidates.

4. Until the mid-1960s, the one group that was overrepresented in state legislatures was
   a. the rural population.
   b. women.
   c. urban dwellers.
   d. minorities.
   e. Southerners.

5. Which of these is INCORRECT?
   a. The Nebraska legislature only has one house.
   b. Although it is the second largest state, the Texas legislature is only scheduled to meet every other year.
   c. All states now limit the terms of their legislators.
   d. Most state legislatures have become much more professionalized over the past thirty years.
   e. Many state legislators are part-timers who have other careers.

6. The fact that most states have a number of elected state executives in addition to the governor
   a. gives the governor greater authority.
   b. reduces the authority of the governor.
   c. reduces the authority of the legislature.
   d. reduces the democratic accountability of the executive branch of state government.
   e. has no effect on the authority of the governor.

7. Except for Nebraska, each state has a
   a. governor and lieutenant governor.
   b. unicameral legislature.
   c. bicameral legislature.
   d. supreme court.
   e. plural executive.

8. The organization of the states' courts reflects
   a. the model of organization set by the national courts.
   b. the judicial preferences of each state's citizens as manifested in state constitutions and statutes.
   c. the will of the executive.
   d. gubernatorial clemency.
   e. both a and b

9. Which of the following statements about selecting judges is TRUE?
   a. Like national judges, state judges are appointed for life.
   b. At the nation's founding, almost all state judges were appointed by the governor or state legislature.
   c. States began selecting judges by partisan ballot during the Jacksonian era.
   d. All of the above are true.
   e. Both b and c are true.

10. Which of the following is provided for by the Merit Plan?
    a. The governor appoints judges from a list of persons recommended by the state bar or a committee of jurists and other officials.
    b. Each appointed judge serves a short "trial run" term before facing a retention election.
    c. Judges are elected in retention elections for life-term appointments.
    d. All of the above.
    e. Both a and b.

11. The recall, referendum, and initiative are forms of
    a. direct democracy
    b. indirect democracy
    c. republican democracy
    d. minority rule
    e. both a and d

12. Iowa Judge John Dillon, articulated Dillon's Rule in 1868, arguing that
    a. local governments were "creatures of the state."
    b. state governments were "creatures of local governments."
    c. local governments were "creatures of the people."
    d. state governments were "creatures of the people."
    e. the national government is a "creature of local governments."

13. Which of the following is NOT a type of local government?
    a. School district
    b. Special district
    c. County
    d. Township
    e. None of the above

14. States' reserved powers are protected by the _____ Amendment to the Constitution.
    a. Second
    b. Fifth
    c. Tenth
    d. Fifteenth
    e. Twentieth

15. County government usually consists of an elected county _____ that makes policy and a collection of "row officers" who run county services.
    a. congress
    b. board of education
    c. directorate
    d. commission
    e. mayor

16. In a council-manager form of government, the implementation and administration of policy is placed in the hands of
    a. the city council itself.
    b. a mayor.
    c. a city manager.
    d. a county manager.
    e. the chief administrative officer.

17. Which of the following do rural residents rely on most for services?
    a. state governments
    b. county governments
    c. the Farm Bureau
    d. special districts
    e. agricultural cooperatives

18. In the past 45 years
    a. many small, often rural, school districts have been consolidated into larger districts.
    b. the number of school districts has dropped 66%.
    c. the number of school districts has increased by 66%.
    d. both a and c.
    e. both b and c.

19. Particularly in rural areas, _____ government is the administrative arm of most state governments, keeping records of births, deaths, and marriages, conducting a system of justice and law enforcement, maintaining roads and bridges, and providing other services.
    a. regional
    b. county
    c. municipal
    d. township
    e. commission

20. Councils of governments have been formed to
    a. reform state and local campaign practices.
    b. improve the public image of local governments.
    c. lobby state legislatures on behalf of localities.
    d. improve cooperation between local governments.
    e. streamline local government bureaucracy.

TRUE/FALSE QUESTIONS

Circle the correct answer:

1. Traditionally, state and local governments have been responsible for most criminal justice policy and maintaining civil order within state borders. T / F

2. The ultimate power of the government comes from its ability to take away the rights and liberties of individuals. T / F

3. Between 1898 and 1998, approximately 80 percent of initiative proposals for constitutional amendments were approved by state voters. T / F

4. Almost one-fourth of state legislators are women. T / F

5. Every state has undertaken a reorganization of the executive branch in the last decade, and most have benefited from enhanced efficiency and effectiveness. T / F

6. Not all state legislatures are full-time bodies. T / F

7. Ninety-eight percent of all litigation in the U.S. is settled in state courts. T / F

8. Growth in subnational governments has lagged behind growth in the national government over the past 100 years. T / F

9. A school district is a part of a county, township, or municipal government, and gets its funding from that government source. T / F

10. The very existence of so many governments to handle complex as well as ordinary services testifies to the health of our democracy. T / F

SHORT ANSWER/SHORT ESSAY QUESTIONS

1. What are the primary characteristics of state constitutions? How are they different and similar to the United States Constitution?

2. Compare and contrast the job of the president of the United States and state governor.

3. Describe the organization of the state court system. Include trial courts, intermediate appellate courts, and courts of last resort.

4. What is the recall and how is it different than the initiative or referendum?

5. What are the functions of special districts? Give an example.

ESSAY QUESTIONS

1. Why are state and local governments important to the American political system? How has this importance increased and changed in recent years? As a citizen of the United States, how would you explain your relationship with—and your expectations of—your state and local governments?

2. Explain in what ways have legislative and gubernatorial elections become similar to congressional and presidential elections? What are the consequences of these changes?

3. Describe what is meant by professionalism of state legislatures, and the trends in professionalism in the past several decades. What are the consequences of these changes? Are these changes ultimately good or bad for democracy?

4. Explain what is meant by "direct democracy." Has the use of direct democracy made state politics more democratic? In what ways might some direct democracy mechanisms be undemocratic in practice, if not in principle?

5. What role do school districts, counties, townships, and special districts play in local governing? Do these add unnecessary layers to government or make for greater democratic control of government? Why, or why not?

ANSWERS TO MULTIPLE CHOICE AND TRUE/FALSE

CHAPTER 1

Multiple Choice		True/False	
1.	b	1.	F
2.	a	2.	T
3.	d	3.	T
4.	e	4.	T
5.	d	5.	F
6.	d	6.	T
7.	e	7.	T
8.	e	8.	T
9.	a	9.	T
10.	e	10.	F
11.	a		
12.	b		
13.	e		
14.	b		
15.	a		
16.	b		
17.	a		
18.	a		
19.	d		
20.	e		

CHAPTER 2

Multiple Choice		True/False	
1.	a	1.	T
2.	b	2.	T
3.	a	3.	F
4.	b	4.	T
5.	c	5.	T
6.	c	6.	F
7.	d	7.	F
8.	d	8.	F
9.	b	9.	T
10.	a	10.	F
11.	d		
12.	d		
13.	a		
14.	b		
15.	a		
16.	c		
17.	a		
18.	e		
19.	a		
20.	c		

CHAPTER 3

Multiple Choice		True/False	
1.	a	1.	F
2.	a	2.	T
3.	b	3.	T
4.	a	4.	F
5.	c	5.	T
6.	e	6.	T
7.	c	7.	T
8.	d	8.	F
9.	a	9.	F
10.	c	10.	T
11.	d		
12.	b		
13.	d		
14.	a		
15.	b		
16.	c		
17.	e		
18.	a		
19.	a		
20.	a		

CHAPTER 4

Multiple Choice		True/False	
1.	b	1.	F
2.	c	2.	T
3.	b	3.	T
4.	a	4.	F
5.	e	5.	F
6.	d	6.	T
7.	a	7.	F
8.	a	8.	T
9.	b	9.	F
10.	a	10.	T
11.	c		
12.	d		
13.	d		
14.	e		
15.	e		
16.	a		
17.	e		
18.	b		
19.	e		
20.	c		

CHAPTER 5

Multiple Choice

1. c
2. d
3. d
4. a
5. c
6. a
7. e
8. d
9. e
10. d
11. b
12. c
13. b
14. e
15. c
16. a
17. c
18. a
19. d
20. d

True/False

1. T
2. F
3. T
4. F
5. T
6. T
7. F
8. T
9. T
10. T

CHAPTER 6

Multiple Choice

1. e
2. c
3. e
4. d
5. c
6. a
7. d
8. d
9. c
10. b
11. d
12. b
13. a
14. b
15. a
16. c
17. b
18. d
19. b
20. a

True/False

1. T
2. T
3. F
4. F
5. T
6. T
7. F
8. F
9. T
10. F

CHAPTER 7

Multiple Choice

1. e
2. b
3. d
4. c
5. a
6. a
7. d
8. a
9. c
10. e
11. d
12. e
13. c
14. d
15. e
16. a
17. a
18. c
19. a
20. c

True/False

1. T
2. F
3. F
4. T
5. T
6. F
7. T
8. T
9. T
10. F

CHAPTER 8

Multiple Choice

1. b
2. d
3. b
4. d
5. a
6. a
7. c
8. e
9. b
10. e
11. b
12. d
13. a
14. a
15. e
16. b
17. d
18. d
19. d
20. d

True/False

1. T
2. T
3. T
4. F
5. T
6. T
7. F
8. F
9. T
10. T

CHAPTER 9

Multiple Choice		True/False	
1.	a	1.	F
2.	c	2.	T
3.	e	3.	T
4.	b	4.	F
5.	a	5.	T
6.	e	6.	F
7.	b	7.	T
8.	c	8.	F
9.	d	9.	F
10.	c	10.	T
11.	a		
12.	a		
13.	e		
14.	b		
15.	b		
16.	e		
17.	a		
18.	b		
19.	d		
20.	e		

CHAPTER 10

Multiple Choice		True/False	
1.	b	1.	T
2.	b	2.	T
3.	a	3.	F
4.	c	4.	T
5.	a	5.	T
6.	a	6.	F
7.	b	7.	F
8.	e	8.	T
9.	a	9.	T
10.	d	10.	F
11.	b		
12.	a		
13.	c		
14.	a		
15.	a		
16.	c		
17.	c		
18.	a		
19.	c		
20.	a		

CHAPTER 11

Multiple Choice		True/False	
1.	c	1.	F
2.	a	2.	T
3.	c	3.	T
4.	c	4.	T
5.	c	5.	F
6.	d	6.	F
7.	a	7.	T
8.	a	8.	T
9.	b	9.	F
10.	c	10.	F
11.	c		
12.	c		
13.	a		
14.	e		
15.	d		
16.	d		
17.	d		
18.	e		
19.	e		
20.	c		

CHAPTER 12

Multiple Choice		True/False	
1.	c	1.	T
2.	e	2.	T
3.	c	3.	F
4.	c	4.	T
5.	d	5.	T
6.	d	6.	T
7.	a	7.	T
8.	b	8.	F
9.	b	9.	F
10.	d	10.	T
11.	c		
12.	d		
13.	e		
14.	c		
15.	b		
16.	d		
17.	d		
18.	b		
19.	e		
20.	b		

CHAPTER 13

Multiple Choice

1. e
2. b
3. c
4. d
5. e
6. c
7. d
8. a
9. e
10. c
11. a
12. b
13. b
14. c
15. a
16. e
17. a
18. d
19. b
20. e

True/False

1. T
2. F
3. T
4. T
5. T
6. T
7. T
8. F
9. F
10. T

CHAPTER 14

Multiple Choice

1. a
2. c
3. d
4. d
5. b
6. c
7. c
8. d
9. b
10. e
11. a
12. b
13. a
14. b
15. b
16. b
17. c
18. a
19. e
20. b

True/False

1. F
2. T
3. T
4. F
5. T
6. T
7. T
8. T
9. T
10. F

CHAPTER 15

Multiple Choice

1. b
2. a
3. c
4. a
5. b
6. c
7. b
8. b
9. d
10. a
11. d
12. d
13. e
14. d
15. b
16. b
17. c
18. e
19. d
20. d

True/False

1. T
2. F
3. F
4. T
5. T
6. T
7. T
8. T
9. F
10. T

CHAPTER 16

Multiple Choice

1. a
2. d
3. c
4. a
5. a
6. c
7. b
8. b
9. d
10. c
11. a
12. a
13. d
14. a
15. b
16. a
17. e
18. a
19. b
20. b

True/False

1. T
2. F
3. T
4. T
5. T
6. T
7. F
8. F
9. T
10. T

CHAPTER 17

Multiple Choice

1. d
2. e
3. b
4. a
5. b
6. d
7. b
8. c
9. b
10. a
11. e
12. d
13. d
14. a
15. d
16. c
17. d
18. b
19. a
20. b

True/False

1. T
2. F
3. T
4. F
5. F
6. T
7. F
8. T
9. T
10. T

CHAPTER 18

Multiple Choice

1. e
2. e
3. b
4. d
5. b
6. c
7. a
8. c
9. a
10. b
11. c
12. a
13. e
14. a
15. a
16. c
17. c
18. e
19. b
20. e

True/False

1. T
2. F
3. T
4. T
5. F
6. T
7. T
8. F
9. F
10. T

CHAPTER 19

Multiple Choice

1. b
2. a
3. b
4. e
5. b
6. e
7. b
8. e
9. b
10. c
11. d
12. a
13. b
14. b
15. a
16. e
17. b
18. a
19. d
20. e

True/False

1. T
2. F
3. T
4. T
5. F
6. T
7. T
8. T
9. T
10. T

CHAPTER 20

Multiple Choice

1. a
2. d
3. e
4. c
5. b
6. a
7. b
8. c
9. a
10. b
11. d
12. d
13. d
14. e
15. a
16. c
17. c
18. b
19. a
20. c

True/False

1. F
2. T
3. F
4. T
5. T
6. F
7. T
8. T
9. T
10. T

CHAPTER 21

Multiple Choice		True/False	
1.	d	1.	T
2.	c	2.	T
3.	a	3.	F
4.	a	4.	T
5.	c	5.	F
6.	b	6.	T
7.	c	7.	T
8.	e	8.	F
9.	e	9.	F
10.	e	10.	T
11.	a		
12.	a		
13.	e		
14.	c		
15.	d		
16.	c		
17.	b		
18.	d		
19.	b		
20.	d		